ZERO CARBON OUR CHOICE

By Chris Lenon

Amazon Kindle Edition

Copyright 2020 Chris Lenon

Contact Chris Lenon at www.zerocarbonourchoice.com

All rights reserved

Licence Notes and All Rights

ABOUT THE AUTHOR

Chris Lenon has a business background. He began thinking about climate change from a business perspective in his role as a senior corporate tax adviser in 2000. He has considerable experience dealing with the OECD, the EC, and governments around the world. This gives him a unique global perspective, combined with an understanding of how major investment decisions are made, and how they can go wrong.

Chris began writing this book because he felt media coverage on climate change and emissions was piecemeal, and, did not really give the public the full picture. While most agree that reducing carbon emissions and tackling climate change is the biggest challenge we currently face, few realise the extent of the decisions and changes required, and how they will impact our lives. Chris's intention is to stimulate debate and facilitate action.

Chris lives in London, with his family, and blogs on Tax and the Environment and Zero emissions at www.zerocarbonourchoice.com .He takes every opportunity to manage the wood in Wiltshire comprising some 7,000 trees he planted in 2012.

CONTENTS

Part 1

Part 2

Part 3

TABLES & CHARTS

THANKS

I wrote this book because there is a real danger that promises that decarbonising the economy is easy will discredit the process when the real difficulties emerge. I spent six years grappling with the issues from the perspective of business as chair of the Green Tax Group for Business Europe. Working with that small group of people helped me to understand the issues and develop my thoughts.

So, this book would not be possible without conversations with Simone Ruiz-Vergote, Kristian Koktvedgaard, Torbjorn Spector, Anna Theuuwes, Theo Keijzer, Krister Andersson and Claes Hammerstedt. And in the UK, Nick Atkinson on trees and John Prior on farming. To Barry Cunningham for his publishing insights.

Finally, thanks to Georgina Lenon for both proof reading this book and polishing its language, and Zara and Stella.

INTRODUCTION

"We've got five years, that's what we've got". David Bowie[i]

We have got five years. Not to reduce emissions to zero as Extinction Rebellion state for the UK – that is impossible. But five years to come up with a plan on how to reach zero carbon by 2050 and then start implementing that plan.

This book is about one of the most, if not *the* most important issues, we face – how do we reduce greenhouse gas emissions to slow and eventually stabilise climate change. It assumes that we recognise the need to reduce emissions and that the question we face is no longer why we need to do this, but how to achieve it. For democracies, with short political cycles, tackling a long-term problem is difficult. Reducing carbon in our economy and will be a real test of democracy as many of the decisions needed will be decisions we make, not government decisions.

The key theme is that to achieve zero carbon, to decarbonise, will require all of us to make changes. This is not something which will be achieved by government regulation or pricing carbon and emissions alone. Look at Sweden; it has virtually decarbonised electricity, but still has emissions and it is these emissions, from housing, transport and agriculture, which will be the most difficult to remove.

There are a number of key themes, to hold in mind. Firstly, change to the dominance of electricity as the fuel source for power, transport and heating. Secondly, the need to control the price of electricity to ensure that this transition does not increase the cost of power, transport and heating, whilst investing enormous sums in the new electricity generation required. And last and most crucially, how change is implemented so that the poorer parts of society do not suffer economically. Each of such changes required is difficult individually, but, combining them makes the task even harder.

This book focusses on how to reduce emissions and the issues this poses. The purpose is not to say that we can't do this, even if it is difficult, and in some sectors very difficult. Based on current technology and lifestyle, it is difficult to see the achievement of zero carbon by 2050, but that should not stop us trying. We need to recognise that this isn't as simple and easy as some would currently have us believe. Instead, we need to focus on how "we", not "they" achieve this. This book is about the fact that this is not "their problem", government can legislate to reduce some emissions, and has been successful in some areas already, but some emissions are "our problem" and therefore only our individual choices will reduce them, and only we can make a difference.

I've been interested in climate change and the mechanisms to address it since the early 2000s. My concern has been that while governments have been focusing on setting targets for reducing carbon emissions over a number of timescales (2020, 2030, 2040 and 2050) with the intention to meet targets to limit global temperature growth, they have not focussed on what needs to be done throughout their economies to achieve these and the scale of that change for both the economy and society in such a short period of time. Experts and politicians who say that achieving zero carbon emissions is easy are misleading the public.

More importantly, they have not explained to their citizens the number of difficult choices and lifestyle changes that will be necessary to achieve these targets. The debate on achieving zero carbon has largely focussed on what the electricity sector and business needs to do, indeed some politicians seem to think that decarbonising the electricity sector solves the problem – it does not. While electricity and business are both a significant part of the issue, they account for less than half of UK emissions and there are many other areas which contribute to emissions which have been largely ignored to date. Making changes to these emissions which affect the standard of living, way of life and aspirations of ordinary people will never be easy. The Gilets Jaune (Yellow Vest) protests in France have shown how difficult it is to introduce reforms to reduce emissions by pricing mechanisms which affect ordinary people and their way of life.

I believe that while the piece below by the Editorial Board of the Financial Times published on 2 May 2019[ii], covers the main issues, it underestimates how the difficulty of the transition to a zero-carbon target and how wide ranging the effects on virtually all aspects of our lives will be:

"In three decades, Britain's greenhouse gas emissions should fall to almost zero, according to the UK's chief advisory body on climate change. In a rigorous report, the Committee on Climate Change proposes Britain adopts the strictest targets for emissions among G20 countries, alongside France. The Net Zero report should be applauded as a blueprint which does not shy away from addressing the costs of transition. The government should seize the opportunity to put Britain on the right path on climate change. The report lays out a clear moral case for the UK reaching net zero by 2050 — meaning any greenhouse gases it does emit must be absorbed through forests or carbon-capturing technology....
Although the 2050 deadline will require sustained government focus, it is by no means unworkable. It is a lot more credible than Extinction Rebellion's proposed 2025 cut-off. While the bulk of the work will be carried out under future administrations, adopting

the report's recommendations is a key first step. The UK has cut emissions significantly from 30 years ago. A decision now could set the path for future administrations to eliminate them 30 years from now. This will require political courage to commit whole-heartedly to net zero. Here is an opportunity for a rudderless government, looking to chart a new path for Britain in the world post-Brexit, to write a place in history."

The approach endorsed by the Financial Times, glosses over the change required in virtually every sector of the economy and focusses primarily on what government can do. To state that *"Although the 2050 deadline will require sustained government focus, it is by no means unworkable"*, is brave. It fails to recognise the scale of change required in such a short period of time. It underplays the technological advances necessary to achieve this target. It ignores the increase in electricity capacity required to achieve these changes and the difficulty in bringing this onstream, exacerbated by the opposition which has already delayed projects like onshore wind and will likely emerge in the future, of people opposed to the changes outlined in this book. While the changes require *"sustained government focus"*, this is not enough as it will show.

It glosses over the difficulties in reducing agricultural emissions while we eat meat. It ignores the emissions from aviation (which are not included in the UK emissions under the UN methodology) for which there are currently no technological solutions. It also fails to mention the largest sector in terms of emissions, transport, whose record on emissions reduction to date has been very poor. The Financial Times is correct that the report from the UK Committee on Climate Change does set out a roadmap, but there are some heroic assumptions in its analysis, Carbon Capture and Sequestration being the major one. Stating that *"Carbon capture and storage systems, which will be central to ensuring that the UK's continued emissions are balanced, are still costly and rare"* is both an understatement and wrong, as the plants are not rare, in actual fact there are currently no commercial CCS plants in the UK.

The danger of the current approach is that time slips by and although the easier decisions are made (such as end coal as a source of power generation), difficult decisions are being postponed and may then made in a rush or panic which is a recipe for bad policy decisions. I have long advocated that a planned policy setting out what is going to change and when that change will happen, is the best method so that all the actors: business, citizens and governments have time to adjust. There is a danger that democracies will arrive at a situation where draconian measures are required, challenging that democracy itself. will democracies be able to make these difficult decisions?

We also need to pose the question whether two pillars of our world order are compatible with zero carbon – urbanisation and globalisation. Metropolitan cities are consistently lagging behind rural areas in aspects of decarbonisation. It is reasonable to ask the question can one really have a zero-carbon metropolis? The logical consequence of decarbonisation is the end of the global trade in carbon (Oil, Gas & Coal) as the role of electricity produced from local source renewables increases. But will it slow or halt the advance of globalisation. Does a zero-carbon economy lead to more emphasis on the local rather than the global economy and not just in power generation?

Diesel emissions – a lesson in the difficulties of change

The current position on diesel emissions in urban areas clearly identifies what happens when a government (in this case local) is not clear about a change and doesn't address the problems that the change causes. In London, the Ultra-Low Emission Zone (ULEZ) was introduced in April 2019. This was signalled in 2013 to help drivers to make the adjustment to either change from diesel or replace old diesel cars with new. Despite signalling this for 6 years in advance, on the day it came into operation, phone-ins were full of "how did this happen?" and "how unfair this is" comments. In 2017, I had a number of conversations with fellow Londoners suggesting that now was possibly the time to sell diesel cars. Most looked bemused, few acted on the advice, and many subsequently complained when the ULEZ was introduced.

Since then people have woken up and smelt the coffee. Sales of new diesel cars within London have plummeted and interest in electric/hybrids increased; some dealers are claiming diesel sales are now only 2% of total sales in London. I think this illustrates the need to set out policy simply and keep reminding people what it is. The charging mechanism in the ULEZ is a transitional measure to reduce particulate emissions and ultimately government policy is to phase out petrol/diesel cars by 2040.

The ULEZ also highlights a key issue in measures to reduce emissions. Many complained that the need to change their car was too costly for the poor. This issue is significant as fuel and energy costs are a larger proportion of the spending of poorer citizens both in western countries and globally, and decarbonisation is largely about fuel source. One of the key policy issues in decarbonising the economy is therefore how do you persuade the less well-off to change their behaviour and buy into a low carbon or no carbon future? Pricing cannot be the whole answer, given the impact of pricing on different income groups, but if pricing is not the driver what is the spur to behavioural change?

This challenge is not helped by the fact that the generation of emissions is greater for the more affluent who spend more on "carbon" goods and services, take more flights, drive larger cars etc. Any solution for reducing emissions, which leads to the more affluent being able to "spend" carbon while the less affluent will have to reduce carbon spending, will rightly raise issues of equity.

This book looks at the choices we will need to make if we are serious about meeting the emission reduction targets our governments have agreed. For a change to zero carbon to take place, we will all have to think about the "carbon cost" of the decisions we make as individuals, in business, in national and local government and in organisations in the widest sense. I have framed this as the decisions which we will all need to make about our carbon budgets.

The first section of the book considers the consequences of economic growth and changes in population on emissions. It argues that we will need to develop a new measure of growth which includes the environmental impact of growth in the calculation of sustainable growth. A measure of raw economic growth is not enough if sustainability is important and the cost of carbon is recognised. Growth based on population increase and power consumption makes reducing emissions more difficult.

Proponents of the "Green Deal" propose a new world where new green jobs are created by decarbonisation. New jobs will be created, but old jobs will also disappear. Sectoral changes on the road to zero-carbon will be significant and the sectors affected may surprise many. The question is will this reduce employment or increase it? It will certainly change employment patterns. Some countries, areas and regions will be adversely affected by the loss of "carbon jobs".

In parallel to this sectoral change, the removal of carbon, the end of the age of carbon, will have geopolitical consequences. Countries which currently have large carbon earnings from oil, gas, and coal will have to adjust as their government revenues and export earnings diminish. In some countries the impact will be on states or provinces, even if the issue is not major at a national level. The most carbon dependent economies may suffer effects which will be de-stabilising for them and their neighbours.

A world which has had to manage the impact of oil on international relations for the last seventy years, will have to adjust to the power challenges of a post carbon world economy. As power supply becomes more focussed on electricity, power issues will become more local and global energy flows will diminish.

We also need to consider the role of the media, influencers and celebrities on the change needed. Is there a whiff of hypocrisy here? Are those who promote and publicise the consumption of goods and travel hindering the changes which are needed? The media are full every day with stories of the conspicuous consumption or travel of celebrities. What is the carbon cost of the goods and services promoted in the "How to Spend it" section of the Financial Times? Should the Financial Times Editorial Board quoted above not consider the contradiction of the income from advertising these items the Financial Times receives that have a high carbon cost and their views expressed above? Other newspapers are not immune, the Guardian which polishes its environmental credentials, promotes travel consumption particularly long haul, amongst other high carbon cost experiences. Looking wider is Instagram, in the travel and consumption it records and encourages, in fact a carbon promoting business?

The role of technology is seen by many as the golden bullet in solving the problems, yet this optimism is misplaced. This view of technology as saviour, is predicated on the successful advance and implementation of technological change in a relatively short period of time, the evidence is that moving from first commercial development to low cost applications to widespread adoption takes decades as is illustrated by solar pv. Some technology is not operating on a scale-able level (i.e. Carbon Capture and Sequestration (CCS)) and the danger is that it will not reach widespread adoption in the period to 2050.

Aviation is a major problem and more so if the target is zero carbon. As the chapter on Aviation and Maritime shows, reducing emissions in these sectors is very difficult. Offsetting is promoted as the solution. The problem is that offsetting works if you're trying to reduce emissions as the financing helps schemes which reduce emissions. With a zero-carbon target however, offsetting only works if it takes you below zero, as emission reduction to zero is already assumed. In a UK moving to zero carbon, does it make sense to build a third runway at Heathrow?

In the second section of the book, I review the various sectors in the UK, which produce emissions and what needs to change in each sector to achieve zero carbon. These changes are not as simplistic as many advocates of de-carbonisation propose. This section looks in detail at the position in the UK based on the official data for 2017[iii]. Each major sector of emissions is considered in terms of the changes in emissions between 1990 and 2017 and how the 2050 targets, which require the decarbonisation of the economy, are to be achieved. These changes will have a major impact in terms of our lifestyle, our standard of living and employment patterns (who will need an oil/diesel car mechanic when all cars are electric / hydrogen and are much simpler cars, etc, etc).

The same issues will apply to other countries even if the specific numbers and the distributional effects amongst sectors are different from those in the UK. While this is a global problem, change will have to start with change in a political unit, be it at national or state level. Anyone expecting a swift international solution, should consider that it has taken the international community seven years to propose a way to tax multinational companies with significant intangible assets, reducing emissions is a much greater challenge than that, and the evidence to date is that the process will be slow. The progress at COP25 illustrates this.

The International dimension is much more difficult. Many see the burdens of reducing emissions as other peoples' problem. When hard choices are needed there will always be resistance to change if it is perceived that others are "getting away with it". In June 2019 The Czech Republic, Estonia, Hungary and Poland, blocked an EU initiative led by 8 predominantly northern European countries to commit the EU to a zero-emission target for 2050. The Financial Times reported:

"Polish prime minister Mateusz Morawiecki told reporters they were very firmly defending their interests. "Poland is one of those countries that must first have a very detailed compensation package. We must know how much we can get for modernisation."[iv]

While countries argue about who shoulders the burden, little progress can be made if the danger for first movers is that their countries will suffer carbon leakage. The industries which compete internationally, and which produce emissions, will simply move to lower compliance countries, whose regimes mean they can emit CO2 and their industry costs will be lower. This will do nothing to reduce global emissions, but merely affect their distribution around the world.

Chapters 5 and 6 use the UK data from 1990 to 2017[v] to explore the significant issues in removing Gas from the fuel mix.

The third section considers the choices we have in transitioning to a low carbon economy from our current position over the next thirty years and the timeline for those choices. First, what can an individual do to reduce emissions? It looks at pricing mechanisms, the balance between lifestyle and living standards and a road map for achieving zero carbon. It also discusses the cost. Conservative estimates get you to £1 trillion for the UK and the probable cost is significantly higher and all to be achieved in thirty years.

My concern has been that the UK, like other countries, has not devoted the energy it should have to examining these choices on what we do to reduce emissions, as they are complex and involve significant if not massive change to our economies, how we live and the natural environment. The process to date has been successful in some sectors (power generation and waste management are good examples). The focus has been on the targets (reduction in the growth of temperature and the reduction in emissions to achieve these temperature targets). This has clearly been a necessary first step, you need to decide what the objective is. You will find many books on why climate change is the major issue confronting us and I will refer to Naomi Klein's book "This Changes Everything". Her book is a great piece of advocacy, but it underplays the actual changes needed to reduce emissions which is the big issue which faces us now.

The real challenge now, is how the world moves to a low carbon or decarbonised economy in a relatively short period of time. I believe we need to do this for following generations. The issue is no longer why, but how do we achieve this. If we continue with the analysis that this is a problem for governments, that "business" needs to reduce emissions, then we ignore the key drivers in this process. It is depressing to hear Green MP Caroline Lucas defending the personal choice of flying, but then continuing to blame industry and oppose nuclear power. Clearly zero carbon won't be achieved if all industry's emissions are removed and we fly more.

If we are serious about reducing emissions, it has to be the focus for governments, organisations and individuals themselves. It is about the actions of individuals. It concerns many decisions that people make in their lives and the impact on emission levels of those decisions which together with Government action and regulation (and pressure from voters on governments to introduce this) which will determine how quickly we reduce emissions.

Life is about choices. This is "Our Choice".

PART 1

INTERNATIONAL

1 QUESTION EVERYTHING

In reading anything it is crucial to understand the perspective of the author, as this bias, at whatever level, needs to be understood in assessing their analysis. Climate Change policy is no different. We should question everything.

The history of climate change deniers has clearly illustrated this. I won't review it in detail as there are plenty of analyses of what has happened. But fake news, selective information and understatement is not the sole preserve of climate change denial. There are plenty of other vested interests in the debate about the process of decarbonisation and we need to be aware of them as they emerge over the following pages. Whether it is a carbon energy company or a renewable energy company, each has their own vested interest and one needs to understand this to analyse what should be done.

Big Oil: Is Gas the saviour?

It is reasonable to question whether the oil and coal companies, which funded climate denial in the 1990s and later, can now be trusted with their proposals today. Exxon Mobil was probably the most aggressive funder of climate questioning. A degree of cynicism might therefore greet its announcement to spend $10m per annum to research technologies that could cut greenhouse gas emissions. Given an annual research budget of $1.2bn this is a paltry sum, it looks like greenwash. Exxon clearly believes in the future of carbon fuels with this proportion of its research budget spent on them.

Darren Woods, Exxon's chief executive, said: *"Unfortunately, the technology does not exist today to meet the growth in demand for energy while reducing emissions in line with the goals of the Paris agreement."*[vi] This statement is misleading. If the UK can reduce its electricity generation emissions by switching to renewables and nuclear then the technology does exist. What Mr Woods may be saying is that *"the technology does not exist today"* to reduce emissions for carbon fuels as Carbon Capture and Sequestration (CCS) is not scalable, meaning it doesn't exist for his company's business model.

The narrative of this book is that reducing carbon is about both government action and personal choices which we make. There are issues with technology in some areas, but if the emission reduction targets for the period to 2050 are to be met, why do we still build carbon energy infrastructure?

The promotion of gas by the oil industry as the saviour of low carbon power generation is an example of what needs to be questioned. Gas does emit less carbon than coal, dramatically less, but it is still a carbon fuel with emissions and without Carbon Capture & Sequestration (CCS see Chapter 7) it won't have a place in power generation after 2050 if a zero emission target is to be met, and yet the oil industry is reticent to make that clear and continues to promote gas as the clean carbon fuel. As Chapter 6 on Gas shows, the UK is dependent on gas at present, and its biggest challenge is to wean itself off this fuel. Adding to gas infrastructure which will be in place at 2050 doesn't make sense given this decarbonisation target, as gas as a fuel source should decline as the UK decarbonises.

The Renewable Industry

The renewable industry is another example where one needs to examine claims with care. Initially, renewables were economic only by governments providing subsidies with feed in tariffs (FiT) and other support mechanisms. The relationship between the industry and government became somewhat incestuous, as the industry needed subsidy and the government wanted renewable investment. The industry sought and became dependent on subsidy and some of the costing of subsidies provided was not well thought through. The change required going forward is that renewables will need to survive in a market, even if that market may be underpinned by a carbon price. Governments will need to be careful that new technologies are supported in the most appropriate way by learning lessons from the past. We all need to be wary of overblown claims about renewables. While they can make a significant contribution to decarbonising the electricity sector, they won't directly deal with other sectors whose emissions need to be reduced as well.

Greenwash.

If you look at most advertising material and company mission statements over the last few years you might believe that a lot of the decarbonisation issues are being dealt with. Car advertising is a case in point. As the sectoral analysis shows, however, the progress in some sectors is extremely slow. It pays to read the T&Cs rather than accept the gloss. Transport has made little progress in reducing emissions compared to other sectors. People still make decisions about buying cars based on kerb appeal and how they will impress customers, colleagues, or neighbours. This is not surprising, watch car adverts and ask yourself the question, have they changed or are they still selling the same dream Do they make any reference to carbon and if they are not electric models? Perhaps as a result of this, in most markets, 30% of us choose to buy SUVs which are bigger, heavier and emit more carbon than smaller cars. We, as consumers, are therefore increasing emissions.

Lorries carry messages about the progress in saving emissions, but road freight emissions are not falling. Indeed, emissions from Heavy Goods Vehicles (HGVs) have gone up marginally. Light Goods Vehicles (LGVs) emissions have nearly doubled between 1990 and 2017. Freight transport will be a very difficult area in which to reduce emissions, particularly for heavier vehicles.

Governments around the world also use greenwash too by the selective use of data. Greta Thunberg has criticised the UK data on emissions reduction because it does not include either aviation and maritime emissions, or the emissions of goods consumed in the UK, but not produced in the UK in its emission figures. Both claims are correct. But the measurement of emissions metrics is decided not by countries, but by the United Nations Framework Convention on Climate Change (UNFCCC) which has mandated the form of reporting. If form of reporting is not acceptable then the UNFCCC needs to change its instructions.

If you examine government websites on emissions, the countries which are reducing emissions less than the average, gloss over why. Two European countries show some examples of government greenwash.

Luxembourg states: *"According to the latest estimates, Luxembourg is set to achieve its CO_2 reduction objective provided for by the Kyoto Protocol by 2020, but will face a considerable challenge when it comes to reducing its emissions by 40% by 2030.* "[vii]. But *"Luxembourg has made a name for itself as the main international climate financing centre."*[viii]

A report by DG Climate Action (European Commission) states *"Luxemburg introduced its first national climate action plan in 2006 and has taken measures on, e.g. energy efficiency, sustainable transport, or renewable energies. However, Luxembourg still has by far the highest per capita emissions in the EU and a slight decrease of total emissions since 2005 can be ascribed rather to the economic recession than to ambitious climate policies, as the Government itself acknowledges."*[ix] Luxembourg's emissions are 20 tonnes per capita (2017 Eurostat), the highest in the EU, and on a par with the US and Canada.

Ireland is one of the few member states which is expected to miss the EU emission reduction target for 2020, and the state expected to miss by the widest margin. Ireland is not on course to hit its 2020 EU targets until around 2040. Government advisers at the Climate Change Advisory Council concluded that Ireland was *"Ireland remains unlikely to achieve its 2020 and 2030 targets"[x] and described future projections as "disturbing". "The continued failure to set out detailed pathways on the cost-effective route to decarbonising the Irish economy by 2050 is a major obstacle to progressing policy on climate change. While Ireland can comply with its EU targets by purchasing emissions allowances, this use of public funds – with no domestic benefit – would impose a current cost on the Exchequer and would leave Ireland with a bigger and more expensive task to meet its future targets to 2030 and beyond."[xi]* Despite its recent performance, Taoiseach Leo Varadkar has said he wants Ireland to become a *"global leader on climate action"*. An example of this is Ireland's decision to become the first country in the world to divest from fossil fuels, with the national investment fund selling €300m of shares in coal, gas and oil companies. This is green wash designed to divert attention from Ireland's emission trajectory, and its failure to plan to reduce its own emissions. Ireland's emissions per head are 13.3 tonnes, slightly lower than US figures. There are examples of other countries where what is said *"we are enthusiastic about reducing emissions"* but that is not born out by the actual statistics. As in all things, don't listen to the spin, look at the numbers.

Advocacy.

There are large numbers of people, and large numbers of organisations telling us that with a little bit of effort we can decarbonise in surprisingly short periods of time. I am a supporter of Greenpeace because I think we need environmental advocacy, someone to hold governments feet to the fire but that doesn't mean I agree with everything they say or do. Greenpeace has a *"10 point plan"[xii]*, to deal the climate emergency.

I can agree with a number of the 10 points; we do need to increase renewable investment (tripling it by 2030 may be difficult, but targets need to ambitious), we need to plant more trees, a frequent flyer tax to reduce air travel should be considered, ending the sale of carbon cars by 2030 rather than 2040 has deliverability issues (see Chapter 11), increasing subsidy to public transport makes sense as does retrofitting homes to be more energy efficient.

But I struggle with *"End carbon emissions from heavy industry like steel and cement – A range of new technologies can make a big difference to industrial emissions – but companies need government support to introduce them"*[xiii]. From this you would think that cement was a significant part of UK emissions. In fact it is about 1% of emissions (on a par with the NHS) and sectors like residential (15%) and transport (27%) need greater absolute reductions and with more urgent action.

Energy intensive businesses do face a difficult transition to no carbon. In effect they need to be powered by non-carbon power, including nuclear, at competitive prices in order to compete globally from a UK or European base. At present the *"range of new technologies"* which *"can make a big difference to industrial emissions"* don't exist at scalable size. There are no commercial CCS plants in the UK. CCS is not working at a scalable level globally and indeed the global total stored using CCS is 32 Mtpa. Global emissions were 35 Btpa in 2015.

If energy intensive businesses cannot compete due to carbon costs which do not apply to their competitors elsewhere, then production will move to countries with lower emission standards. That does not address global emissions but merely moves them. The challenge is to produce non carbon electricity at a competitive price in global terms to power industries like cement and the rest of the economy. As the Committee on Climate Change report puts it *"Carbon capture (usage) and storage, which is crucial to the delivery of zero GHG emissions and strategically important to the UK economy, is yet to get started. While global progress has also been slow, there are now 43 large-scale projects operating or under development around the world, but none in the UK.[xiv]"*

Greenpeace is being somewhat economical with the truth, *"A range of new technologies can make a big difference to industrial emissions – but companies need government support to introduce them"* is inaccurate. This isn't about government support, it is about making CCS work for large scale industrial plants, which as the numbers show it doesn't do yet.

The Green Deal

The green deal mantra also needs to be questioned. This often runs along the lines of creating millions of new jobs in a new green economy by helping workers gain the skills they need for the future. That might mean helping people switch from offshore oil to offshore wind, or from car engine manufacturing to battery production for electric cars. This all sounds great.

"THE GREEN TRANSFORMATION: LABOUR'S ENVIRONMENT POLICY" states *"The potential benefits of transitioning to a sustainable economy are significant – whether in cheaper energy, growing global markets for green tech, or new high quality jobs in renewables industries – but it will take concerted action by government to ensure that these potential benefits are both realised and widely shared.[xv]"*

While new jobs will be created in new industries, some old jobs however will also disappear and the net result on employment may be negative, (as is shown in the OECD graphic below). One only need reflect on the employment issues posed by the closure of the UK coal mining industry, to see that such transitions are not necessarily smooth for the individuals or regions involved. A carbon car is more complex

27

than an electric car to manufacture and service, and it has far more parts. Electric cars require smaller supply chains for those fewer parts and a simpler assembly process involving fewer jobs. The likelihood is that electric car production will reduce employment in the automotive industry rather than increase it.

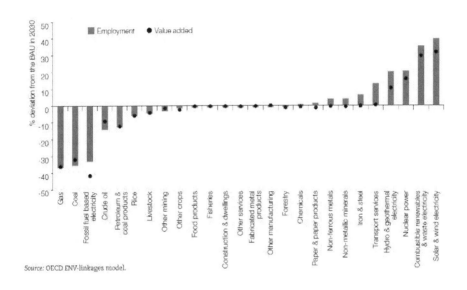

Oecd: Job gains and losses decarbonisation

A report for DG Energy (European Commission) states: *"From a sectoral perspective, the report suggests a decline in fossil-fuel de- pendent sectors towards those related to electrification, renewable energy sources and energy efficiency installation and equipment. This tendency highlights the challenge of replacing the lost jobs and the need to retrain workers as relevant industries are typically geographically concentrated. With regards to level of skills, a move towards higher-level occupations and qualifications is expected. This shift may stretch the demand for high-skill occupations to levels that the supply may not be able to keep pace with. Finally, the impact of stronger decarbonisation may be felt more in spe- cific "greening" occupations for which new competences will be needed.*[xvi]"

The emphasis here is on new technology and higher-level jobs. A report by the IPPR on Northern England notes a *"significant risk with around 28,000 job losses in the coal, oil and gas industries expected "by 2030. "These figures do not include the other potential job losses in high-carbon, energy-intensive industries, and the wider economic and social implications that the loss of industry can bring about, with the IPPR highlighting the history of poorly managed industry transitions in the north.*[xvii]"

Battery production may be widely distributed around the world or it may be focussed in a few global locations, so the UK or other countries may not benefit from the employment in battery production. Currently, battery cell production is concentrated in Japan, Korea and the US. Battery pack assembly centres on South Korea, Hungary and the US. The likelihood is that battery production will be concentrated to achieve economies of scale. Tesla's decision to build batteries near Berlin for Europe, not Germany, is an example of this.

The location of "green jobs" is highlighted by the recent dispute at the BiFab construction yards in Methil and Burntisland on the Fife coast in Scotland. This illustrates some of the challenges for new green jobs. It's worth quoting the Guardian report to illustrate the challenge which globalisation poses to the location of "green jobs".

"There has been almost £5bn of investment in offshore renewables in Scotland that, if properly managed and negotiated, could amount to several thousand sustainable and skilled jobs. According to the GMB, only 100 temporary jobs currently derive from this. In this global sector, we are often taking a penknife to a gunfight, with for-eign-owned outfits heavily backed by governments that underwrite losses. Thus, our contracts need to be watertight and stringent.

The Scottish government spent a great deal of money securing all the necessary consents for the wind farm and said that jobs would be created in the Fife yards. That was before EDF bought the project from the previous owners for £500m, before crudely jettisoning all prior commitments to local jobs. How the Scottish government failed to get these jobs nailed down legally, even in the event of the contract being bought out, may yet be scrutinised in court. Scotland faces the bizarre and humiliating prospect of a French firm riding on the crest of our spanking new green energy revolution by moving it to the other side of the world, before towing it back on diesel-burning ships to stick it 10 miles off the coast of Fife as a permanent insult to the communities that must look at them every day.

UK taxpayers are entitled to ask why they are paying fortunes to subsidise green energy and create jobs everywhere else in the world except here. EDF and the other global firms that have filled their boots on Scotland's energy potential will make a lot of money from this. Gary Smith, secretary of GMB Scotland, said: "The electricity produced by this work will be very expensive. As a society, we are entitled to insist that the jobs created should be made here in Scotland.[xviii]"

It is interesting that the Guardian didn't draw the logical conclusion from this, and ask whether the same issue would affect the promised green jobs in the UK? What proponents of the green deal don't explain is how they can guarantee that these jobs will be distributed evenly to countries which decarbonise. While we need the investment in new non carbon infrastructure, it is naive to believe that this will lead to an increase in net employment per se or that it will produce the same type of jobs.

To quote Naomi Klein *"Fortunately, it is eminently possible to transform our economy so that it is less resource-intensive, and to do it in ways that are equitable, with the most vulnerable protected and the most responsible bearing the bulk of the burden. Low carbon sectors of our economies can be encouraged to expand and create jobs, while high carbon sectors are encouraged to contract.[xix]"*. This is aspirational but ignores the challenges of decarbonisation like the increase in the cost of energy for the less well off. It is not backed up by numbers and the sectors which will be affected by decarbonisation are significant. It was encouraging to hear Labour MP Jess Phillips recognise that decarbonisation would affect the two biggest employers in her constituency, the airport and the motor industry, while acknowledging that there were uncertainties about which green jobs would replace them for her constituents. We need to be realistic about the loss of jobs in decarbonisation and the green jobs which will replace them. We also need to recognise that the jobs lost may be disproportionately lower skilled, and that new jobs proportionally higher skilled resulting in different effect of decarbonisation on different sectors of society. To quote the EC, *"With regards to level of skills, a move towards higher-level occupations and qualifications is expected"*. Will those with lesser qualifications therefore be left behind.

Government

Government has a difficult line to tread in managing a transition of this magnitude. Setting targets is the easy part; how to achieve those targets is the difficult part. As the scale of the change necessary becomes clear, the problem for democratic governments will be how to take us, their citizens, along with the decisions they make, and encourage us to make the decarbonisation decisions we need to make. We have seen the Gilet Jaune protests about fuel price increases and the ability of traditional or populist politicians to seize the agenda generally. It is not surprising therefore that governments seek to play down the changes which will be necessary to achieve zero carbon.

This is not a long-term strategy, however it is a short term tactic, and eventually the issues will have to be faced if the economy is to decarbonise. The next time a minister, businessperson, commentator or expert reassures you as to how easy a transition to zero carbon will be, or an advocate of the green deal talks about new jobs, try to focus on the things they are not saying about that transition...

Question Everything. And always ask for the numbers.

2 GROWTH VS SUSTAINABLE GROWTH

There is a potential conflict between growth and reducing carbon emissions which is underplayed in discussions about the transition to a low carbon or no carbon economy. In simple terms growth as we know it is a problematic unless it becomes growth in low carbon terms, so that it is sustainable growth.

"Growth" is the mantra of politicians. Governments laud it and promise it. Oppositions criticise the lack of it as a failure of the government. Very rarely does any politician make a distinction between good and bad growth or seek to describe sustainable growth. The focus is on growth (any growth) leading to an increase in living standards for us the voters. This is perfectly understandable if you focus on a short-term political cycle. The following recent quotes illustrate this:

In 2018 former **President Obama** said that he deserved more credit for the current economic landscape, telling the crowd: "By the time I left office … the economy was growing. And by the way that growth has just kept on going."
"Right now, Republicans are all 'Look the economy is so good' he said. "Where do you think that started? When did that start?"

Chancellor Merkel in November 2018 said Germany is well

positioned economically and is on course to achieve 1.8 percent growth in the coming fiscal year. She added that German policymakers would *"need to remain vigilant to ensure the country's decade of economic growth continues"* in the face of a slowing global economy.

She also lauded the country's 4.9 percent unemployment rate — the lowest since 1980. Merkel stated that economic growth was the result of German exports, which are heavily dependent on the country's mid-sized companies, and domestic policy decisions that have led to an increase in consumer spending at home. The chancellor also noted that the World Economic Forum in Davos ranked Germany the most innovative place in the world to do business.

This exchange at Prime Ministers Questions between **Corbyn and May** on Bank of England economic forecasts 27 February 2019 sums up how key

growth is in the current political debate:

Jeremy Corbyn asked the Prime Minister if "shambolic handling of Brexit, or her failed austerity policies" were to blame for growth forecasts from the Bank of England. She told the Labour leader the UK is forecast to have higher growth than Germany, before giving him a list which showed the UK economy was "fit for the future". The Brexit debate in the UK led to the charge that Brexit will make people worse off leaving the EU, and that no one voted to be poorer.

It is worth noting the mission statement of the Organisation for Economic Cooperation and Development (OECD) which repays some attention. Originally it read:

"Pursuant to Article 1 of the Convention signed in Paris on 14th December 1960, and which came into force on 30th September 1961, the Organisation for Economic Co-operation and Development (OECD) shall promote policies designed: --

*to achieve the highest sustainable economic growth and employ-
ment and a rising standard of living in Member countries, while
maintaining financial stability, and thus to contribute to the development of the world economy;"*

In the 60 years since the founding of the OECD, its mission
has changed and now includes *"environmentally friendly
'green growth' strategies"* works *"with governments to understand what drives economic, social and environmental change"*,
but also seeks to *"promote policies that will improve the economic and social well-being of people around the world"*. This is
still fundamentally predicated on growth which is hardly
surprising given its members and their government policies.

The EU has a similar Mission Statement. Again, the emphasis is on *"sustainable development based on balanced economic
growth and price stability, a highly competitive market economy
with full employment and social progress, and environmental protection"*.

I would suggest that while both these statements do make
reference to both environmental change and environmental
protection, they are still fundamentally driven by the aim of
growth, and not sustainable growth in environmental terms.
The same holds true for business. Corporates are judged on
their future earnings and on an increase in sales and earnings,
on growth per se.

The challenge in reducing carbon emissions is that it will fundamentally change the basis of growth (which we have used
to for centuries) and this will have winners as well as losers.
Altering our lifestyle in a consumerist political system is a
challenge.

Reducing Carbon Emissions – the Baseline

The targets which governments have agreed and set for themselves for reducing carbon are absolute targets with a fixed
basis in terms of both emissions and time. They are quoted in

terms of reducing emissions from the amount that existed at a fixed point in time (the baseline) with the object of achieving a percentage decline in emissions from this point of time to a date in the future (the target date).

The EU Energy Roadmap 2050 states:

"The EU has set itself a long-term goal of reducing greenhouse gas emissions by 80-95%, when compared to 1990 levels, by 2050. The Energy Roadmap 2050 explores the transition of the energy system in ways that would be compatible with this greenhouse gas reductions target while also increasing competitiveness and security of supply.

To achieve these goals, significant investments need to be made in new low-carbon technologies, renewable energy, energy efficiency, and grid infrastructure. Because investments are made for a period of 20 to 60 years, policies that promote a stable business climate which encourages low-carbon investments must start being made today."

This is a target of between 80-95% rather than a fixed target, but this is the target for the EU and at its upper end it equates to virtually removing carbon emissions in Europe in the next 30 years. The means to achieve these goals are primarily related to power generation and distribution. As will become clear, however, achieving emissions reduction targets for national and regional emissions goes beyond power into many sectors. This strategy, in the Roadmap, does not address emissions from transport, residential, aviation, maritime or agriculture.

The target is based on a baseline date (here 1990) and implicitly on the nature of the economy at that time. This is an absolute target, so during the period from the baseline to the target date, if the growth in the economy is based on carbon, it will increase emissions compared to the 1990 baseline. In other words that growth, based on carbon, increases the size of the task of reduction as the target is based on a fixed base of emissions in 1990. Growth will not increase emissions if that growth is based on non-carbon sources. Consequently, any growth based on carbon makes it more difficult to achieve the absolute target by the target date as it adds emissions to the total which need to be removed to achieve the original target.

If growth is built on carbon free economic activity, then the emissions reduction target required remains the same. To achieve this means creating additional carbon free power at least equal to growth, just to stand still in meeting carbon reduction targets.

In number terms, this requires that UK renewable power generation increases from 155 TWh (Terra Watt Hours) to either 540TWh or 645TWh depending on whether the Core of Further Ambition cases (used by the Committee on Climate Change)[xx] are used. This is an increase of 385 or 490TWh over 30 years. This means that in addition to the replacement of roughly 150 TWh consumption currently met by fossil fuels, there will be additional demand of between 230 to 335TWh from new electricity demand as the economy becomes more dependent on electricity.

Population

Population is a key driver to both economic growth and emissions. In any country an increase in population increases emissions unless it decarbonises.

Falling population should lead to a reduction in personal emissions (heating, transport etc) and to the economy becoming smaller generally if the decrease reduces the economically active population. The flip side to this is that any increase in population will increase the level of emissions particularly if it leads to an increase in the economically active population, unless it is balanced by creating additional carbon free power at least equal to the needs created by that growth in population.

Migration from one country to another, moves the problem of carbon emission reduction between countries. It may exacerbate the level of emissions both in the new country and overall, if the movement of population is from a lower emission per head country to a higher emission per head country and the migrant's emissions per head adjust to the new country level. A direct consequence of the current migration to Europe and North America will be an increase in emissions globally if the immigrant's emissions per head adjust to the new country level.

The European Investment Bank survey[xxi] shows that 41% of young Europeans, think they will have to move to another country due to climate change. If this applies within Europe, it is equally likely that young people outside Europe may think they will need to move to another country or Europe due to climate change.

If we look at World Population from 1990 to 2020, the increase will be 2,306,000,000 or an increase of 43.7%.[xxii] Even at the current levels of carbon emissions in developing countries this will have added emissions. If we assume 1 tonne per person (sub Saharan Africa is 0.8 tonne per person) then this population growth adds 2,306,000,000 tonnes per annum by 2020. At the average rate of 4.8 tonnes, the contribution of population to emissions growth is therefore 11,068,000,000 tonnes per annum.

The World Bank has reported that *"Global emissions of carbon dioxide, a major greenhouse gas and driver of climate change, increased from 22.4 billion metric tons in 1990 to 35.8 billion in 2013, a rise of 60 percent. The increase in CO2 emissions and other greenhouse gases has contributed to a rise of about 0.8 degrees Celsius in mean global temperature above pre-industrial times."*

The Scientific American reported in December 2018 that *"The scientists project that fossil-fuel-related carbon dioxide emissions will hit a record high of 37.1 billion metric tons by the end of this year."*

If we look at the parallel growth patterns of population and emissions there are similarities, between population and then emissions. Both have a take-off point in 1950 with emissions growth of 700% and population increase of 270%. This is not to suggest that population growth per se explains the growth in emissions, but that population growth does explain some of the growth in emissions. The combination of population growth and economic growth (when the geographical distribution of economic growth since 1990 under globalisation is factored in) is certainly a major contributory factor and poses the question whether the world can control emissions if it does not stabilise population? Of course, there are a number of reasons for this increase in population growth, including those religions which do not support stabilising population. If one looks at the forecasts above from the U.S. Census Bureau, International Database, future population growth will continue at a similar rate with a corresponding increase in emissions (based on per capita emissions).

The consequences of the geographical distribution of economic growth since 1990 under globalisation are also illustrated by the graph below which shows the distribution of cumulative emissions between countries/trading blocs. While the graph shows that current emissions are mainly generated outside the EU and America, the graph for cumulative data shows that if trends continue the cumulative contribution will also shift towards China, India and developing economies and away from the EU and America over time.

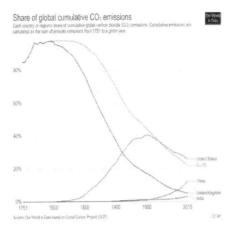

Measures to reduce emissions which do not address this consequence of current economic and population growth will not be successful in global terms. The IEA chart below shows that future growth in energy demand is almost exclusively concentrated in Asia and Africa, indeed most OECD countries will see an actual fall in primary energy demand.

The question which needs to be asked therefore is whether the current model of globalisation and global economic growth can be maintained at the same time as a restructuring to a low or zero carbon global economy? Whatever Europe does to reduce emissions will be potentially overshadowed by the actions of India, China, Africa and South East Asia.

Statistics

My first experience of the importance of the use of statistics in this question was at a meeting at the OECD in 2006. It was a meeting between government representatives and business ostensibly about emission trading systems. The meeting spent all its energy discussing which year was the best baseline year for measuring emissions and the corresponding allocation of emission trading permits. Each country present argued strongly for the date which suited their data. They saw competitive advantage in finding a baseline which reduced their need to decarbonise and unfortunately, but understandably, this continues today.

Many wonder "Are we even looking at the correct figures?" The BBC Reality Check posed the question about the fall in UK emissions after they were challenged by Greta Thunberg. UK government figures show that greenhouse gas emissions have fallen by 42% since 1990 (see Chapter 3). Ms Thunberg claimed that the true reduction was more like 10%.

The reason for the difference is that the 42% figure excludes emissions from international aviation, shipping and imports. The UK's figures refer to the UK's "territorial emissions" - that is a measure of what happens within the country's borders, including emissions associated with heating and powering homes, transport, domestic industry and agriculture.

The UK is not unique in producing figures like this. Indeed, it is using the internationally agreed standards. Reporting made to the UN under the Kyoto protocol is done on a territorial basis, excluding international aviation, shipping and imports. The UK is in effect complying with the UN standard. One may wonder if the UN have the best standard to monitor emission growth or reduction?

The Department for Environment, Food and Rural Affairs (Defra), does produce figures on "consumption emissions". This measure of emissions based on everything the UK uses, including imports, but are not used as official figures. Using this measure, the UK's estimated overall carbon footprint in 2016 was about 10% lower than in 1997 when it first published these figures.

In 2016, the UK consumed an estimated total of 784 million tonnes of carbon dioxide, more than one-and-a-half times the 468 million tonnes from territorial emissions alone. In 2017, international aviation to and from the UK was responsible for an estimated 35 million tonnes of carbon dioxide, according to the Department for Business, Energy and Industrial Strategy (BEIS). International shipping from the UK produced about 8 million tonnes. That has not changed dramatically since 1990.

What is clear, however is that consumption emissions figures are less accurate because tracking the total use of emissions through complex global supply chains is very difficult and can lead to double counting. It also means countries are measuring things they do not always control, for example, if the UK imports products from China, and China starts making things in a more carbon-intensive way, the UK's consumption emissions will go up despite consuming the same amount.

Territorial emissions should represent a clearer measure of how government is acting to tackle emissions in their territory, which it can be argued, are the emissions over which it ultimately has control. There are continuing debates about how responsibility for the emissions associated with global supply chains should be allocated between countries, particularly as many developing countries are responsible for manufacturing goods then used in developed countries.

In the end, this is an accounting and allocation issue, and both sets of figures are useful allocations of global emissions. However, a country which has a balance of payments surplus in carbon emissions due to exports, will appear to have higher emissions than one which has a balance of payments deficit. One can claim that this country is exporting or outsourcing its emissions to those countries from which it imports goods with carbon content. This is indeed the argument advanced by China.

For the purpose of this book, I have used territorial emissions and those specifically from international aviation and shipping for the section on them. I have not included consumption emissions.

Per Capita

Much is made of per capita emissions and of the carbon intensity of different countries. As the chart above on cumulative global emissions shows the rebalancing of the global economy is changing the main generators of emissions and the cumulative scorecard in terms of emissions.

While OECD countries mainly occupy the top positions of emissions per head, China is there too and in due course India is likely to join them. The key driver in emissions is economic activity and population growth so the pattern is likely to change over time.

The chart is in metric tonnes per capita. (Some measures are in metric tons (see below) some in tonnes so care needs to be taken in handling these statistics).

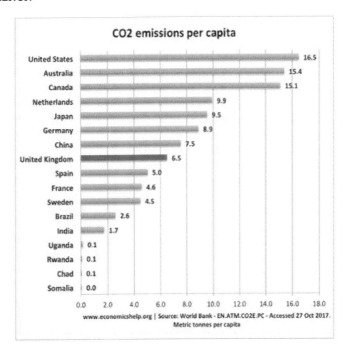

Growth is a major challenge in emission reduction

Economic growth and population growth are both contributors to emissions. To achieve the targets for emission reductions and decarbonisation in a zero-carbon scenario, the way we look at and measure growth will need to change to embrace growth focussed on low or zero carbon. The geographical distribution of economic growth and primary energy demand means the key decisions about the impact of growth on reducing carbon emissions in the next thirty years will be made in Asia.

This challenge is increased if global population continues to rise as forecast and it makes the reduction in global emissions even more difficult. Unless the economy is de-carbonised, global population growth will increase global emissions. The largest increase in population will be in Africa and Asia. While this doesn't get the UK or Europe off the hook, it does mean that their policies and actions need to be seen in the perspective of the trajectory of global emissions.

Global Population share

A letter in the Financial Times 6th May 2019 from Ali Athar posed all the right questions about how we measure growth in a world faced with the need to decarbonise and move towards sustainable development and growth. He asked "Our notion of wealth and gross domestic product is directly related to how quickly we pull natural resources out of the earth and then trash them. If I bought five cars and trashed them in a year, GDP would go up. That is true across all sectors. Fast fashion, for example, is exactly that[xxiii]." He points out that "If I bought something and did not replace it for 10 years, our economy would be poorer, but the environment safer."

This goes to the heart of the question. Unless we change our measures of value (income and growth), we will keep trashing our planet. The current notion of GDP is inconsistent with climate and ecological protection. It would be interesting to hear the views of economists on this subject."
This letter seems to sum up the enormous challenge facing us. If one of the criteria for sustainable growth is the environmental impact, then the production of short life goods or goods with built-in obsolescence is counter to sustainability. So when you hear a politician blithely say that growth is compatible with decarbonisation, we should be asking them which type of growth? If it is business as usual, they are either lying, a charlatan or a fool, as they are not discussing sustainable growth.

3 SECTORAL CHANGE

It's not about just electricity

While most of the commentary is on the quantum of emissions and emissions by country there is very little discussion of the sectoral distribution of emissions. Most people (and most politicians) either assume or create the impression that if you decarbonise electricity generation you solve the problem. But this is far from the case.

It is interesting to compare the distribution between sectors at a Global, EU and UK level to see common themes. Although the data sets are different (global 2010, EU 2016 and UK 2017) they show some similarities. In particular it is clear that Electricity (which has been the main focus of emission reduction) while significant, is not enough to achieve the emission reduction targets for 2050.

The following from www.epa.gov shows a global analysis by sector. It is from the Fifth Assessment Report to the Intergovernmental Panel on Climate Change:

Global Emissions by Economic Sector

Global greenhouse gas emissions can also be broken down by the economic activities that lead to their production.[1]

Global Greenhouse Gas Emissions by Economic Sector			
www.epa.gov			
Electricity and Heat Production			25
Agriculture, Forestry and Other Land Use			24
Buildings			6
Transportation			14
Industry			21
Other Energy			10

Source: IPCC (2014); based on global emissions from 2010. Details about the sources included in these estimates can be found in the *Contribution of Working Group III to the Fifth Assessment Report of the Intergovernmental Panel on Climate Change.*[xxiv]

The comparable figures for the EU are:

EU Sector	2016	% of Total
Energy supply	1,280.0	26%
Industry	849.0	18%
Transport	931.0	19%
Biomass	557.0	12%
Residential	575.0	12%
Agriculture	511.0	11%
Land use, land use change and forestry	-301.0	-6%
Int Aviation	148.0	3%
Int Shipping	147.0	3%
Waste management	138.0	3%
Grand Total	4,835.0	

And those for the UK:

Sector	2017	%	% reduction from 1990
Energy supply	112.6	24%	59.5
Business	80.1	17%	29.7
Transport	125.9	27%	1.7
Public	7.8	2%	42.1
Residential	66.9	15%	16.4
Agriculture	45.6	10%	15.5
Industrial processes	10.8	2%	81.9
Land use and forestry	-9.9	-2%	3763.9
Waste management	20.3	4%	69.5
Grand Total	460.2		42.1

47

Unfortunately, in addition to different year sets, there are differences in the analysis of sectors (both inconsistencies are problems which seems to bedevil emissions statistics, one set of data would be welcome), but despite this, although these data sets are not directly comparable, some broad trends emerge.

Energy supply accounts for approximately 25% of emissions in the EU and UK and data from the OECD shows that this is consistent with their members who are developed economies. The figures for countries at different stages of economic development will obviously differ.

The other significant sectors in terms of emissions are transport, business/industry, residential and agriculture.

In terms of trends, the overall picture is that more regulated areas like energy supply, business/industry and waste management have declined the most, while those which are more consumer orientated have shown much smaller falls in emissions. Despite this, politicians continue to steer the public towards the idea that business is the sector which needs to reduce emissions. The Financial Times reported Ed Davey, Lib Dem Treasury spokesperson and former environment minister as stating : *"The party would introduce regulations to force companies and financial institutions to be transparent about their carbon investments and legislation requiring them to say how their business strategy moves them towards net zero carbon."* [xxv]

Transport has shown the smallest fall. Agriculture struggles with emissions around meat production and housing in the UK is largely based on gas as the fuel for heating. Politicians rarely suggest the same strictures for consumers as they do for Industry and Business.

To quote Jonathon Ford in the Financial Times:

"The first thing is that this war will not be won in Britain, or even

Europe and the US. Almost all emissions growth is in developing countries, where the priorities are understandably weighted towards economic development. Indeed, our own approach to decarbonisation has deactivated some levers we could have pulled. So, we have cut our own emissions by outsourcing production to cheaper, more emitting locations in the developing world. What is needed now is a different approach. Some sort of carbon tariff would be a more effective mechanism for driving down CO2 — either by repatriating production to developed countries or establishing equivalent environmental standards in middle-income ones (as the price of tariff-free access). It would not have to apply to everything; just energy intensive industries, such as steel and petrochemicals. After all, we are presently in the daft position of subsidising domestic players in these sectors to keep them from shutting down.

Second, we need to accept we have not yet got the technologies to get to the desired destination. That means a smarter approach to using public money. We have spent a lot on existing technologies that can help but will not ultimately solve the problem, such as offshore wind and solar panels. About 20 per cent of electricity bills go towards legacy subsidy costs, a significant burden for poorer households (and one that fuels a brand of populist politics that is hostile to environmentalism). We need to de-link spending from corporate interests, and fund more R&D in promising but as-yet-uncracked areas such as hydrogen, nuclear and solar film. None may come off, but if just one did it would give us much more bang for the buck. Haste would only make sense if we genuinely did not have time. But although the UN's Intergovernmental Panel on Climate Change has become more insistent in its pressure for action, it has yet to truncate its timetable drastically. Extinction Rebellion is in one sense a mirror of the climate change "deniers" in rejecting expert opinion, albeit pushing in the opposite direction. Given the complexity of the problem, going off scientific piste makes little sense.

Lastly, there is the charge that democratic systems are too conflicted to take action. Sure, decarbonisation will be costly — which requires politicians to have the guts to spell out the price to achieve the benefit. But history shows we can move fast when we need to. After the oil shock in the 1970s, Sweden responded by building a fleet of nuclear reactors that cut emissions per capita by 75 per cent in just 16 years. Would an unaccountable regime do better? Who knows, but melancholy experience suggests otherwise. All too often, environmental degradation and authoritarian politics have gone hand in hand."[xxvi]

What is clear is that any attempt to reach zero carbon, will require more than regulation by government or pricing mechanisms for emissions. One of the most obstinate sectors in terms of not reducing emissions is transport and that is already subject to levels of taxation (albeit in the form of fuel duty) which far exceed any proposed level of carbon tax. Yet despite these levels of taxation, people still buy petrol and diesel to drive. It is reducing emissions in transport, residential and agriculture which will provide the greatest challenge because the reduction of these emissions will be down to consumer decisions and will affect the costs which consumers bear.

Brexit and the reaction to the problems identified in a "No Deal" scenario illustrate that people worry about not being able to enjoy what they are used to. In no deal it is food imports from Europe, etc. The sectoral change required to move to zero carbon will raise all these issues about coping with change. The second part of this book looks in detail at the scope of these changes and how they will affect our lifestyle which is currently based on a carbon economy.

How do these sectors change to zero carbon?

All those sectors which depend on carbon to facilitate their products will not transform easily into low or zero carbon businesses. The travel business is based on carbon (aviation, shipping, cars, buses and some trains) and is a significant sector of economic activity (it is estimated that tourism is 10% of global GDP) as Chapter 17 shows. But it is not just about planes, etc, it's about hotels, restaurants and ancillary services like tours, conferences, etc, which depend on air travel based on carbon. If carbon is properly priced for aviation, what effect will this have on global tourism?

UK residential emissions are largely related to gas, and to a lesser extent oil. As we move away from these carbon fuels the business built around them will diminish. In parallel to electric cars, electric heating has a much lower service requirement than gas heating (just look at an electric boiler or an air source heat pump compared to a gas boiler). Think about how many times you see an electricity service engineer compared to a gas service engineer. Moving to air source heat pumps or ground source heat pumps requires a different set of technical skills (plumbers can't service these pumps without further training). These changes will affect the businesses which service gas and the employment which gas requires in its import, distribution and maintenance.

As the chapters on agriculture and land use shows, the changes here will be significant and require new skill sets and employment patterns if the benefits of forestation are to be realised. Forestry will become a growth sector in UK employment if the target of 3 billion additional trees is to be met and will require a training programme for the new jobs. Agriculture will need to weather the calls created to reduce or remove meat and dairy products as a business sector.

Whichever way you add them up, all sectors will need to change significantly in a very short timescale if, zero carbon in 2050 is to be achieved. The arithmetic means that while there are further steps to reduce carbon, there is no easy route to zero carbon and difficult choices will need to be made over a short period of time by governments, business, organisations and citizens. It also means that the distribution of those changes will relate to the significance of carbon either directly or indirectly in an economy, country, or region. The decline of the UK Coal industry in the last decades of the twentieth century had major effects in former coal mining areas, but over the country as a whole, the effects were not significant. Moving to zero carbon will lead to a similar pattern where some areas suffer major impacts.

The other question is which businesses will lead the change to zero carbon. The oil industry is trying to reinvent itself as either the gas industry or the renewable energy industry. This is possible; Danish energy company DONG Energy decided to change its name in 2017, following the completion of the sale of its upstream oil and gas business, which marked the company's exit from the oil and gas business overall. Danish Oil & Gas (DONG) become Orested the business leader in wind turbines (see chapter 7). Can the oil industry follow this path when the comparative size of its existing business is so much greater than its renewable power interests. DONG was a small national oil company not one used to global power which big oil has exercised. Also, can big oil transform itself to what is primarily a local business with a significant customer interface – which is the nature of the electricity business.

Car making is another interesting sector. Why should carbon car manufacturers have an advantage in producing electric cars where the power system (the battery) is made outside their control. An internal combustion engine car has more than two thousand parts in its drivetrain, compared to around twenty in an electric vehicle. The resulting change for parts supply both to manufacturers and for spare parts will be dramatic with corresponding decreases in employment. It is interesting to look at the comparable recent history in another sector. In 2000 IBM was the third most valuable brand with a value of $53bn. Fast forward to 2018, and its value has fallen to $43bn and its position declined to twelth. It has been overtaken by companies involved in software, the internet etc (Google, Amazon, Apple, Microsoft. One wonders if is this a parallel for carbon to electric cars?

While the proponents of the Green Deal emphasise the positive, they also need to recognise the impact of the negatives and the change involved. A decarbonised economy will look very different to what we have now. The stock market will reflect declining carbon share prices if zero carbon bites. This will affect pension funds and share or stock investments.

However, if there are countries which do not follow new investment policies for low carbon, then the investment in carbon power sources will continue to be attractive in terms of returns, even if it is risky in terms of longevity so there will be carbon investment opportunities. Larger companies may exit due to reputational concerns and investor and ngo pressure, but private capital may still invest in carbon. Carbon investment will continue while there is still a demand for carbon fuels, particularly from Asia.

Unless there is some global agreement, it is unlikely that zero carbon will be global by 2050 or even 2080, however much the UK and Europe pursues this goal. This will cause instability in business planning.

4 GEO-POLITICAL CONSEQUENCES

Carbon Wealth at Risk

Wealth at risk

Fossil-fuel-rich developing countries face a drop in demand for their oil, gas, and coal reserves if the world succeeds in reducing use of carbon-emitting products.

Sources: BP Statistical Review 2015; and authors' calculations.
Note: Fossil-fuel-rich developing countries are in red. These are developing countries in which the value of fossil fuel production is 10 percent or more of GDP or the value of fossil fuel reserves is 25 percent or more of a country's national wealth.

Most commentaries on climate change focus on the winners

not the losers of decarbonisation. What they don't focus on, however, are the consequences of these changes in Geo-Political terms on the losers. The changes which will occur in the world economy with the decline of hydrocarbons and the political consequences of this decline at a regional, national, and local level on those countries which have significant carbon wealth. Clearly, the primary outcomes of decarbonisation leading to the reduction of carbon wealth relate to the oil, gas and coal revenues for the owners. There is a further impact on the GDP of countries, on their balance of payments and government revenue, at the national, state and local levels. This obviously has an impact on their ability to provide public services.

But there are also secondary consequences for those businesses whose sales have a large petro-dollar component (oil & gas) or are made to coal rich economies. As those carbon economies adjust to reduced sales of carbon products, and their carbon wealth is as a result reduced, the purchases of those economies will decline. If they are a significant market for goods and services, then the providers of those goods and services will also suffer.

The loss of sales revenues, export earnings and government revenues will all impact on the political and social stability of carbon rich states. This potential instability may also lead to consequences for neighbouring states if the fall in oil, gas and coal revenue leads to instability in their hydrocarbon rich neighbours. Although not related to decarbonisation, the effect of instability in Venezuela on its neighbours and of Syria on both Jordan and Lebanon are recent examples of such instability contagion. As a result, it is possible that the spread of political and social instability could encompass both carbon rich states and a significant contagion zone around them.

The map from BP Statistical Review (above) is of Fossil fuel rich developing countries, it does not include Saudi Arabia and the Gulf states. Based on this analysis, only North America, Europe and Australia as regions will not directly be affected by any contagion (although Australia has issues given the role carbon plays in its economy).

The obvious consequences are that those countries which have a high percentage of fuel exports as a percentage of merchandise exports, will suffer economically over time. Their balance of payments will deteriorate with probable decline in their currency exchange rate leading to inflationary pressures. These countries span the Middle East, Africa, South America, and Asia.

The following chart shows the issue in terms of oil rent as % of GDP. Oil rent is the value extracted by the state from oil production. It includes all payments that the government receives for the exploitation of the resource including permit payments, royalties, taxes and oil entitlement. Any country with an oil rent over 10% of GDP will find adjustment very difficult given the effect on government spending, unless, like Norway, an Investment fund has been set up to accumulate Hydrocarbon revenues for the state to be used for the benefit of the state.

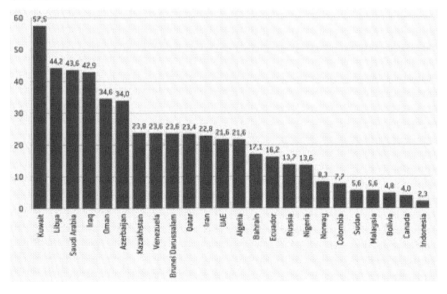

Source: Breugel

Aside from the Gulf region, there are implications for Libya, Algeria and Nigeria in Africa, Venezuela and Ecuador in South America and Azerbaijan, Russia, and Kazakhstan.

But it is not just oil producing countries which will be affected. oil and gas distribution infrastructure will decline with the decline of oil and gas in international trade. As examples, both the Netherlands and Singapore will suffer. The Netherlands as the entre port for Europe and Singapore as the entre port for Asia. Both have a significant part of their respective economies based on hydrocarbons. Global shipping will be affected in the longer term as discussed below.

It is not just oil producing countries that will be affected, but also countries that export gas both as gas and as Liquified Natural Gas (LNG). Russia's is the largest exporter of natural gas and its economy benefits from gas exports to Europe. If that flow of gas diminishes as Europe decarbonises, then the Russian economy will decline with effects on GDP, exports, currency and government revenues. In addition, the leverage which Russia currently exercises over its customers in Europe and the Ukraine will diminish. The second largest producer of Gas is Qatar which will be similarly impacted.

If we consider how significant hydrocarbon producing countries have been in geo-political terms in the period since the Second World War, it would be surprising if their economic decline did not lead to tensions. Over time, US, UK, Europe, Russia and lately China have directed foreign policy in the Middle East towards protecting their respective access to oil, given its crucial role in the global economy. The 2015 film Bitter Lake by Adam Curtis traces the twists and turns of the relationship between the USA and Saudi Arabia since the meeting of King Ibn Saud and President Roosevelt on the USS Quincy in 1945. Oil has dominated US foreign policy during that period. In thinking about Russian gas, one might question whether

European sanctions against Russia would have been stronger if Europe had not been dependent on Russian gas?

Figure 7. Russia's natural gas exports by destination, 2016

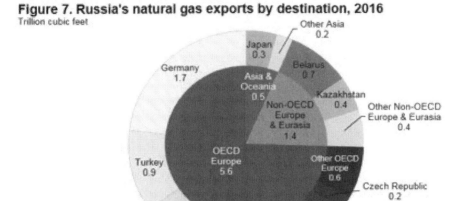

Trillion cubic feet

Source: U.S. Energy Information Administration, based on Russian export statistics and partner country import statistics, Global Trade Tracker

In due course the significance of carbon economies in diplomacy and foreign policy, may diminish but it is unlikely to be a smooth transition on the road to zero carbon.

There is a secondary economic consequence in terms of the current importance of Petro dollars in sectors such as defence procurement and luxury consumer goods. As an example, BAE systems makes just under a fifth of its sales to the Middle East. It is difficult to quantify the percentage of sales to Petro dollar countries in the luxury consumer goods sector but it is clear that there are significant sales for LVHM and other groups. In each case a new market will need to replace such sales.

If we look at coal a similar pattern emerges.

The producer countries most at risk are the top six countries in the chart by value.

Major Coal IMPORTING Countries 2017		
Country	Value $m.	World %
Japan	22,900	17.5
China	18,500	14.1
India	15,200	11.6
South Korea	15,100	11.5
Taiwan	6,800	5.3
Germany	5,900	4.5
Netherlands	5,600	4.3
Turkey	3,900	3.0
Brazil	3,400	2.6
Ukraine	2,700	2.1
Malaysia	2,500	1.9
France	2,200	1.7
Spain	1,860	1.4
Italy	1,850	1.4
Poland	1,500	1.2
TOTALS:	109,910	84.1

Major Coal EXPORTING Countries 2017		
Country	Value $m.	World %
Australia	40,600	36.6
Indonesia	17,900	16.1
Russia	13,500	12.2
U.S.A	9,900	8.9
Colombia	6,800	6.2
South Africa	5,700	5.2
Canada	5,100	4.6
Netherlands	4,100	3.7
Mongolia	2,200	2.0
China	1,100	1.0
Poland	816	0.7
Kazakistan	445	0.4
North Korea	404	0.4
Philippines	337	0.3
Czech Republic	332	0.3
TOTALS:	109,234	98.6

"Coal is expected to become Australia's most valuable export for the first time in nine years in fiscal 2018 ending June this year, as increasing concentration in the mining industry pushes up prices and exports to China and other countries in Asia rise"[xxvii].

Coal is 19.3% of Australia's exports[xxviii] Removing these exports would turn Australia's balance of payments negative from their current positive position. The largest export for Indonesia is Coal and Lignite at 11.5%[xxix]. Russia has 4.7% of exports from coal. In total its carbon exports are roughly 55% of exports by value[xxx]. In Colombia, 20% of exports are coal, only exceeded by Oil at 27%[xxxi].

These are significant numbers for all the countries involved and the effect on government revenues, economic activity and balance of payments will be pronounced. These numbers have to be aggregated with other carbon exports to measure the full exposure for each country to carbon exports.

But there is also an issue for major coal importing countries. If we look at the dependence of Japan, China, India and South

Korea on coal imports, the problem with zero carbon is replacing coal with zero carbon power generation. Given the role that these countries play in the current globalised economy, these changes may lead to a slowdown in the global economy. The level of investment required to replace coal powered generation for these countries will be enormous.

To focus on countries is only half the story. Natural resource distribution means that sub national areas (states, provinces, etc) are often dependent on carbon more than the country within which they sit. Consider the coal producing states of the US, New South Wales and Queensland in Australia, South Sumatra and Kalimantan in Indonesia. The US provides a good example in terms of Wyoming.

While coal in the US is in decline, Wyoming demonstrates how dependent states or provinces have been and are. Using 2012 figures coal provided 12% of gross state product, 9.3% of labour income, 5.9% of employment and 12% of government revenues. *"Wyoming has one of the lowest tax burdens in the nation. In Wyoming, the extractive industries play a major role in generating revenues for state and local governments. In fact, it is estimated that minerals directly contribute roughly two-thirds of the State's revenue."*[xxxii]

"Wyoming state government gets money from coal in four primary ways. Companies pay severance taxes to Wyoming on the coal they remove from the ground. Roughly half the federal mineral royalties paid to Washington D.C. on the coal owned by the federal government, returns to Wyoming. Then there are coal lease bonuses — lump sum payments the state receives on the sale of new coal leases. Finally, revenue comes from ad valorem taxes, a form of property tax paid at the county level, but which is redistributed throughout the state. In 2012, according to that math, Wyoming collected approximately $586 million in coal from federal lands. Coal's contribution made up 72 percent of the $809 million total Wyoming collected in federal mineral royalty money that year. In 2018, Wyoming collected only approximately $202 million in coal

royalties. The drop in collections of $384 million put the state at a level last seen in 2005."[xxxiii]

WyoFile goes on to state: *"Coal's dwindling prospects carry dire impacts for Wyoming workers and towns. Coal company bankruptcies impact workers' retirement and health care benefits. Mine and plant closures are an even larger threat that could dry up livelihoods for Wyoming families and put entire communities dependent on coal jobs at risk. For state government coffers, coal's decline is a slower-moving catastrophe. But the decline has already had an enormous impact and will leave lasting change, lawmakers and analysts say. Wyoming pays for state government — everything from public schools and road maintenance to public health and the criminal justice system — primarily with revenue collected from the oil, gas and coal industries. Of those three, coal has been both the stable bedrock — not prone to the up-and-down swings of the oil and gas markets — and at times the largest contributor.*"[xxxiv]

This pattern would apply to many carbon resource rich states in the US or states and provinces elsewhere. The problem for these countries is how to replace the government revenue from carbon sources over time while maintaining public services. Whilst Wyoming is an extreme example, the issue is generic and those who trumpet a green deal dividend fail to discuss the issues which the absence of carbon revenue will produce at both national and local level.

In geo-political terms the changes which will arise when countries which consume carbon no longer have to secure fuel supplies, will have an effect both on the diplomatic balance between countries and regions with large carbon resources and the defence needs of countries more generally. The major powers including China, the US, Russia and Europe will need to reassess their defence spending and purpose in the light of the new world order a decarbonised economy produces. The adjustment necessary, particularly in the transitional phase as carbon declines in the world economy, will provide multiple new challenges.

Shipping Carbon

Shipping carbon is a major part of the global shipping business. Using UN figures for 2017, the total of all trade shipped globally was 10,702 million tons. Of this, crude oil, petroleum products and gas total 3,146 million tons and coal 1,208 million tons, a total for carbon of 4,354 million tons or 40% of world shipping by weight. The obvious consequence in a zero-carbon world is that international freight shipping reduces by 40%. The emissions associated with it will decline correspondingly.

In the meantime the demand for shipping in the future will be both smaller and influenced by factors such as the pace of decarbonization and electrification to drive the energy transition, new fossil fuel production methods such as hydraulic fracturing, increasing liquefaction of natural gas (LNG), regional shifts in fossil-fuel demand and supply, and geopolitical changes. These changes to international shipping will have consequences for all the major shipping hubs (what happens to oil terminals, etc if oil is not being shipped?).

The New Oil – Zero Carbon minerals

While a zero-carbon world will remove the geo-political issues relating to oil & gas over time, it will make the world more dependent on other natural resources. The focus will shift to those minerals which are important in the electricity business and in applications which use electricity like batteries.

Battery dependence on cobalt is discussed in the Chapter 11. Electricity currently uses copper in transmission. But this underestimates the importance of new minerals. The seven key minerals for wind, solar and batteries are nickel, lithium, cobalt, copper, graphite, aluminium and vanadium. As an example, a 3Mw wind turbine contains up to 4.7 tons of copper. To build a Mw of wind power offshore takes 21,607 lbs of copper – 9.6 tons. A carbon car has 48 lbs of copper, but an electric battery car has 183 lbs – nearly four times as much.

Where these minerals are in short supply, control of that supply will be important. It would be wrong to dismiss the possibility that these minerals could lead to the same sort of geo-political tensions that oil has caused. No doubt we may be hearing more about the Democratic Republic of the Congo in the future given its dominance in the supply of cobalt. Some sectors of the Mining Industry will become more significant and higher profile, and governments will need to focus on securing supply of key minerals. Ironically then, a zero-carbon world will actually need mining more than a carbon one.

Power as a domestic political issue

The other consequence of the decarbonisation of power is that the global energy business will be in retreat. For a long period, fuel supply has been a global business with oil, coal and gas (in liquified form) able to be supplied anywhere in the global market. Sophisticated financial instruments have been developed to facilitate this efficiently such as swap arrangements which allow producers to supply a competitor's product to a customer while supplying their own product to the competitor's customer where transport costs are high. Hedging the price of these commodities is a major financial business for businesses. The public doesn't question where our fuel and power come from, and the arrangements to facilitate this; we just expect it to be delivered to us. Attitudes to Russian gas in Europe is a good example, whatever the doubts about Russia, Europe still buys the gas primarily because of the need for that fuel and power. Similarly, while there are objections to arms sales to Saudi Arabia, oil is still bought from the Saudis.

As we become less reliant on hydrocarbons, we inevitably

become more reliant on the energy we produce either domestically or from our immediate neighbours. Electricity is not a global business, due to transmission loss issues. To state the obvious, you can't ship electricity around the world like oil or coal. As a result, zero carbon fuel markets will be national or regional, their size determined by the transmission loss issues. The U.S. Energy Information Administration (EIA) estimates that electricity transmission and distribution (T&D) losses average about 5% of the electricity that is transmitted and distributed annually in the United States (2013-2017). This figure is low as coal can be shipped by train to power stations close to demand. The US will face a challenge in replicating this model in a zero-carbon electricity system. "In the UK Energy is lost during transportation from production to consumption. Electricity distribution losses on average account for 8% of transported volumes and vary between 3.1% to 10%".[xxxv]

The UK in part relies on subsea interconnector cables. These link Great Britain to France, Ireland, the Netherlands and Northern Ireland. These links, total 4 gigawatts (GW), and represent around 5% of the UK's existing electricity generation capacity. The Anglo/French Inter-connector (2GW to France), the Brit-Ned Inter-connector (1GW to the Netherlands), the Moyle Inter-connector (500MW to Northern Ireland) and the East-West Inter-connector (500MW to the Republic of Ireland). Interconnector technology currently limits the effective length of interconnectors to 1500km due to transmission losses.

As a result, our perspective on power will become more local/regional as the ability to transmit electricity over long distances is limited and finite. Another consequence of this, is that electricity generation and the security of electricity generation and supply becomes more important as electricity becomes the key power source. As it assumes the key role in power, it also becomes the responsibility of national government. The process to provide that power becomes more transparent to citizens; power, in effect, becomes a domestic political issue because electricity becomes the dominant fuel source in zero carbon. No longer can changes in price be blamed on foreign interests, or supply failures be blamed on other country suppliers. Ensuring supply becomes government responsibility either directly or through regulation.

Like decisions about land use that need to be made with regard to tree planting (see Chapter 14), decisions about increased electricity generation capacity need to be made sooner rather than later. Those decisions may require citizens to accept changes to our landscape to enable larger, secure electricity production from new plants, the most obvious ones being onshore wind, solar, biomass plants, nuclear power stations and hydro schemes big and small.

While globalised trade will continue, the globalised trade in energy will decline as electricity assumes a larger role, leading to winners and losers in terms of power supply dependent on location. A country's power generation capacity will depend on its natural resources (both above and below ground). The UK appears to be in a good position given its resources of wind (particularly offshore), together with the transmission distances not being long either offshore or onshore. Not all countries will be in such a fortunate position; the issues for large countries may be significant due to transmission losses (Argentina faces problems with its hydro assets being situated in the Andes a long way from its metropolitan centres of demand for electricity).

Conclusion

The changes in the geo-political landscape will be profound as decarbonisation occurs. Trade in goods and services will continue, but energy will become a national or regional issue. The global trade in hydrocarbons will slowly come to an end.

The impact on hydrocarbon rich countries and states will

be dramatic. There will be an uncomfortable transition for hydrocarbon rich countries with implications for the services they can provide to their citizens. The instability that will result, may impact on their neighbours.

One of the current drivers of foreign policy, oil, will decline as access to hydrocarbons becomes less important. The instability caused by the decline in government revenues for hydrocarbon rich states could lead to regional contagion and cross border tensions.

One might start to wonder that if oil is not a driver of US or Chinese foreign policy, what will those policies look like?

5 COAL

Coal's decline

In February 2019 the closure of Cottam Power station in Nottinghamshire became the latest step in the decline of the UK coal industry, following that of three other plants in 2016. Only six coal-fired power stations are now operational in the UK, and coal has declined from being the country's principal energy source in 2014, to being sixth on the list. Coal was responsible for less than 10 per cent of Britain's power output in 2018, behind gas, nuclear, wind, imports, and biomass. The scale and size of this change is remarkable. But it is in consultancy terms "low hanging fruit" – an easy to achieve change as gas has been substituted for coal. The next steps in removing carbon are more difficult.

UK emissions from Coal in 2017 were 25.5 MtCO2 (6%) of the total compared to 180 MtCO2 in 1990. Coal is being gradually eliminated from the UK power mix. It is the black sheep of carbon reduction for the simple reason that it produces more carbon per British Thermal Unit (BTU) than other fuels. To quote the US Energy Information Agency (EIA):

"The amount of heat emitted during coal combustion depends largely on the amounts of carbon, hydrogen, and oxygen present in the coal and, to a lesser extent, on the sulfur content. Hence, the ratio of carbon to heat content depends on these heat-producing components of coal, and these components vary by coal rank.

Carbon, by far the major component of coal, is the principal source of heat, generating about 14,500 British thermal units (Btu) per pound. The typical carbon content for coal (dry basis) ranges from more than 60 per cent for lignite to more than 80 per cent for anthracite. Although hydrogen generates about 62,000 Btu per pound, it accounts for only 5 percent or less of coal and not all of this is available for heat because part of the hydrogen combines with oxygen to form water vapor. The higher the oxygen content of coal, the lower its heating value. This inverse relationship occurs because oxygen in the coal is bound to the carbon and has, there-fore, already partially oxidized the carbon, decreasing its ability to generate heat. The amount of heat contributed by the combustion of sulfur in coal is relatively small, because the heating value of sulfur is only about 4,000 Btu per pound, and the sulfur content of coal generally averages 1 to 2 percent by weight. Consequently, vari-ations in the ratios of carbon to heat content of coal are due pri-marily to variations in the hydrogen content.

The carbon dioxide emission factors in this article are expressed in terms of the energy content of coal as pounds of carbon dioxide per million Btu. Carbon dioxide (CO_2) forms during coal combustion when one atom of carbon (C) unites with two atoms of oxygen (O) from the air. Because the atomic weight of carbon is 12 and that of oxygen is 16, the atomic weight of carbon dioxide is 44. Based on that ratio, and assuming complete combustion, 1 pound of carbon combines with 2.667 pounds of oxygen to produce 3.667 pounds of carbon dioxide. For example, coal with a carbon content of 78 percent and a heating value of 14,000 Btu per pound emits about 204.3 pounds of carbon dioxide per million Btu when completely burned. Complete combustion of 1 short ton (2,000 pounds) of this coal will generate about 5,720 pounds (2.86 short tons) of car-bon dioxide." [xxxvi]

Again, it produces some nasty products during combustion:
"Sulphur dioxide (SO2), which contributes to acid rain and respiratory illnesses. Nitrogen oxides (NOx), which contribute to smog and respiratory illnesses. Particulates, which contribute to smog, haze, and respiratory illnesses and lung disease. Carbon di-oxide (CO2), which is the primary greenhouse gas produced from

burning fossil fuels (coal, oil, and natural gas). Mercury and other heavy metals, which have been linked to both neurological and developmental damage in humans and other animals. Fly ash and bottom ash, which are residues created when power plants burn coal." [xxxvii]

Coal has been a part of British life for centuries. In 1970 the National Coal Board employed 700,000 people in the UK coal industry. It has been a part of my family history too. My grandfather was a coal miner cutting 17 tons of coal a day by hand in County Durham and my mother a coal miner's daughter. I myself went down a deep pit coal mine in Derbyshire in 1970 and ended up working for a mining company which was one of the largest producers of coal globally in the 1990s but which has sold all its steam coal assets in response to the trajectory of carbon. It is hardly surprising that the UK is removing all coal from the power mix by 2025 given carbon dioxide and other outputs.

However, the picture in Europe is a tale of two Europes, to quote IEA:

"Western Europe is accelerating its coal exit – action on climate change and air pollution, combined action to specifically phase out coal-fired power generation, are all impacting coal demand. Along with the expansion of renewables, these policy efforts will eventually push coal out the Western European power mix." (with the exception of Spain and Germany where it is "under discussion").

"By contrast, most countries in Eastern Europe have not announced phase-out policies and a handful of new coal power plants are under construction in Poland, Greece and the Balkans. Some countries in Eastern Europe are among the few places in the world where lignite remains the cornerstone of the electricity system." [xxxviii]

Surprisingly, some European countries have high coal shares in power generation. Denmark's share is 30%, Netherlands 35%, Germany 45% and Poland 80%. This is also reflected in consumption around the world.

Global Coal

And yet, as shown below, we don't appear to have reached peak global coal production as this chart shows.

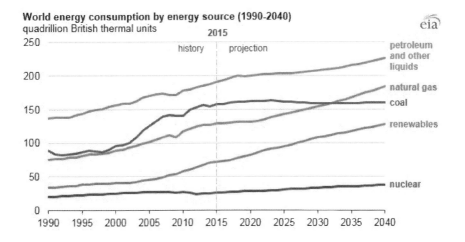

In world power terms while global coal energy consumption levels off, the EIA forecast that it will still be more significant than global renewables in 2040, and all three carbon fuels will exceed renewables with both petroleum and natural gas with increasing consumption.

In BP's "Evolving Transition scenario", global coal consumption broadly stagnates around current levels, with falls in China and OECD countries offset by gains in India and other emerging Asian countries. This is in sharp contrast to the past 20 years or so when coal was the largest source of energy growth.

BP reported that in 2019, however, that Coal consumption actually grew by 1.4%, double its 10-year average growth. Consumption growth was led by India (36 million tons oil equivalent (mtoe)) and China (16 mtoe). OECD demand fell to its lowest level since 1975. Coal's share in primary energy fell to

27.2%, its lowest in fifteen years. Global coal production rose by 162 mtoe, or 4.3%, with China (82 mtoe) and Indonesia (51 mtoe) providing the largest increments.

"The global market for coal continues to be dominated by China, where coal consumption falls for much of the Outlook as the economy adjusts to a more balanced, sustainable pattern of growth. The weakness in global coal consumption is compounded by significant falls in the OECD, as countries switch to cleaner, lower-carbon fuels. In contrast, coal demand within India and other emerging Asian economies increases. India is the largest growth market for coal, with its share of global coal consumption more than doubling to around a quarter in 2040. The majority of the increase in coal consumption in India and other developing Asian countries is used to meet robust growth in power demand as these economies grow and prosperity increases. The potential trade-off is between the growth of power demand and the ability to decarbonize the power sector as this power demand increases." [xxxix]

This illustrates the dilemna of zero carbon. Coal consumption will continue to increase in global terms largely driven by Asian demand and in particular India. What the UK has already done is dwarfed by this increase in demand by India, doubling in the period to 2040. While Europe removes coal, Asian demand increases so more coal will be mined. This poses the question as to whether the UK and other countries should be changing if other countries do not? Given the qualities of coal described above, the answer has to be yes. The UK has shown a successful transition away from coal to date.

Conclusion - The end of coal in the UK, but not the World

Those who think that coal is finished in global terms are wrong, reports of its demise are premature. It is in the UK. The closure of the last coal plant in 2025 will occur due to regulations which limit the carbon that plants can emit to 450g CO_2 per KW hour, which could only be met by installing carbon capture and storage (CCS) equipment. No operator is currently considering using CCS for coal plants, the focus of the fledgling CCS industry having switched to capturing emissions from industrial plants and biomass power stations.

Coal should be a model for the future of gas. Coal is the first carbon fuel to be squeezed out of the UK energy mix. The logical course is that other carbon fuels will follow (unless CCS is operational for them). Gas too needs to follow this trajectory, if the UK is to remove carbon from power. The question is over what timescale will it follow coal's decline?

Coal companies are now only an investment if the market into which they sell is not reducing coal fired power generation, and predominantly if their long-term customer base is in Asia. Logically, the same trajectory will apply to the oil and gas sector as carbon fuels are squeezed out of power supplies in Europe. Carbon fuel producers will be competing to supply the Asian market as Europe decarbonises. Until the market in India turns, there will still be profitable investments in mining coal which can be transported to these markets at a competitive price. The world will go on burning coal while there are countries which still use coal for power generation.

How should countries seeking to reduce carbon respond to the continued use of coal for power generation when those countries are removing coal in their power mix? Some argue that they should apply tariffs to those which do not reduce emissions in future negotiations on the shared responsibilities for tacking climate change. Currently the EU has a not insubstantial problem with this argument given that its eastern members are not removing coal from their power mix. Having said that, India's cumulative emissions are growing rapidly so that in the 2020s, it will overtake the cumulative emissions of Russia and in due course the EU. Coal is still very "big" in the world. While it is, carbon may become the basis for trade wars of the future. (See Chapter 20)

6 OIL AND GAS

UK Oil & Gas Emissions

Oil & Gas			
Oil & Gas	1990	2017	Reduction (Increase)
Petroleum	202.4	152.4	25%
Gas	146.7	184.1	-26%

UK Domestic Power Use

UK Domestic power use		
Million tonnes oil equivalent		
	Domestic	% of Total
Coal	0.6	1%
Gas	25.5	63%
Oil	2.5	6%
Electricity	9.1	23%
Bioenergy	2.5	6%
Total	40.2	
Domestic as % of Total emissions	28%	

The table on UK domestic power use above shows how large an issue gas is in the UK's pursuit of decarbonisation. It is 63% of domestic power use. Gas has replaced coal to reduce emissions, but it will in turn need to be replaced to reduce emissions itself. **The emissions from gas have increased by 26% since 1990.**

Oil and gas are a large part of most investor's portfolios, when looking at the FTSE 100 or any other major stock market index, but in the world of decarbonisation how long will this last? The Financial Time's Lex column summed up the difference between oil and gas – "Thanks to climate change, the dash for gas now comes with a whiff of the odour of sanctity." Perhaps we will see the oil industry rebranding itself as the gas industry. Despite the credentials of gas as the least worst carbon fuel in carbon emissions, however, to describe it as the best is inappropriate. In a decarbonised world, gas has no future without carbon capture and storage (CCS).

UK Oil & Gas Emissions		% of Total
Petroleum	152.4	33%
Gas	184.1	40%
Total	460.222766	

This encapsulates the dilemma for policy makers. We have become more dependent on gas with the first stage of decarbonisation as the switch from coal to gas has been made, but how do we remove gas from the energy supply over the next 30 years? The table above shows that gas is the carbon fuel whose emissions have increased most since 1990, despite the change from coal to gas having reduced emissions overall but.

UK oil & gas emissions as % of UK total emissions

Gas is now 40% of the total of UK emissions and accounts for 63% of UK Domestic power use. These are large numbers and show how great the task is to remove gas from the fuel mix, unless it is replaced by biogas. The challenge for the UK and other countries (the share of **natural gas** in EU primary energy consumption in 2016 was 23.9 %), is how to wean the economy off gas.

This is an urgent issue given the size of gas's share of emissions. The average life of a gas-powered power station is 25 to 30 years, so decisions taken now to build gas-powered power stations mean they will be coming to the end of their life in 2050 (when the emissions target means they need to be out of commission). One could view new gas-powered power as part of a useful transition to 2050 when new technology will take over. However, given average life, should we be building new gas-powered power stations beyond 2025? It is at best questionable, but the answer is probably not if the zero-carbon target is serious.

The other problem for the UK, is the dominance of gas in domestic heating with a 63% share. The UK government has announced that from 2025, new homes will not be permitted to use gas as a heating source. The bigger problem, however, is existing gas heating systems in current dwellings. They will come to the end of their life (boiler life is roughly 10 years) but existing small-bore central heating pipes are not compatible with air or ground pump source heating (they need bigger bore pipes to establish an ambient temperature). A proportion of the existing housing stock will therefore need costly retrofitting.

The gas lobby has been very successful so far in promoting gas as the easiest step to carbon reduction and with the budgets of the oil industry major players this is hardly surprising. But the key word is reduction not elimination, as replacing coal reduces emissions. Gas currently plays a key role in base load power generation ensuring that it meets demand when renewable power dips. As such it competes with nuclear as the provider of base load power. Some commentators assert that gas will be much cheaper than nuclear and indeed figures have been quoted that gas-fired power stations cost £0.5bn/MW to build, whilst nuclear can be as much as £6.9bn/MW. This is only part of the story. Given the need for base load power, making the right decisions on investment is very important.

These figures don't represent a fair comparison, however, as they don't compare the different construction costs together with running costs to provide a comparable cost of the investment and price of power produced during the life of the power station. The cost of nuclear is largely upfront but the cost per MW produced must include an apportionment of capital costs and running costs to produce the total cost. Any investment decision needs to include the discounted costs of both investment and running costs over the life of the project. Gas power stations have a thirty year life, nuclear towards sixty years, so the initial cost needs to be depreciated over different time scales.

The two power sources are also subject to different risk profiles. There are criticisms that nuclear has cost overruns on construction and this is undoubtedly its primary risk (if of course one accepts the safety profile of nuclear is acceptable), but gas is subject to price risk, supply risk and carbon risk.

To establish the total cost for a gas plant one needs to forecast gas prices over the operating life of that plant which is usually thirty years. Forecasting price created by supply and demand over a thirty year investment period is very difficult, and there are plenty of examples from the recent past where prices have fluctuated. Consider for example when Russia cut supplies to and through Ukraine in 2008 with a corresponding spike in gas prices.

Related to price risk is supply risk. Does the UK have a secure supply of gas which will ensure that gas is available for power generation? Historically that has been the case with North Sea gas providing a largely secure supply mix. But that halcyon period has nearly passed and will do so during the next 10 years. By 2030, 90% of gas will be imported.

Like the change in coal's place in power generation, these changes to the source of supply are dramatic. To go from self-sufficiency, to almost total import dependency over thirty years is a massive change. Additionally some of that gas does come from Norway, but the issue of dependence is about how secure the sources of supply are going forward, how secure is the price and will it have geo political consequences (can you have a foreign policy which stands up to a country which is a major power source supplier, one thinks of about Saudi Arabia and oil since the 1970s, and the equivocal policy of European countries who are dependent on Russian gas in regard to Russia).

The UK Energy Research Centre put it thus: *"European Commission (2018) data show that in 2017 Russia accounted for 43% of extra-EU imports (Norway was 34%) at around 162 billion cubic metres (bcm). This means that although the UK is not directly dependent on Russian gas supplies the significance of Russian imports to wider EU gas security means that any disruption of Russian supplies to the EU market would have a knock on effect on prices in the UK and in the future may impact the ability of the UK to attract gas from EU markets."*

There is a further supply and related price issue. In Chapter 3, we saw that decarbonisation policies will have a significant impact on those countries with reliance on fossil fuels for government income, exports and balance of payments. It is likely that those countries will resist decarbonisation because of its economic effects. There is therefore a risk that there will be shocks to the system as these hydrocarbon dependent countries react. The Tv drama "Occupied" on Netflix dramatises the potential relationship between Norway and Russia when Norway decides to decarbonise. Fiction yes, but it poses some interesting questions as to how Russia would react.

Then there is carbon price risk. What assumption does one include in the pricing of a gas power station for the cost of carbon to be included in the cost base? Carbon pricing (by whichever mechanism) is very difficult to forecast as its driven by political will. Governments de facto set the carbon price. Markets respond to government actions not vice versa. Government regulation will lead to the closure of the last coal plant in 2025 due to limits on the carbon that plants can emit. Government will increasingly, regulate gas power plants by a mixture of regulation and carbon pricing which makes forecasting very difficult.

Forecasting carbon prices is inherently hard, but the carbon price will affect the price the consumer pays for gas going forward. Between 2012 and 2017 the price of carbon under the EU emission trading system (EUETS) remained below 10 euro. By July 2019 the price had risen to 29.30 euro due to political decisions about the operation of the EUETS. A Point Carbon report for the EC shows a "Base case: EC proposal" producing a carbon price in 2030 0f 50 euro[xl].

As regards estimates for the longer term the UK government comments: *"In the July paper, we used the GLOCAF and other models to set the 2030 and 2050 carbon values. The emission trajectories used reflect the long term climate change objective of the EU and UK Government of limiting the expected rise in temperature to no more than 2 degrees C. Two emission trajectories were used (475ppm and 500ppm) consistent with this stabilisation goal and translated, in the GLOCAF model, to an average global carbon price of £65/tCO2e in 2030 and £255/tCO2e in 2050. 3 These model-based estimates were then refined through a model comparison exercise (using models that were also consistent with the 2 C target) that led to the finally-adopted central values of £70 in 2030 and £200 in 2050."* So, which forecast carbon price should be used for assessing the cost of a new gas power station?

This poses the question of who bears the risk of this carbon cost. Is it the investor, the gas supplier or the consumer of the power? The investor will assess the project in terms of how long the financial payback period is, i.e. how long will it take to recover the investment cost from the cash flows from the plant discounted for inflation and its cost of capital. When payback is achieved, the investor will then look at the operating profit (which from their perspective) will only be affected by carbon price to the extent that it reduces sales or which it is forced to bear. The gas supplier is exposed to the risk of the carbon price to the extent it affects sales. The main bearer of risk for the carbon price is the final consumer as they will have to bear this cost if gas remains a significant part of the energy mix for power generation.

The EU Energy Roadmap 2050 contains no indication of a forecast carbon price in 2050, but it does make these comments about the role of gas.

"Gas plays a key role in the transition. Gas will be critical for the transformation of the energy system. Substitution of coal (and oil) with gas in the short to medium term could help to reduce emissions with existing technologies until at least 2030 or 2035. Although gas demand in the residential sector, for example, might drop by a quarter by 2030 due to several energy efficiency measures in the housing sector, it will stay high in other sectors such as the power sector over a longer period. In the diversified supply technologies scenario for example, gas-fired power generation accounts for roughly 800 TWh in 2050, slightly higher than current levels. With evolving technologies, gas might play an increasing role in the future.

The gas market needs more integration, more liquidity, more diversity of supply sources and more storage capacity, for gas to maintain its competitive advantages as a fuel for electricity generation. Long term gas supply contracts may continue to be necessary to underwrite investments in gas production and transmission infrastructures. Greater flexibility in price formula, moving away from pure oil-indexation, will be needed if gas is to remain a competitive fuel for electricity generation. Global gas markets are changing, notably through the development of shale gas in North America. With liquefied natural gas (LNG), markets have become increasingly global since transport has become more independent from pipelines. Shale gas and other unconventional gas sources have become potential important new sources of supply in or around Europe. Together with internal market integration, these developments could relax concerns on gas import dependency.

However, due to the early stage of exploration it is unclear when unconventional resources might become significant. As conventional gas production declines, Europe will have to rely on significant gas imports in addition to domestic natural gas production and potential indigenous shale gas exploitation. The scenarios are rather conservative with respect to the role of gas. The economic advantages of gas today provide reasonable certainty of returns to investors, as well as low risks and therefore incentives to invest in gas-fired power stations. Gas power stations have lower upfront investment costs, are rather quickly built and relatively flexible in use. Investors can also hedge against risks of price developments, with gas-fired generation often setting the wholesale market price for electricity. However, operational costs in the future may be higher than for carbon-free options and gas-fired power stations might run for fewer hours.

If carbon capture and storage (CCS) is available and applied on a large scale, gas may become a low carbon technology, but without CCS, the long-term role of gas may be limited to a flexible backup and balancing capacity where renewable energy supplies are variable. For all fossil fuels, carbon capture and storage will have to be applied from around 2030 onwards in the power sector in order to reach the decarbonisation targets. CCS is also an important option for decarbonisation of several heavy industries and combined with biomass could deliver 'carbonnegative' values. The future of CCS crucially depends on public acceptance and adequate carbon prices; it needs to be sufficiently demonstrated on a large scale and investment in the technology ensured in this decade, and then deployed from 2020, in order to be feasible for widespread use by 2030."[xli]

Admittedly this is written as part of a policy for an 80% reduction in emissions, but the statement that "gas-fired power generation accounts for roughly 800 TWh in 2050, slightly higher than current levels" is odd in an emissions reduction "roadmap". Given the other challenges in emission reduction in other sectors, why would one increase gas power generation, unless CCS was widespread? Just using gas to generate as much electricity as Hinkley Point C would increase carbon dioxide emissions by around 9 million tonnes per year. At broadly comparable prices and with both sources having risks, why is gas therefore seen as desirable? The **EU Energy Roadmap 2050** does not provide a pathway to an 80% reduction in emissions let alone zero carbon and shows the real limit of EC ambitions, but poses the question as to whether the EC is serious about carbon reduction targets?

Indeed taking into account all these costs, including fuel and carbon taxes, one can make a reasonable case that the average lifetime cost of a new gas-fired power plant opening in 2024 is slightly higher than that of Hinkley Point C, based on DECC's central assumptions for gas and carbon costs, at an estimated £94/MWh. One might ask if governments been seduced by gas, or does the gas industry just lobby very well? A further example is that in London currently there is the currently large-scale gas main replacement project in London. Unless Biogas becomes feasible, is this investment justified, or wise? Should we really be investing in gas infrastructure, and if not, when does it cease to be justified.

While the Industrial Strategy White Paper[xlii] mentions a National Retraining Scheme, it provides no specific regarding government plans to transition coal workers to other employment. Similar concerns have been raised in relation to the government's approach to oil and gas, which is anticipated to play a prominent role in the UK's transition to a low carbon economy for several more decades at least. The Vision 2035 strategy being developed by the Oil and Gas Authority with input from industry stakeholders aims to double the

UK's share of global oil and gas supply chains by 2035. This vision received a boost in January, when Glengorm, the largest UK gasfield in a decade, was discovered under the North Sea.

This discovery was welcomed as *"very exciting news"* by the Oil and Gas Authority. It prompted fierce criticism from environmental groups. *"We've known for years that we need to leave fossil fuels in the ground if we're to tackle climate change,"* said Friends of the Earth Scotland Climate campaigner Caroline Rance. *"It's a disgrace that oil and gas exploration is still going ahead in the seas off Scotland. It's high time our governments stopped supporting fossil fuel development and get serious about planning a just transition away from this industry."*

Indeed, questions remain over whether the Government's strategy of maximising the production of indigenous hydrocarbon reserves is aligned with domestic and international climate policies. The government's plans are supported by statutory changes in the 2015 Infrastructure Act, and have been backed by the Committee on Climate Change (CCC), which concluded that "we need gas - the cleanest fossil fuel - to support our climate change efforts by providing flexibility and helping us to reduce the use of high-carbon coal."

Business Green reported CCC boss Chris Stark acknowledged that the development of the UK gas industry as part of a net zero economy was subject to considerable uncertainties. *"What will happen to the oil [and gas] industry is largely dependent on two things: what is the global demand for the products they are producing and what is the UK's own strategy?"* he observed. *"If for example we were to use hydrogen at bigger scale to achieve this kind of outcome, it is very likely we would still need hydrocarbons, but with the carbon removed, of course. So natural gas plays a role in that hydrogen supply, if that's the choice that the UK government wants to take for supplying heat in future. That's why we're cautious about it, because it would be very easy for the Committee to say that we should ban new developments or end extraction, but actually that doesn't necessarily flow from this analysis. What matters is that we can't be burning them."*

He also argued the development of CCS could yet throw a lifeline to the gas industry. *"It's very simple,"* Stark explained. *"The simplest bit of science is that fossil fuels burned unabated are what's causing this. So that's the issue we'll have to address. But if the choice is to go big on carbon capture and storage, for example, then that will address the climate issue as long as we can safely store it. We do have the science to support that, and indeed we have the infrastructure in the North Sea, so I know there are many who would love to see the CCC make an easy recommendation like that, but it doesn't necessarily flow from this analysis."*

As both investors and governments look to cut emissions in line with the Paris Agreement, however, the feasibility of the government's oil and gas strategy is facing ever more questions. In February, Andrew McDowell, vice president of the European Investment Bank, said: *"As we prepare our new energy lending policy, we believe that the gas industry must now explain its decarbonisation strategy and show how it is consistent with EU emissions reduction targets."* Plenty of other investors are making similar demands on oil and gas giants, at the same time as quitting coal companies altogether.

The UK's continued success in ending its reliance on coal power is welcome to anyone serious about slashing the country's carbon emissions. But tough decisions remain to be made about the UK's energy mix as it moves towards ending its contribution to climate change altogether, including how to ensure a just transition to a zero-carbon economy that does not strand workers currently employed in fossil fuel industries.

As Josh Burke warned in February: *"If there is a failure to adequately prepare, the socio-economic ramifications will be far-reaching and long-felt - analogous to the impacts of coal mine closures in mining areas, which continue to experience labour market imbalances and, consequently, high levels of unemployment."* Those advocates of the Green Deal should take note. Removing first Coal then Gas will affect economic activity and employment in those locations where these sectors are significant. We need to plan for both the removal of carbon power sources and the employment consequences of this.

Conclusion

The UK is not alone in its dependence on gas for power generation and heating. To reach zero carbon, will require a dramatic change in both sectors. It seems that the industry isn't preparing for this, but for a growth in gas's position in the global power mix. Governments need to develop their roadmaps to remove gas and in a short time scale if gas is to be removed from the power mix by 2050 unless CCS is available on a scale for that gas) or Biogas production increases significantly. This is probably the single largest issue in achieving zero carbon the UK faces.

The other conclusion that the removal of gas leads to, is the need to invest in a nuclear sector of sufficient size to act as the source of base load power for the National Grid.

7 TECHNOLOGY

Can technology solve the problems and achieve zero carbon?

Most people believe that we can reduce emissions because there are technological fixes which will facilitate the transition, and by implication that the process of decarbonisation will be painless as a result. Is technology the golden bullet, however, and can we rely on it in a thirty year timescale to 2050? This is perhaps questionable. There are issues with the time lag in getting technology from first commercial development to widespread adoption. For example, mobile phones were technically feasible in the late forties, but it took fifty years for them to become widespread.

We need to look at which technologies we can rely on in the next thirty years and to move to widespread adoption by supporting commercial research.

Delivering Technology to market

I was first made aware of the gap between scientific discovery and commercial application and adoption in a talk on technology and renewables at Imperial College, London at an early stage of the research which is described below.

The graphic below shows the timescale from initial commercial development to low cost and then widespread adoption.

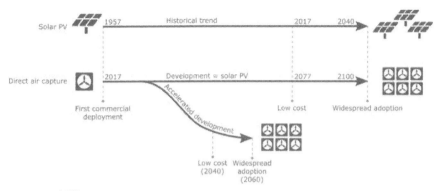

Source [xliii]

"If air capture follows a similar timeline to solar, it won't be low cost until 2077 or attain widespread adoption until 2100". (William Lamb)
The study "How long does innovation and commercialisation in the energy sectors take? Historical case studies of the timescale from invention to widespread commercialisation in energy supply and end use technology" by Robert Gross et al 2018 exactly describes this.
"This raises an important question: how long might it take for individual technologies to emerge from research, find market opportunities and make a tangible impact on emissions reductions?

The authors consider historical evidence for the time a range of energy supply and energy end-use technologies have taken to emerge from invention to enter into the market and reach widespread deployment. They found considerable variation, from 20 to almost 70 years. Their findings suggest that the time needed for new technologies to achieve widespread deployment should not be overlooked, and that innovation policy should focus on accelerating the deployment of existing technologies as well as research into new ones.

The two renewable generation technologies, solar PV (55 years in Germany) and wind (40 years in Denmark), also have amongst the longest timescales of the 13 innovations included in our study. Another insight from this analysis concerns the potential for more rapid commercialisation of end-use products when com-

pared to electricity generation technologies. However, the products reviewed here suggest that consumer products such as phones and flat screen TVs have tended to commercialise relatively rapidly. There is also evidence to suggest that replacement products which can benefit from established infrastructures and institutions commercialise more rapidly than those which are entirely new concepts.

As we look to the future it is important that innovation policy continues to recognise that sustained support for low carbon technologies is likely to be required over many decades. Policy efforts to promote 'breakthrough' technologies are important, particularly in areas where low carbon substitutes for existing products or processes are yet to be found. However, it would be unwise if this were to focus excessively on RD&D[xliv], neglecting the time and effort needed to ensure that low carbon technologies find a route to market. Climate policies will need to continue to ensure that lower carbon options are given the support that they may need to compete with incumbent technologies until they become established and secure widespread use."

These words of caution illustrate that while technology may have the answer, the bigger question is if it doesn't now, when will it? The review of technology below suggests that there are known technologies which have capability for expansion with the right financial infrastructure and that this should be the focus of policy together with making electric grids compatible with greater renewable inputs. This also demonstrates the wisdom of relying on proven technology rather than future technology given the time it usually takes to move from initial commercial development to low cost and widespread adoption.

Base Load Power and Renewables

Renewables have seen a dramatic increase in their contribution to the energy mix over the last ten years. However, with the exception of hydro, and biomass/biogas, they provide intermittent power supply dependent on wind patterns for wind turbines and sun for solar. Indeed, this intermittent power supply and power surges provides challenges for grid management when wind or solar production dwarfs demand.

To deal with such surges and gaps in power supply from intermittent renewables, energy producers need to be able to turn on base load power to ensure power supply meets demand.

Historically this has been done by carbon fuel power stations, increasingly by gas rather than coal as gas is less carbon intensive.

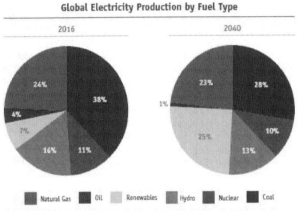

Figure 1. Source: 2018 BP Energy Outlook, BP Statistical Review of World Energy (67th edition)

The chart above from the BP statistical review 2018 shows how small the contribution of renewables was in 2016.The second chart shows a forecast of global electricity with 52% from carbon sources in 2040 together with 25% renewable and 23% from nuclear/hydro.

This need for base load power in the electricity mix will continue with intermittent renewables. The challenge will be to find non-carbon power sources to provide this. At present the only scalable sources of non-carbon power for base load are nuclear and hydro. Bio methane and gas may be able to contribute as described below. In terms of achieving carbon reduction targets or decarbonisation, there is a need for nuclear both to provide base load (although nuclear cannot be turned on and off like gas) and as a constant base in the electricity mix in the absence of any other non-carbon source. This will pose issues for those countries which have removed nuclear from their power mix, (for example Germany and Japan). The scale of the challenge is clear with these forecasts of both current and 2040 sources of fuel for electricity production. BP forecast 28% coal and 24% oil and gas in global electricity production in 2040.

Existing scalable technology

What then are the scalable operating non carbon technologies which can be deployed now? One might question how wise it would be to be dependent on any technology which is currently not scalable. In envisaging the roadmap for zero carbon, what would happen to the target if these technologies don't work in the 2050 timescale? It is therefore important to focus on what we have.

Solar PV

Like wind power, solar pv has developed over the last fifteen years with both improved technology and lower costs. It will be a growing part of the zero-carbon power mix if the correct balance is found between support price and solar's competitive position within the power mix. The technology has improved over the last decade and the price has fallen dramatically.

As the graphic at the start of the chapter demonstrates, solar PV is now low cost, but the question is when will it achieve widespread adoption and how much can its total contribution grow to beyond the 3.4% of power generation in 2017?

Onshore Wind

Onshore wind generation has been restrained in development in the UK by the local objections to planning permission for proposed development. Since 2015 and the removal of on-shore wind from the Renewable Obligation subsidy scheme[xlv] there has been a decline in the adoption of this technology, with the number of applications for new onshore wind farms in England declining by a massive 94% between 2015 and 2018.

Despite this, the UK's onshore capacity is currently at 13.8GW, enough to power 7.6 million homes in the UK. The technology works and would benefit from larger turbines, as offshore has shown, in terms of both efficiency and cost. This is not just a UK issue, in Germany onshore wind has declined, again due to bureaucracy and citizens' opposition, hampering efforts to build up renewable energy and meet climate targets. The question is when will the government review and liberal-ise the regime for onshore wind to encourage further develop-ment?

One might wonder what onshore wind could provide as a per-centage of the power generation mix if it was not restricted in this way?

Offshore Wind

Europe installed 2.6 GW of new offshore wind energy capacity in 2018. The UK and Germany account for 85% of the instal-lations: 1.3 GW and 969 MW respectively, or, in other words the UK installed 50% of new European capacity. Indeed, the largest turbine in the world was connected in the UK (the V164-8.8 MW from MHI Vestas Offshore Wind) and the world's biggest wind farm came online in 2018 also in the UK (Walney 3 extension, 657 MW).

Offshore Wind (as the chapter 9 shows) has been both a particular focus and success story for the UK. Operational ex-perience has allowed the development of the technology for larger turbines and there seems little doubt that if costs con-tinue their downward trend that Offshore Wind will be a large part of zero carbon power generation, given prices bid in current power auctions.

The question is how much can these three sources of renewable energy contribute? In addition, how can the grid be made stable enough to incorporate use of these intermittent renewables? How do they interact with baseload generation?

Hydro

Hydro is the oldest form of renewable electricity generation. Total global installed power has doubled since 1980 as the chart below shows. Hydro provides both low cost generation and a low cost form of storage for renewable energy. This is important because in common with battery technology, storage of renewable power generation to match demand will be a key challenge in maximising the contribution of renewable power generation.

Storage mechanisms used to date mainly involve hydro with pumped schemes using electricity surpluses to pump water uphill to release as hydro power at a different time of day. This mechanism would certainly lend itself to the storage of surplus renewable power generation.

Around the world, China is investing in pumped hydro at a rapid rate, deploying 15,000MW or about one-tenth of global capacity over the past decade. It is forecast to build 50,000 of the 78,000MW of pumped storage capacity due to be installed worldwide over the next decade, according to the International Hydropower Association.

In the UK, however, investment in pumped storage remains elusive because of a lack of long-term contracts and a regulatory framework that does not adequately value the stabilisation services provided by the technology. ILI Group, is planning a £500m project in Loch Ness, and has joined other hydropower operators in calling for a shake-up of market rules to help them attract more funding. *"Prior to market liberalisation in the UK you had more central planning and investment in pumped hydro storage but no new facilities have been built since the late 1980s,"* [xlvi]Karen Turner, a professor at Strathclyde University's Centre for Energy Reform.

As an example, the Lochaber power plant has been in operation since the 1920s.The scheme harnessed the headwaters of the Treig and Spean Rivers, and the River Spey. A dam contains the flow of the Spean in a reservoir. The plant's main tunnel, was until 1970 the longest water-carrying tunnel in the world, at 24 km (15 miles) long and 5 m in diameter. The water is channelled down five massive steel penstocks to the power house producing 65MW of generation capacity. This was used to power an Aluminium smelter in Scotland. Quebec Hydro has similar hydro plants in Quebec province in Canada, which have powered Alcan (Aluminium Company of Canada).

A good example is provided in Australia by the Snowy 2.0 project in New South Wales, scheduled to be completed by 2025. It is described as a showcase for the technology and encouragement for other nations to begin the shift to a grid based 100 per cent on green energy.

The plan is to build an additional 2,000 megawatts of generation. *"The beauty of hydro is that it is a renewable energy supply that is available on demand. So, when the market needs electricity we simply use the water that we have in our upper storage to drive the turbines in this power station, providing electricity to the market,"* says Mr Boardman, the area manager for Snowy Hydro."[xlvii]

Re-building the grid is also essential to deal with a different spatial distribution of generation and also the different time patterns of generation from many renewable sources. Tthe Snowy Hydro project by lacks an adequate high-voltage transmission network to carry electricity to parts of the energy grid that consume it. An additional A$2bn investment is required in the grid, a cost that is likely to be borne by consumers. This and the problems with hydro in Argentina (hydro in west, demand in east) illustrate that future proofing the transmission infrastructure is a key element in using stored hydro.

It is particularly interesting that Australia is making this investment, a country which has a schizophrenic attitude to climate change demonstrated by the fact that coal still generates 60 per cent of the nation's electricity and was its top export earner last year worth A\$69bn. The UK needs to introduce long-term contracts for stored hydro providing a framework for substantial investment in this technology.

Small scale hydro

large scale hydro isn't the only option, however and small-scale hydro has a place. I have followed the Whitby Esk project since its inception, and it is a perfect example of small is beautiful as well as the impact a community of local people, can have on delivering renewables. There is no nimbyism, nor is moving to low/non carbon power regarded as other people's problem, they have just got on with it!

Based on their website: *"Esk Energy (Yorkshire) Limited, run by a team of local people, worked hard to raise funds for their **Whitby Esk Energy** project. The funds were used to install a 50kw hydro-electric turbine, using a 'fish friendly' Archimedes screw, on the River Esk at Ruswarp, near Whitby. The group worked with the Environment Agency, North York Moors National Park, and River Esk Action Committee to develop a scheme which will generate green electricity over at least 20 years and support local carbon reducing projects. By buying shares, shareholders had a chance to act locally to offset their carbon emissions and help promote renewable energy. Investing in the Whitby Esk Energy project should be seen as a social investment, not a financial investment. Shareholders were not able to withdraw ... money in the first five years, but could thereafter."*[xlviii]

Given the location in the North York Moors National Park, planning permission and water abstraction licence and flood defence approval from the Environment Agency needed to be sought. The National Park in support of the project installed a fish pass alongside the site of the turbine which will also enhance the River Esk as an important salmon and sea trout river. The Environment Agency has started a programme of monitoring movements of migratory fish over the weir.

In the first 5 years of operation (2012 – 2017) the project generated approximately 120,000 kWh / annum or approximately enough energy for 40 homes, and by July 2017 reached the 500 MWh milestone. The carbon used in the production and installation of the turbine was recovered within three years of starting to generate.

This illustrates that low carbon infrastructure does not have to always be part of some grand project and that small scale and local can sit side by side with larger projects. Facilitating local communities to establish renewable energy projects like this should be a policy objective for both national and local government. It is always worth remembering that local production for local markets reduces the transmission losses of large projects more distant from their markets.

Nuclear Energy

Nuclear is the other main example of non-carbon power. It has been demonised by the Green movement for some time. A good example is Naomi Klein's book "This changes everything", *"lowering emissions.does not have to involve building a global network of new nuclear plants. In fact, that could well slow down the transition, since renewable energy is faster and cheaper to roll out than nuclear, critical factors given the tightness of the timeframe"*.[xlix] The problem with this approach, is that it ignores the need for base load non carbon power sources (and does not provide an alternative to play this role), which is why nuclear should remain a key building block in non- carbon power generation for the foreseeable future.

Sweden has used nuclear as part of its low carbon strategy

for some time and is the most successful country to date in reducing carbon in power generation. It has three operational nuclear power plants, with ten operational nuclear reactors, which produce about 35-40% of the country's electricity. The Ringhals power plant, generates about 15 percent of Sweden's annual electricity consumption. Sweden aimed to end nuclear power generation in Sweden by 2010. But in 2009, effectively ending the phase-out policy. Sweden has recognised that Nuclear is needed for scalable non carbon power.

Professor Joshua Goldstein from the American University in Washington, and the Swedish engineer, scientist and consultant Staffan Qvist, in their book, "A Bright Future", have a simple recommendation: *The world just needs to be a bit more like Sweden. That means slashing our reliance on fossil fuels as ruthlessly as possible, continuing to build up our renewable energy resources, and above all else, build "kärnkraft""*[1]. That is Swedish for nuclear power plants.

It will take a period of time to build solar and wind power that is both of a scale and can be integrated into the power demand schedule. There is therefore a requirement for baseload electricity and the obvious known and reliable technology is nuclear power generation. In short, it provides a safe and cost-effective route to fully decarbonised power generation within a time frame that allows other technologies to be developed. So why the dichotomy between the respect for Sweden (which implicitly includes in its low carbon economy baseload power from nuclear power) and the recent developments in nuclear power? In the UK the government does not appear to have a coherent nuclear policy, instead vacillating between new plants and then backtracking. This is illustrated by the Wylfa plant on Anglesey or Ynys Mon. This plant provided power to the Anglesey Aluminium plant from 1971 to 2009 when it was shut down. Since then, a number of proposals to reopen it have been considered, but Hitachi recently pulled out of the Wylfa Newydd plant project.

In the eight years since the **Fukushima disaster in Japan**, forty two nuclear plants across Japan have been idled and the inclusion of the Green Party in the German grand coalition government, has led to the closure of eight plants in Germany, and stalled government nuclear plans in many other countries. The irony is that partially as a result of the closure of nuclear plants in Germany that country has increased its reliance on coal, so the Jänschwalde coal-fired plant, almost as big as the Ringhals nuclear plant in Sweden, burns 50,000 tonnes of lignite a day, and throws up into the atmosphere about 22 million tonnes of carbon dioxide a year. Jänschwalde is part of Germany's energy transition policy which has gambled all on renewables, abandoned nuclear power, and resorted to coal-fired power. Today, Germany is praised for lifting renewables to around 38 per cent of its power supply, but resort to coal to provide reliability in supply means its carbon dioxide emissions today are as high as they have ever been. *"Coal burns on,"* Goldstein and Qvist note, *"Germany talks the talk, but Sweden walks the walk."*[li] Goldstein and Qvist contrast Germany's showpiece Solarpark Meuro with nuclear. It covers 200 hectares and was until recently Europe's largest solar facility, with a capacity of 166MW. To put this in perspective, there would need to be at least 24 Solarparks to match the capacity of Ringhals, without factoring in the lack of continuous production by solar.

The greens complain that nuclear is too costly and too dangerous. However, in the face of complaints in the UK and the US at the expense of nuclear facilities, the authors note that South Korea and China are reliably building nuclear plants for about US$2 billion per GW, compared with US$8 billion in the UK and US$12 billion in the US and selling power at less than 7 US cents per kWh, far cheaper than average US costs of around 10 cents per kWh, and almost on a par with the 3-4 cent cost possible at coal-fired plants.

Goldstein and Qvist contrast the concern over nuclear power safety (based on three incidents at Three Mile Island, Chernobyl and Fukoshima) with coal pollution. They claim that more than one million people a year die or are sickened worldwide by the environmental harm done by burning coal. It is for this reason that Sweden provides a model for their decarbonised future. Sweden is among the world's top 10 per capita consumers of power, and yet manages a quality of life that ranks high worldwide without affecting our climate. The authors propose that we set aside our anxieties about nuclear power and build nuclear plants as fast as possible, over one hundred a year, to get rid of fossil-based power generation that is the true and existential threat to our future, and to provide a bridge to the day when renewables can fill the breach.

Their advice to China, which is building more nuclear, more wind, and more solar than any other nation, but is still by far the world's worst emitter of carbon dioxide: "*Solving the world's climate problem without solving the China coal problem is flat-out impossible. So, China must do what Sweden did, but on a bigger scale.*"[lii]

The International Energy Authority report in 2019[liii] expresses concerns that we are abandoning nuclear when it still has a role to play. "*Nuclear is the second-largest low-carbon power source in the world today, accounting for 10% of global electricity generation. It is second only to hydropower at 16%. For advanced economies – including the United States, Canada, the European Union and Japan – nuclear has been the biggest low-carbon source of electricity for more than 30 years and remains so today. It plays an important role in electricity security in several countries.*"

However, the future of nuclear power is uncertain as ageing plants are beginning to close in advanced economies, partly because of policies to phase them out but also as a result of economic and regulatory factors. Without policy changes, advanced economies could lose 25% of their nuclear capacity by 2025 and as much as two-thirds of it by 2040. This lack of further lifetime extensions of existing nuclear plants and new projects could result in an additional 4 billion tonnes of CO2 emissions. Some countries have opted out of nuclear power in the light of concerns about safety and other issues. Many others, however, still see a role for nuclear in their energy transitions but are not doing enough to meet their goals, according to the report.

With its mission to cover all fuels and technologies, the IEA hopes that the publication of its first report addressing nuclear power in nearly two decades will help bring the topic back into the global energy debate. *"Without an important contribution from nuclear power, the global energy transition will be that much harder,"* said Dr Fatih Birol, the IEA's Executive Director. *"Alongside renewables, energy efficiency and other innovative technologies, nuclear can make a significant contribution to achieving sustainable energy goals and enhancing energy security. But unless the barriers it faces are overcome, its role will soon be on a steep decline worldwide, particularly in the United States, Europe and Japan."*[liv]

The new report finds that extending the operational life of existing nuclear plants requires substantial capital investment. Its cost is competitive, however, with other electricity generation technologies, including new solar and wind projects, and can lead to a more secure, less disruptive energy transition. Nevertheless, market conditions remain unfavourable for lengthening the lifetimes of nuclear plants. An extended period of low wholesale electricity prices in most advanced economies has sharply reduced or eliminated profit margins for many technologies, putting nuclear plants at risk of shutting down early.

In the United States, for example, some ninety reactors have sixty-year operating licenses, yet several have already retired early and many more are at risk. In Europe, Japan and other advanced economies, extensions of plants' lifetimes also face uncertain prospects. Investment in new nuclear projects in advanced economies is even more difficult. New projects planned in Finland, France and the United States are not yet in service, and have faced major cost overruns. Korea has been an important exception, with a record of completing construction of new projects on time and on budget, though government policy aims to end new nuclear construction. A sharp decline in nuclear power capacity in advanced economies would have major implications. Without additional lifetime extensions and new builds, achieving key sustainable energy goals, including international climate targets, would become more difficult and expensive.

If other low-carbon sources, namely wind and solar pv, are to fill the shortfall in nuclear, their deployment would have to accelerate to an unprecedented level. In the past twenty years, wind and solar pv capacity has increased by about 580 gigawatts in advanced economies. But over the next twenty years, nearly five times that amount would need to be added. Such a drastic increase in renewable power generation would create serious challenges in integrating the new sources into the broader energy system and maintaining a stable grid. *"Policy makers hold the key to nuclear power's future,"* Dr Birol stated. *"Electricity market design must value the environmental and energy security attributes of nuclear power and other clean energy sources. Governments should recognise the cost-competitiveness of safely extending the lifetimes of existing nuclear plants."*[lv]

These reports emphasise the key role which nuclear can play as a bridge to a non-carbon future by providing baseload generation in the period until renewables and power storage can fill that space. In contrast to other technologies which are mooted as the solution, nuclear is practical and scalable. Its costs may be high, but as an insurance policy this is a reasonable cost to pay.

Bio Methane/ BioGas

Biogas is a mixture of around 60% methane, 40% carbon

dioxide and traces of other contaminant gases. The exact composition of biogas depends on the type of feedstock being digested. It requires technology which scrubs out carbon dioxide and it is based on anaerobic digestion (AD). (See the diagram below. www.adbioresources.org)

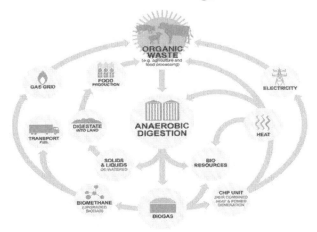

Biomethane is a clean form of biogas that is 98% methane. Also known as green gas, it can be used interchangeably with conventional fossil-fuel natural gas. The benefits include, net zero emissions, interchangeability with existing natural gas usage and infrastructure and the ability to capture methane emissions from other processes such as landfill and manure production.[lvi] Biogas can be combusted to provide heat, electricity or both. Alternatively, the biogas can be 'upgraded' to pure methane, often called biomethane, by removing other gases. This pure stream of biomethane can then be injected it into the mains gas grid or used as a road fuel. One cubic metre of biogas at 60% methane content converts to 6.7 kWh energy.

Heat only
Biogas can be combusted to produce heat alone. Some of this energy can be used on site to maintain the temperature of the digester and to heat nearby buildings. However, even small plants will have an excess of heat. The heat can be transferred

via hot water to remote users by a district heating system, a concept widely used in European countries like Denmark, or in the UK used by horticultural and industrial businesses in the vicinity. Using biogas for heating requires investment in new infrastructure, and installations can benefit from the Renewable Heat Incentive (RHI) support. The RHI includes support for biogas combustion and for biomethane injection into the national grid at all scales.

Electricity only

Electricity generation is a relatively straightforward use for biogas and it can be the most profitable. Biogas requires minimal investment in cleaning and upgrading and electricity. The electricity produced is easier to transport than heat and supply is easily measured. Electricity storage, however, is not so simple and connecting to the electricity network may be costly.

Combined Heat and Power (CHP)

Combined heat and power (CHP) is the simultaneous production of useable heat and electricity. As the process of anaerobic digestion (AD) requires some heat it is suited to CHP and this is currently the most popular option for UK plants. Whilst coal and gas-fired power stations have an efficiency of around 34% and 55% respectively, CHP plants can achieve overall efficiencies in excess of 80% at the point of use given the use of heat. The ratio of heat to power varies dependent on the scale and technology, but typically 35-40% is converted to electricity, 40-45% to heat and the balance lost as inefficiencies at various stages of the process. This typically equates to over 2kWh electricity and 2.5kWh heat per cubic metre, at 60% methane. Obviously while CHP makes power generation more efficient, it only decreases emissions if non carbon fuel is used. Greater use of CHP could increase the effectiveness of non carbon fuel sources in power / heating.

Biomethane Injection

Biogas can be upgraded to biomethane and injected into a gas grid. This can be the national high-pressure gas transmission grid or a local low-pressure gas distribution network. To be used in the gas grid in the UK, biogas needs to have impurities removed, be dried, and upgraded to a higher methane content (> 95%) so that it resembles the qualities of natural gas. The benefit of this is that it is known technology and can be used on a scalable basis so smaller plants can be used. A good example is the Wensleydale Creamery which agreed to supply the waste whey from its cheese factory to a local bioenergy plant that produces enough renewable biogas to heat 4,000 homes. The Leeming biogas plant, which currently runs on ice-cream residue, uses anaerobic digestion to turn the dairy-based waste into renewable biogas.

This process has been used since the 19th century to capture gases that are created naturally when food waste breaks down. Modern anaerobic digestion plants can inject the gas directly into the local gas grid and produce bio-fertiliser too.

Biomethane for Transport

Biogas can be cleaned to remove impurities and upgraded to pure biomethane. It can then be used as a renewable transport fuel in vehicles designed to run on compressed natural gas (CNG) or liquefied natural gas (LNG). Biomethane is eligible for support under the Renewable Transport Fuel Obligation. The greenhouse gas savings of biomethane fuelled vehicles can be significant. Methane fuelled vehicles can also have extremely low emissions of local pollutants, including NOx and particulates (PM2.5 and PM10) when compared to modern petrol and diesel vehicles. There are currently few biomethane or CNG vehicles in the UK, and infrastructure to supply biomethane road fuel is sparse. Other countries, for example Sweden and Germany, have invested heavily in supply chain infrastructure and have biomethane strategies. There are only around 15 CNG or LNG refueling sites in the UK compared to around 800 in Germany.

What is the potential for Biomethane?

Currently the top biomethane producing countries are Germany, the UK, Sweden, France and the United States. A report in 2017 by Euractiv claims that by 2050 renewable gas could provide 76% of gas demand in Europe. This would require significant investment as current production produces 18 bn cu m out of a market of 450 bn cu m. This expenditure in production plants while large will allow continued use of the existing gas distribution infrastructure.

Bioethanol

Bioethanol is promoted by the oil industry as a way to reduce emissions. But like many oil claims on decarbonisation this is questionable. Is it the most efficient use of land to reduce carbon given the energy involved in production, or is this merely a piece of green wash to justify the sale of petroleum? The land use required competes with other uses described in Chapter 14.

BioGas and Anaerobic Digestion are therefore known technologies, with a number of different applications. Their utilisation would require significant investment but a government policy for this sector is required urgently. Given the ability to produce gas which can then be distributed through the grid, this is an important opportunity to move away from natural gas and carbon.

Potential scalable technology

Potential new technology is available, but as the graphic at the start of this chapter shows the issue is how long each takes to become both scalable and capable of roll out. The issue with the following technologies is whether they can reliably be rolled out in the next thirty years to meet a zero-carbon target by 2050? Also, it is questionable a policy framework which relies on them is responsible.

Carbon Capture (CCS)

Carbon capture has long been touted as the technological saviour in the transition to a low or non-carbon future for a long time. I can remember when the coal industry saw it as a lifeline to continued production in a low carbon environment after 2000. Governments have sought to find the silver bullet for CCS with grants and R&D support. Despite many fanfares, however, progress has been very disappointing. The key question is where, after nearly twenty years of effort are the industrial scale plants?

In the US, the coal-fired power station in Kemper County, had many expectations when construction began in 2010. If the plant could cleanly burn lignite coal reserves, the most heavily carbon-emitting of all coal types, then the future of lignite in American energy production would be assured. Costs have overrun to $7.5 billion, $4 billion over its planned budget and the carbon capture scheme is three years behind schedule. The plant was supposed to gasify the soft brown lignite coal to create a fuel that emits similar amounts of carbon dioxide as natural gas when burned. The gasification system has not worked as planned, however, and the plant has been burning natural gas. It will continue to do so. Southern, the plant's owner is *"immediately suspending start-up and operations activities"* for coal gasification at the plant.

It is worth reviewing the 2017 report of The Global CCS Institute which describes itself as *"the world's leading authority on carbon capture and storage (CCS) – an international climate change organisation whose mission is to accelerate the deployment of CCS as an imperative technology in tackling climate change and providing energy security."* This organisation is not going to underplay the potential of CCS.[lvii]

That report states that *"since 1972, more than 200 million tonnes of CO2 has been captured and injected deep underground. Early application of CCS technologies in the 1970s and 1980s involved processes in which CO2 was already routinely separated, such as in natural gas processing and fertiliser production. This was then augmented with the demand for CO2 for use in Enhanced Oil Recovery (EOR). Today, the portfolio of CCS facilities is much more diverse, including applications in coal-fired power, steel manufacture, chemical and hydrogen production and Bio-Energy Carbon Capture and Storage (BECCS). While CO2-EOR remains a key business driver for CCS, wider geological storage solutions are now represented among operating projects. Much has been achieved over the last four decades, capture technologies are now widely employed at scale globally, and costs are falling rapidly as new facilities come onstream and next generation technologies are unleashed. More than 6,000 kilometres (km) of CO2 pipelines are operational with an excellent safety record. CO2 is injected securely into a variety of strata with no evidence of leakage to the atmosphere. There are 17 large-scale CCS facilities in operation globally, capturing more than 30 Mtpa of CO2. Four additional large-scale facilities are currently in construction, all planned to be operational in 2018, and capable of capturing an additional 6 Mtpa of CO2. There are around 15 smaller scale CCS facilities in operation or under construction around the world. The CO2 capture capacity of these individual facilities ranges from around 50,000 to almost 400,000 tonnes per annum. In total, these facilities can capture over 2 Mtpa of CO2. All this carbon capture capacity adds up to the equivalent of over 8 million motor vehicles taken off the roads.*

In the US, key large-scale facilities became operational. On 29 December 2016, Petra Nova Carbon Capture, a joint venture between NRG Energy and JX Nippon Oil & Gas Exploration, began CO 2 capture operations on Unit 8 at the W.A. Parish power plant near Houston Texas. At a capture rate of 1.4 Mtpa, this is the world's largest post-combustion capture facility at a power plant. In April 2017, the world's first large-scale bio-energy with CCS facility was launched into operation in Illinois. This facility can capture and store approximately 1 Mtpa of CO 2. It is operated by Archer Daniels Midland and administered by the US Department of Energy's (US DOE's) Office of Fossil Energy. Other significant milestones around the world included. In Norway, the offshore Sleipner and Snøhvit facilities exceeded 20 million tonnes of CO 2 captured and stored, and the EFTA Surveillance Authority (ESA) approved a three-year extension of Norway's aid scheme for carbon capture testing at the CO 2 Technology Centre Mongstad.xix. In Canada, the Shell-operated Quest CCS facilities exceeded 2 million tonnes of CO 2 captured and stored since operations began in 2015, a milestone that is being approached by the capture facilities at the Boundary Dam Unit 3 generating plant in Saskatchewan. In the US, CCS facilities at a refinery in Port Arthur, Texas, have captured approximately 4 million tonnes of CO 2. In Brazil, the Santos Basin offshore facilities have injected over 4 million tonnes of CO 2."[lviii]

This is a long quote, but it is important to examine it. This all sounds very impressive. However, the total stored including the 2018 plants is 32 Mtpa. Global emissions were 35 Btpa in 2015. So CCS is a start, but the need to scale up is huge, a thousand fold increase. In the UK, the project at Tata Chemicals in Cheshire demonstrates the potential for CCS plants, but again it will remove only 40,000 tonnes of CO2 from the air. The size emphasises the need to scale up.

The Climate Change Committee has summed up the position: *"Carbon capture (usage) and storage, which is crucial to the delivery of zero GHG emissions and strategically important to the UK economy, is yet to get started. While global progress has also been slow, there are now 43 large-scale projects operating or under development around the world, but none in the UK."[lix]* The question is should this be a cornerstone of the UK's carbon reduction policy given the practical experience to date? The UK government has announced new proposals to promote CCS in the Queen's Speech (December 2019)

Battery Storage

Chapter 11 focuses on the challenges in changing to electric cars from electric battery production. The same challenges apply to batteries used for electricity storage, because in the components of batteries for either cars or storage, the key issue is supply of cobalt. The demand for cobalt for car batteries will compete with demand from electricity storage batteries while supply is dominated by the Democratic Republic of the Congo (DRC) and proved reserves are going to be stretched by this new demand. This reliance on the DRC and the need for more cobalt reserves and production suggest that there may be both supply and price problems for battery technology.

Hydrogen

Hydrogen has been largely under the radar in the public discourse on decarbonisation. But it does offer some possibilities. In the UK, the University of Birmingham is testing prototype hydrogen trains and two such trains are currently running in northern Germany. on a 100km route between the towns and cities of Cuxhaven, Bremerhaven, Bremervoerde and Buxtehude, a stretch which formerly used diesel trains.

Hydrogen trains are equipped with fuel cells that produce electricity through a combination of hydrogen and oxygen, a process that leaves steam and water as the only emissions. Excess energy is stored in ion lithium batteries on board the train. The trains can run for about 600 miles (1,000km) on a single tank of hydrogen, similar to the range of diesel trains.

This technology can be used for road vehicles as well with a fuel-cell car similar to an electric vehicle in that it uses its hydrogen to charge on-board batteries that power an electric motor that turns the wheels. The fuel-cell car has a hydrogen tank that can be refilled with pressurised hydrogen in minutes. When this hydrogen is passed through a 'fuel-cell stack', electricity is generated for the car's batteries and motor. A fuel-cell stack is essentially a three-dimensional wire mesh in a liquid that triggers a reaction. It has a positively charged anode at one end and a negatively charged cathode at the other.

The hydrogen atoms split into protons and electrons within this stack; the protons combine with air to make water vapour, while the electrons are fed into the car's batteries, powering the wheels using a motor. At high speeds, the electricity produced by the hydrogen can power the motor directly, rather than being stored in the battery first. In addition, during heavy acceleration, the batteries and the hydrogen can power it simultaneously. The beauty of hydrogen fuel-cell cars is that their only exhaust emission is water, and they effectively have their own power station to recharge their batteries. Unlike pure electric cars, which can take hours to recharge, a hydrogen fuel-cell car can be refuelled in a matter of minutes, making it far more practical for long journeys.

That's the good news. However, there are problems with the technology too. First cost, the only hydrogen car on sale at present costs £66,000. Then there's the issue of refuelling, as there are only a handful of hydrogen stations dotted around the UK as hydrogen is also difficult to transport and store, compared to conventional fossil fuels. Those problems are understandable, because new technology needs 'early adopters' to forge a path for the rest of us to follow as infrastructure catches up and costs come down.

The biggest challenge is how hydrogen fuel is produced in the first place. Despite its abundance, hydrogen makes up just one part per million of our atmosphere. There's a huge amount of hydrogen on the surface of the planet, but the majority of it exists in chemical compounds such as water and – ironically, crude oil. It is necessary to produce hydrogen fuel industrially and, in the commercial world, as much as 95% of all hydrogen is produced by burning fossil fuels. This leads to a quandary: for a hydrogen fuel-cell car to work, it's necessary burn oil, gas or coal to produce, store and use hydrogen in sufficient amounts to power a number of cars.

Given this dilemma, clearly until large-scale hydrogen production becomes environmentally friendly, it makes more sense to either burn petrol or diesel directly to power the car, or use electricity straight from the grid to charge an electric car's batteries, rather than store the energy as hydrogen in between. A low carbon way to produce hydrogen does not currently exist. Research is underway, however to find low carbon methods of producing Hydrogen. Honda has been developing experimental home hydrogen stations powered by sunlight, as well as slightly larger stations that can be powered by waste or organic biomass. Toyota has taken more than two decades to perfect its fuel-cell car, so the question with this technology is whether it can be developed in a way which isn't based on hydrocarbon and is capable of widespread rollout within the timescale to 2050. This currently looks unlikely.

The Grid for a low carbon world

All of these variants and new products pose different challenges for the power grids, compared to large scale production from fossil fuels and a key challenge will be the planning to re-engineer the grid to adjust over time to different technologies and the relative use of those technologies. This is already operational with the hydro storage of power, however, the use of intermittent renewables has posed new issues for grid management.

In the UK the government's announcement to remove emissions by 2050 has led to National Grid, the listed company responsible for balancing power supply with demand, to discuss their planning for an electricity system capable of operating with net zero carbon emissions. This would incorporate much higher levels of intermittent power from wind and solar than the current system.

Julian Leslie, head of national control at the National Grid Electricity System Operator, an independent unit of National Grid, said shifting to a net zero carbon system meant *"funda-*

mentally changing the way we think about electricity". He posed the question, "*Can a superplant save the planet?*"

This would include more energy storage, different energy use patterns, and new technologies to keep the grid stable. It would require quadrupling the amount of energy storage such as batteries connected to the grid, to help balance out the irregular power supply from renewables and to provide back-up if a large power plant fails, he said. National Grid estimates it would need about 1.3GW of energy storage, equivalent to the Sizewell nuclear plant, to safely operate an electricity system with net zero carbon emissions.

Another change needed to operate a net zero carbon power system is to be able to control the demand for electricity, with a centralised system that links up to thermostats and factories across the country. "*At the moment we dispatch generation to meet demand, but at some point in the future we need to switch that around, to dispatch demand to meet generation,*" said Mr Leslie. That could include an automated system that would use incentives to shift the timing of factory operations or household appliances, such as running dishwashers at night, to times of high winds.

A low-carbon system also needs new technologies to maintain the stability of the electrical grid and the frequency of the voltage. While renewable costs have been falling, the cost of implementing a zero-carbon electricity system was still likely to run into the billions per year. Mr Leslie said a zero-carbon grid would be cheaper to operate and maintain after the initial improvements were made, but the National Grid has not yet estimated how much the upfront investment cost would be.

Conclusion

This chapter began with the adoption timescale for renewable technologies. The timescale indicates that historically, technologies have taken decades to move from first commercial adoption to low cost and then to widespread application. Given the timetable for de-carbonisation is less than thirty years, it would be a high risk strategy to rely on technologies which are now at the first commercial adoption stage. They may develop more swiftly than is the norm, but equally they may not, leaving a gap in the de-carbonisation strategy and a failure to achieve the target.

The Washington Post in a recent article stated *"we need a new emphasis from the research community on innovation beyond research and development. We need serious work on early deployment, niche markets, scale-up, demand and public acceptance"*[lx]. This should be the process but the base for a de-carbonisation strategy needs to be built upon known technologies which will deliver a workable transition rather than a hit and hope approach that something will turn up.

Using this approach, the obvious technologies to decarbonise are hydro, nuclear, wind and solar and biogas variants. Investment in adjusting the electricity grid to cope with a different set of power sources is crucial and perhaps the technology which needs the most investment is power storage to configure renewable production to demand.

Other technologies will play their part (CCS being clearly one) and may contribute and increase over time, but they are not the key elements of this strategy, they are add-ons. We need to focus on what we know works as the core of a zero-carbon roadmap.

PART 2

UK EMISSIONS

8 UK – THE NUMBERS

All the tables on UK emissions in this book are from data in 2017 UK GREENHOUSE GAS EMISSIONS, PROVISIONAL FIGURES Statistical Release: National Statistics 29 March 2018.

The three tables below show the breakdown of emissions by sector, final user and fuel type.

(These figures are based on the UN Framework Convention on Climate Change (UNFCCC) methodology and do not include Aviation and Maritime emissions).

Sector	2017	%	% reduction from 1990
Energy supply	112.6	24%	59.5
Business	80.1	17%	29.7
Transport	125.9	27%	1.7
Public	7.8	2%	42.1
Residential	66.9	15%	16.4
Agriculture	45.6	10%	15.5
Industrial processes	10.8	2%	81.9
Land use and forestry	-9.9	-2%	3763.9
Waste management	20.3	4%	69.5
Grand Total	460.2		42.1

By final user		
Business	125.6	27%
Transport	140.9	31%
Public	12.4	3%
Residential	100.4	22%
Agriculture	47.2	10%
Industrial processes	11.2	2%
Land use and forestry	-9.9	-2%
Waste management	20.3	4%
Exports	12.1	3%
Grand Total	460.2	
By fuel type		
Coal	25.5	6%
Other solid fuels	7.7	2%
Petroleum	152.4	33%
Gaseous fuels	184.1	40%
Other emissions	90.5	20%
Grand Total	460.2	

The Government's target is to cut emissions by 100% by 2050, i.e. within the next thirty years. The figures above illustrate how difficult this is. There are key decisions to be made, and to be made quickly to achieve as much of the reduction as is possible. Top of those is removing gas from the fuel mix and replacing it with renewables and nuclear. We will need a dramatic rise in tree planting/sequestration to sequester carbon. An enormous increase in non-carbon electricity generation capacity is required to take the place of gas. Lastly, we need to think about flying and eating meat.

The numbers are stark; if we remove emissions from power generation and industry which are the emissions most politicians talk about, this deals with 41% of emissions. While this work needs to obviously continue, the other sectors should be the priority as these emissions arise from decisions and choices that we as individuals make, related to transport, residential and agriculture. The car we drive, the way we heat our homes and what we eat.

The previous target was to move closer to a reduction of 80%. This would have required us to largely eliminate emissions from transport, but the lack of reduction since 1990 means that this is challenging and indeed Sweden (one of the role models of decarbonisation) has struggled to reduce transport emissions. If the current rate of reduction prevails for transport, we will need to cut emissions from the other sectors to virtually nil to even meet this 80% target.

With a target of a 100% cut in emissions, this becomes more and more difficult. It would, for example, mean virtually no emissions from agriculture. In this sector roughly 5% of emissions come from livestock (or 50% of agricultural emissions) and that poses the question as to how much meat we can produce and still meet the target? (The position in the EU and world is worse than in the UK with higher levels of agricultural emissions). It also calls into question dairy production and dairy products. This looks to be a challenge for the population to accept, but the ability to offset emissions of this size is immensely challenging.

The only good news in reducing emissions is land use, where increased tree planting and other carbon sequestration planting may reduce emissions, but this, by itself, will not achieve all the reductions required, unless the area of land involved is enormous. Changes in land use will be the most significant visible change in achieving the target reduction in the UK. The scale of change will challenge a wide variety of institutions who, at present, act as guardians of the landscape. They will have to prioritise zero carbon over their vision of "natural" landscape, which requires changes in planning law which many communities will not accept easily. It will also starkly expose the dependence our urban lifestyle has on the rest of the country. A tension which already exists between these two tribes, metropolitan and rural, could be exacerbated by this. A theme which runs through this book is how little metropolitan areas do to reduce emissions.

Whichever way you cut the figures the challenge to achieve the old 80% target is considerable and even greater with the 100% target. The change illustrates how unrealistic Extinction Rebellion are in their proposed timescale. We actually need five years, not to remove emissions, but to work out exactly what we are doing to remove emissions. It is difficult to see how this can be achieved without significant changes to our lifestyle in the UK, as we all need to significantly reduce all of our carbon guilty pleasures. Looking at emissions by end user, business, residential, transport and agriculture will have to eliminate emissions if the reduction target is to be met, and given progress to date, this will be an enormous challenge as I will show later.

Finally, the table on fuel type above, illustrates the need to eliminate both gas and oil to achieve the target. They currently contribute 73% of emissions. Power generation will need to be carbon free from 2050, requiring huge investment in additional renewable and nuclear power. The end of residential gas central heating and oil central heating (the UK government has announced plans that new housing from 2025 cannot have carbon powered heating) and the transformation of transport to electric power will all be significant (see Chapter 11). Given the acceptance of gas central heating as the preferred form of space heating in the UK and a lifestyle and housing distribution supported by car use, these changes will be unpopular and difficult to achieve.

What is clear from these various permutations, is that decarbonising power generation is a good start, but achieving the 100% target will require changes to our individual lives and the choices and decisions about how and where we live and what we consume in the widest sense of the word. This isn't

116

a problem the government can solve by regulation or legislation (unless they had the level of powers which a democracy would struggle to permit). This mostly concerns the personal choices we make and the actions we take. It's not the government's problem, it's our problem. It is therefore interesting to see the reactions of a group of ordinary people at the Camden Peoples Assembly on Climate Change. According to the Guardian report:

"Some participants said that although they were keen to do something, they felt the real scope for action lay with the national government. After all, aircraft do not take off in Camden, there are no large power plants, and container ships do not pass through."

This myopic world view illustrates just how difficult this is going to be while people believe that reducing emissions doesn't involve them personally. It is these very people who take flights, buy goods which container ships transport to the UK and consume the electricity which is still 50% generated from carbon sources. We all need to think about our personal carbon budgets.

The UK population (and those in other countries) will need to accept that achieving zero carbon is not something government does, but something both government and we, the people, do together.

How does the UK shape up?

These issues are not unique to the UK, and it is worth looking at some comparative data on how other countries will be affected. The data shown for emissions per capita in tonnes for European countries from Eurostat.[lxi]

The UK sits below the EU average of 8.8 in 2017. The countries which are surprising in their size of emissions are Luxembourg (the country with the highest gross domestic product/person within the EU), Ireland, Cyprus and the Netherlands. The remaining countries above 10 tonnes per person, are Belgium, the Czech Republic, Germany, Poland, Finland and Norway. All these countries have a significantly harder journey in achieving net zero. What is also interesting is the pace of reduction, as no European country has exceeded the UK's reduction per capita (39%). This reduction has also occurred in a period when the UK's population has risen. Five eastern European countries have increased their emissions per head and Germany, the Netherlands and Norway have all achieved below the EU average level of reduction.

The UK is the first country within the EU to announce a target to achieve zero carbon emissions and specify a date. The EU as a whole can only move at the speed decided by its slowest member in agreeing a zero-emissions target date. It is clear that Eastern European members will resist this change for as long as possible given their reliance on carbon sources for electricity generation. With hindsight the original decision which gave Eastern European members countries a period of time where they were not required to reduce emissions may have been ill thought through, and will have consequences going forward. This divide within the EU will also weaken its voice in emission reduction negotiations.

It is also worth comparing the UK to the "real" bad boys of climate change: Saudi Arabia 16.8, Australia 15.8, USA 15.5 and Canada 15.3. Luxemburg is on a par with them all and Ireland isn't far behind.

If one compares the carbon intensity of EU electricity generation then a similar pattern emerges, the UK has reduced the intensity by 59%, compared to Germany's 34% reduction and the Netherlands which has only reduced by 17%. Again, the UK has reduced by more than the EU average.

The UK has further challenges which are not shown in the figures. The emission numbers only include the emissions generated in the country under UN methodology, as the UK produces fewer goods than it did in 1990 and has a greater proportion of service income in its GDP. Arguably, it has exported some of its emissions to countries which produce the goods which the UK then imports from them. In addition, the UN methodology does not include either Aviation or Maritime generated emissions which is dealt with in chapter 17. On this basis, the UK's reduction is not as impressive.

In conclusion, the UK faces major challenges to achieve the government target of zero emissions by 2050. Having said that, however, it is also fair to say that other countries (in Europe and elsewhere) have larger challenges to reach the same target. It is also clear that in progress to date the UK has outperformed many countries.

9 ENERGY SUPPLY & POWER GENERATION

All the tables on UK emissions in this book are from data in 2017 UK GREENHOUSE GAS EMISSIONS, PROVISIONAL FIGURES Statistical Release: National Statistics 29 March 2018.

Energy supply	1990	2017	Reduction (Increase)
	277.9	112.6	59.5%
Power stations	204.2	73.1	64.2%
Refineries	17.9	13.6	24.0%
Manufacture of solid fuels	14.2	15.7	-10.9%
Solid fuel transformation	1.7	0.4	78.7%
Coal mining and handling	21.8	0.5	97.8%
Exploration, production of oils	1.4	0.3	75.6%
Power station desulphurisation	0.0	0.1	-100.0%
Exploration, production of gas	11.2	4.0	64.3%
Offshore oil and gas - Flaring	4.6	4.2	8.2%
Offshore oil and gas - Venting	1.1	0.7	35.3%

Energy Supply is 24% of UK emissions – the success story to date

The progress on reducing emissions in Energy Supply (and Power Generation in particular), has been one of the success stories in reducing emissions and can be explained by a number of factors over the period 1990 to 2017.

What immediately stands out is the growth of renewable power, but the really significant change in the fall in emissions has been due to the switch from coal to gas. In 2012 oil and coal accounted for 42% of electricity generation, six years later 12.1%. A significant proportion of that 59% reduction in power supply emissions has been achieved by switching from one fossil fuel to another with lower emissions. This is discussed in the chapters 5 & 6. In contrast electricity consumption has grown from 320 Twh in 1990 to 339Twh in 2017 demonstrating that the reduction in carbon is not caused by a decrease in production, but by the sources of that production. In addition, the UK population increased from 57m in 1990 to 66m in 2017. Electricity use has actually decreased per head in this period, as have emissions from electricity.

The UK currently has a power generating capacity of around 80GW, and during the winter has a maximum demand of around 60GW, leaving a head room of 20GW. The UK is going to lose 12GW of generating power from old coal fired power stations, however, and 7.5GW of nuclear generating capacity is due to come to its end of life. Security of supply requires a headroom in excess of maximum demand. New nuclear power is not planned to come online until 2023 or later. This gap clearly illustrates the importance of offshore wind energy. In addition to the capacity already installed, a further 5.7GW of offshore wind is either in construction or has planning approval, and a further 12.3GW is in the planning system. Against this, 20% of the generation capacity we had in 2010 has already ceased and a further 35% will close by 2030. Given the increase in demand which will arise from changes to electricity demand from the decarbonisation of other sectors there will be a need for large investment in energy infrastructure and the planning and implementation of this are urgent priorities.

The three main sources for electricity are now gas, renewables and nuclear. This poses a real challenge in the strategy to decarbonise, as the challenge going forward is the removal of gas from electricity generation. This means that a policy decision needs to be made shortly on a moratorium on new gas-powered generation, to avoid, given the average thirty year life of gas power stations, and the 2050 target.

Between 2012 and 2018, electricity generated from coal fell by 88 per cent, with a 25 per cent decrease occurring from 2017 to 2018 alone. Gas is the largest sector of Electricity generation with 40% of the total. This means that while emissions have been reduced by the switch to gas, the next stage of removing emissions (which will largely relate to gas) will be more difficult. The latest milestone marks further progress towards the goal of phasing out unabated coal-fired power generation entirely by 2025, one of the Conservative government's flagship green policies.

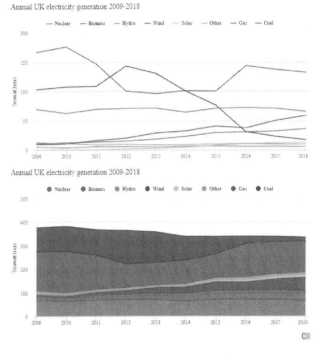

To achieve zero emissions in 2050 the 40% of power generated from Gas needs to be replaced by non-fossil fuel. We can continue to use gas for power, however, to the extent that CCS works for gas used for that electricity production, or natural gas is replaced by BioGas. As the section on Technology shows, it would also be possible to substitute biogas using existing gas infrastructure. The key question is whether the capability to replace all or part of current gas with biogas is available.

How does the UK move to zero emission power generation? Part of the reduction in emissions to date is due to the combination of the stability in electricity generated over the period from 1990, combined with the switch to gas. Going forward, new increased electricity capacity will be needed to provide the power to replace carbon power and the increased use of electricity in other sectors resulting from decarbonisation, electric cars being an example.

Decarbonisation means that electricity will assume a dominant role in our economy and life. The price of electricity will be a major part of the cost of living. The challenge of controlling that price and making electricity cost effective for heating, transport and business will be significant.

New Generating capacity

The UK will need to install new generation capacity both to replace carbon generation but also to increase power generation. The Committee on Climate Change (CCC) report (2019) states that

"The Further Ambition options we consider for electricity generation result in emissions of 3 MtCO2e in 2050, which are residual emissions from CCS facilities operating as part of a fully decarbonised electricity supply. Fully decarbonising electricity supply can be achieved through increasing the share of renewables and from low-carbon power from around 50% today to around 95% in 2050, whilst meeting additional demand for electricity from electric vehicles and heat pumps. Decarbonised gas – via CCS and hydrogen will be required for the remaining 5%. Renewable generation could be four times today's levels, requiring a sustained and increased build out between now and 2050, complemented by firm low-carbon power options such as nuclear power and CCS (applied to biomass or gas-fired plants). Overall, these changes could be made at an average abatement cost of around £20/tCO2e in

2050."[lxii]

This means that renewable power generation increases from 155 Terrawatt Hours (TWh) to either 540TWh or 645TWh depending on whether the "Core" or "Further Ambition" cases in the report are used. This represents an increase of 385 or 490TWh over thirty years. In addition to the replacement of roughly 150 TWh consumption met by fossil fuels, there will be additional demand of between 230 to 335TWh from new electricity demand. Put another way, to hit net zero by 2050, the electricity network will have to cut emissions to almost zero. At the same time, aside from the replacement of carbon in power generation, capacity will have to grow substantially to decarbonise heating and transport, doubling its annual output from 300 TWh at present to 650TWh.

The question therefore is where does this capacity come from? The CCC suggests a combination of decarbonised gas (biogas / CCS gas and hydrogen) for 5%, and the rest from nuclear and renewables. Amazingly, this crucial part of the decarbonisation strategy is covered in the eleven lines quoted above. In many ways, because of progress to date the road map for electricity is simpler; more of the same, nuclear, renewables, an improved grid with greater capacity and storage for renewable production that doesn't match demand.

What the CCC report doesn't address is that communities will have to accept nuclear power stations, onshore wind and solar installations of some size under this scenario given the scale of new capacity required. This is something which has produced significant opposition to date and hasn't lent itself to rapid deployment. In the same way that land use will need to change dramatically, New electricity generation facilities will need to be rapidly approved (see Chapter 14).

Nuclear

As Chapter 7 outlines, the UK has flip flopped on new nuclear generation capacity in response to a concerted campaign of opposition by the Greens against it and the cost of new generation. The parallel campaign by the Greens in Germany has seen the closure of nuclear capacity becoming government policy. However, it is impossible to see the UK achieving the government targets without nuclear power offer not only continuing with its current contribution in the high teens in percentage terms but indeed increasing as the baseload provider. Nuclear provides, a completely different type of power generation option based on longer life and a different set of risks.

It has few friends in green politics and as green votes increase there is a danger that the potential benefits of nuclear described in Chapter 7, will not be realised. Green opposition to fracking for gas does not seem to extend to gas as a whole, and particularly to new gas power stations (I can't find details of protests but there are plenty about fracking, but this is not to advocate fracking either).

The key risk with nuclear is the upfront cost, but once constructed, commissioned and in production, nuclear has low production costs (2019 - $0.775/KWh EIA). The UK government is reviewing whether it can act as lender of last resort by guaranteeing funding. Under these plans, the government would propose a similar financial structure to that already allowed in other infrastructure projects. It allowed the London super-sewer's developers to charge customers upfront for the project. It has also agreed to cover cost overruns above 30% of the budget and step in as a lender if funding dries up. Nuclear, requires uranium so like cobalt for electric cars, supply needs to be reliable and secure.

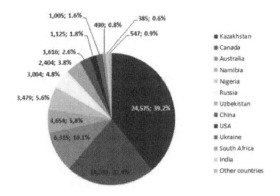

Uranium also has a limited geographical distribution like cobalt. The chart (Source: Eniscuola) shows that in production terms, there is a significant role for Kazakhstan, with total production equal to that in the next four countries by size (Canada, Australia, Namibia and Nigeria). This production distribution is far less risk exposed compared to cobalt where the DRC is dominant in both reserves and production. The security of supply is greater than cobalt given the stability of these producers. Security of supply concerns both current production and proven reserves for future production. If one looks at the distribution of uranium reserves, (Source: Researchgate) then the risk profile is smaller. There is both a greater number of countries with reserves and a significant proportion of the reserves are in stable countries.

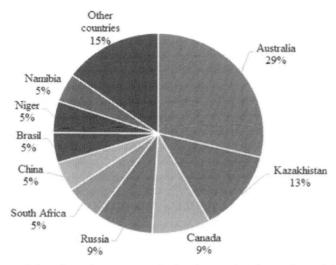

As I stated in the Chapter 7, "The key...is the role which nuclear can play as a bridge to a non-carbon future by providing baseload generation in the period until renewables and power storage can fill that space. In contrast to other technologies which are mooted as the solution, nuclear is practical and scalable. Its costs may be high but as an insurance policy this is a reasonable cost to pay." UK policy should be to invest in sufficient new nuclear power stations, to provide a baseload capacity that allows the grid to cope with the intermittent supply of power from the much larger renewable sector required to meet the CCC targets. It will be interesting to see how Germany increases the proportion of power to renewables without the support of nuclear baseload given the political antipathy to nuclear and plans to close the sector.

Renewables

As is clear from the Chapter 7, the future for renewables is bright and its role in power generation will continue to increase so long as the storage and grid issues of matching production to demand are managed. Improving battery storage is a key technological advance required to do this and if battery storage prices fall in a similar way to both solar panels and wind turbines, then the potential of smaller renewable installations will increase.

Solar

For the UK, there will be more solar pv investment and if my experience is common, then the yields from existing and future solar will grow given the changing climate. Our small domestic installation produced new records each year of the annual Kw produced due to more hours of sunshine. In 2017, solar accounted for 3.4% of Britain's total electricity generation.

There has been considerable investment in solar farms in the UK. By 2015, there were 426 solar farms located in the UK. The largest, at the time of writing, is Shotwick Solar Park in Flintshire, North Wales. Shotwick Solar Park is a 250 acre site, with a total capacity of 72.2 megawatts and each year contributes to reducing CO_2 emissions by over 202,000 tonnes, powering over 11,000 homes.

Metropolitan demand but little production

What is interesting is the distribution of these solar farms. The MyGrid UK Renewables Map is very informative, and shows distribution is skewed with rural areas dominating and metropolitan areas making a negligible contribution to solar farms. There are 5 within the M25 out of that 426, amounting to only 1.1% of the total. Notably there are none around Brighton, none in the Bristol metropolitan area, two on the edge of the Oxford metropolitan area, one within eight miles of Cambridge. None within the Manchester ring road, in Liverpool, in Newcastle, near Leeds or Sheffield, near Edinburgh or Glasgow, Cardiff and Swansea. One in Birmingham.

Clearly, the metropolitan areas (whose electorate is more pro green) are making an insignificant contribution to solar generation. Those fifteen areas contribute 2% of solar farm generation while their population is over 26 million (about 40% of the UK population). While cities trumpet their aim to be carbon neutral, it does not seem to extend renewable energy production. The same pattern applies for wind power, however, this is not surprising given the dominance of off-shore wind. We need to focus on sites within metropolitan areas which could be used for "farms", given the transmission loss over distance, it makes sense to build solar farms within metropolitan areas, and polls show 80% support for solar farms.

The London "Solar Action plan for London" (June 2018) states that

"London has a large amount of potential space for solar PV and solar thermal technologies. Greater London covers an area of around 1,600 km2, around one third of which is comprised of building rooftops. But rooftops are not the only suitable area for solar technologies. London has a potentially huge, but unquantified, opportunity for installing renewable technologies on vacant land and open space, building facades, and alongside thousands of kilometres of roads and railway sidings. However, London's economic potential for solar is less strong. The GLA assessed the economic potential for solar PV and solar thermal technologies on buildings as part of its zero carbon pathways modelling to inform the London Environment Strategy. This took into account the economic constraints resulting from current government policies – predominantly the reduction to FiTs – and trends in deployment between 2010 and 2017. This study estimated that under an ambitious scenario17 solar PV installations could reach around 550 MW capacity by 2025, 850 MW capacity by 2030 and 2 GW capacity by 2050. Solar thermal could potentially contribute the equivalent of around an additional 100 MW by 2030.

In 2016 solar PV registered through the FiT is estimated to have generated 80 gigawatt hours (GWh) in London, 0.2 per cent of the capital's total electricity demand, from a capacity of around 108 MW as of the end of 2017

The most recent data (to December 2017) shows that London continues to lag behind other regions in the UK in relation to solar

PV installation. London has only three per cent of total domestic capacity registered through the FiT for England and the **lowest of any region** in the UK20. As of November 2017, London had 258 accredited solar thermal schemes, out of a national total of 8,508."[lxiii]

The excuse for this is *"The upfront capital cost of installing solar PV is still fairly high (around £4,000 - £6,000 for a typical family home in the UK). This can discourage Londoners from investing in the technology."* London is the most affluent region in the country, yet the Mayor claims that the cost is putting Londoners off installing solar. Oddly it doesn't put off people in the poorer regions, and London has the lowest take up of solar PV on residential. To criticise Government policy when the uptake is lower in affluent London than poorer areas is to obfuscate the issue. London is not doing enough to reduce carbon in power generation and consumption.

This mismatch between supply and demand also poses the question as to how sustainable the increasing dominance of metropolitan area living is in a zero-carbon world? How compatible are cities with a sustainable zero carbon economy?

Areas of Outstanding National Beauty (AONB)

While metropolitan areas are not doing enough, neither are certain rural areas. Again, the MyGrid UK Renewables Map is very informative. There is a virtually 100% negative correlation between solar farms and AONBs. Indeed, the solar farm map almost defines the boundaries of AONBs. There are a few outliers such as the four farms in the Cotswold AONB.

There are forty six AONBs in Britain, (thirty three wholly in England, four wholly in Wales, one that straddles the Anglo-Welsh border and eight in Northern Ireland). The AONBs of England and Wales together cover around 18% of the countryside in the two countries.[lxiv] A significant part of the UK's landmass appears to be quarantined from renewable energy in terms of solar pv.

The designation of and control of AONB is the responsibility of Natural England. Before Natural England proposes an area becomes an AONB, it must meet the 'natural beauty criterion'. This can be a combination of factors, such as: *"landscape quality, where natural or man-made landscape is good quality; scenic quality, such as striking coastal landforms; relative wildness, such as distance from housing or having few roads; relative tranquillity, where natural sounds, such as streams or birdsong are predominant; natural heritage features, such as distinctive geology or species and habitat; cultural heritage, which can include the built environment that makes the area unique, such as archaeological remains or historic parkland."*[lxv]

"Only local authorities or the Secretary of State can give permission for development in, or affecting, an AONB. As a local authority, you must make sure that any proposals have regard for the purpose of conserving and enhancing the natural beauty of the AONB, for example when either adding utility services, like gas pipes

and telecommunications cables or creating public access as part of rights of way improvement"[lxvi]

The question this poses for me is whether the criteria for AONBs mean that we are forgoing the opportunity to expand solar PV power due to our elevation of the "visual quality"of some areas of countryside which may ultimately make the achievement of zero carbon more difficult or unachievable, quarantining large parts of the countryside from renewables. It is also worth noting that a high proportion of the AONB land area lies south of a line through Stratford on Avon, in other words the area of the country with the highest sunshine hours. In this area, the proportion of land in AONB is far higher than 18%. I have discussed this more extensively in the Chapter 14 and it is another example of how we need to re-examine our view of the "natural" landscape in the light of the needs for renewable power to achieve zero carbon.

Residential and Commercial Solar

It is interesting to look at the policy for encouraging and paying for electricity from smaller Solar pv installations, be they residential or commercial. The first policy was that small scale renewable electricity generators, including households with solar pv panels on their roof, received the Feed in Tariff (FiT) subsidy for the clean energy they generate. The FiT consists of two payments. The generation tariff, a payment for every kilowatt hour (kWh) of clean electricity generated by the household's system and the export tariff, a payment of roughly 5p/kWh for the clean electricity the system exports to the national grid.

For most homes under the FiT, the amount exported isn't measured directly, but instead assumed at 50% of the total amount of electricity generated. The new policy is that the FiT will no longer be available for new installations of renewable energy (existing installations will continue to receive it, including the export tariff). An Energy Saving Trust analysis[lxvii] predicts a big impact: for the large majority of homes, solar PV will cease to be a cost-effective improvement and it is likely that there will be a drop in the number of home-owners adopting it.

For small scale renewable electricity systems after the FiT, the government have now proposed introducing the Smart Export Guarantee (SEG) – a new version of the export tariff. SEGs may have a fixed price, or they may have an element of 'smartness'. Some tariffs on solar exports may vary depending on how valuable the export is to the electricity system at the time, i.e. if the export of electricity is at a time when the system needs more power, the price paid for exporting power is higher than when demand for power is weak.

There are already 'smart' tariffs which use the varying prices to encourage individuals to shift their electricity use away from times when others are also using a lot of electricity ('peak' times). Similarly, some SEG tariffs may try and encourage houses to export at times when the electricity system needs more power. These smart tariffs could operate on half-hourly windows i.e. prices paid may vary each half hour with recordings of exports on a half-hourly basis, or suppliers offering different day/night rights or even weekday/weekend. The price paid will not fall below zero at any point. These tariffs also permit battery storage systems as the payments are for exported electricity not produced electricity.

Undoubtedly, the FiT tariffs were over generous at certain points in time, but it will be interesting to see whether SEG payments will be sufficient to encourage further investment in the residential market for solar installations.

Onshore Wind

Onshore wind is another example of the tussle between investing in renewables and the "natural" landscape. The facts are simple and show that onshore wind was developing successfully before the current hiatus. There are 7913 onshore turbines in over 2000 projects with an operational capacity of 13,061.700 MW. The Department for Business, Energy and Industrial Strategy's recent public attitude survey highlighted that 79% of people support onshore wind.

Despite this, the regulatory and policy vacuum around onshore renewables means that the deployment of new projects is at its slowest for a decade. As examples, Onshore wind is excluded from capacity auctions for new power generation, has had subsidy support and other incentives removed, and must meet rigorous planning requirements. These requirements are often more onerous than those applied to fracking for shale gas.

Under the English planning regime, new wind farms must be located within areas allocated under Local Plans, and to be approved they have to have met severe planning tests. The rules are not as strict in Scotland, Wales and Northern Ireland. In England, as a result, the need for a proposal to meet these requirements alongside demonstrating full public support has led to an effective moratorium on onshore wind, with no new developments applying for permission in the past four years.

The second restriction relates to repowering. This is a key element in sustaining and increasing onshore wind capacity in terms of the re-design of existing wind energy sites when wind turbines reach the end of their operational life after 20-25 years. This is achieved by replacing older wind turbines with new, highly efficient technology in a more effective layout across the site, increasing the wind farm's generating capacity whilst utilising an area where planning permission has previously been granted. A recent report from Renewable UK, the renewable energy industry's trade association, found that over 8GWs of the UK's existing 13GW onshore wind capacity is set to be retired in the next ten years, amounting to almost a fifth of the UK's entire renewable energy output.

First-generation wind farms were the pioneer projects for the industry, often located in areas with the best wind resource, and repowering these turbines with modern technology could lead to an increase of over 300% in generating capacity. This zero- carbon power gain from the efficiency gains from technology development is the sort of low hanging fruit which should be a priority. Instead, local councils can refuse applications to repower existing wind farms despite positive recommendations from planners. This is often because under Government guidelines where new proposals are required to demonstrate unfettered community support, any local opposition – no matter how small – will see a project challenged and may result in refusal.

Finding the right balance is key and broad support from councils and their constituents is essential in planning for new projects and repowering existing ones. *"Policy currently favours this small, vocal minority who oppose the development of renewable energy infrastructure such as wind power, often for spurious reasons and regardless of the high level of public support that the government's own statistics illustrate"*.[lxviii] The wind industry said if a bar on onshore windfarm subsidies was lifted it would allow the construction of 794 projects which have won consent through the planning system and are ready to build. Together they would generate around 12 terawatt hours of energy a year.

Technical reports also support the contention that although the fabrication of onshore turbines is largely conducted offshore, there are significant local economic benefits in terms of maintenance and local supply chain support once the turbines are installed. A report by Vivid Economics in 2019[lxix] shows that growing onshore wind from 13GW today to 35GW by 2035 would reduce the cost of electricity by 7%. This would reduce average bills by £50 per annum. This is because onshore wind is expected to be cheaper than gas-generated electricity due to plummeting turbine technology costs coupled with the rising cost of carbon emissions, as described Chapter 6.

To achieve zero carbon, onshore wind needs to be a significant building block in the strategy. It will need to be favoured in terms of the auction and planning system. Government policy needs to change dramatically in favour of onshore wind.

Offshore Wind

The UK benefits from having a long coastline and a large area of relatively shallow sea-bed, which are combined with short distances from offshore windfarm landing points to major areas of consumption. Britain currently has the largest installed offshore wind capacity in the world. Although it still accounts for a small proportion of overall electricity generated, its share is growing. In 2018 it was 8 per cent, compared with 6.2 per cent the year before. Offshore Turbines total 2016, 37 Projects and Offshore Operational capacity of 8,483,420 MW.

Onshore wind offers the most cost-effective choice for new electricity generation in the UK. It is cheaper than gas, nuclear, coal and other renewables, subject to the comments below on system costs to cope with variable power (comparable size onshore wind would match this if permitted). A recent report from Cornwall Insight[lxx] suggest that the emergence of a new generation of giant offshore wind turbines coupled with on-going planning restrictions for onshore turbines not permitting this size of turbine onshore, could see offshore projects undercut their onshore equivalent on a level cost of energy (LCOE) basis by around 2028.

The company stated that the projections are based on projected capital costs by technology, fixed and variable operational costs, expected hurdle rates, and locational factors such as transmission losses and connection fees. They use the current load factors for both technologies, currently at

58.4 per cent for offshore wind and 38 per cent for onshore wind. Overall, the UK has installed over 12 gigawatts of onshore wind capacity, which supports jobs and local economic growth. The cumulative investment impact of the UK's 1,500 operational onshore wind farms is over £35 billion.

Offshore Wind has developed swiftly since inception. The world's first offshore array, Vindeby, was built in Danish waters in 1991 and consisted of eleven 0.45 megawatt turbines that were 54 metres high, had a blade length of 17 metres and were capable of powering 2,200 homes a year when the wind was blowing.

In 2019 Orsted, the Danish energy company that built Vindeby constructed the Hornsea 1 wind farm 120km off the coast of Yorkshire, with 174 7MW machines that are 190m high and have a blade length of 75m. Their project will power more than 1m homes.

"Now you don't even need half a turbine basically to make that same project [as Vindeby]," said Martin Gerhardt, head of offshore platform and portfolio management at Siemens Gamesa, one of the main turbine manufacturers. The technology is developing rapidly. According to Siemens Gamesa, a 10MW model will be in the UK "in the mid-2020s", while some in the industry are betting on future machines reaching 15MW. Turbines have developed to become more sophisticated and capable of operating in harsh marine environments, reducing maintenance and repair costs, thanks to the changes in the early part of the decade when machines which were designed for offshore conditions became available. They are now controlled remotely, cutting down on vessels going out to sea, while sensors amass data, allowing operators to manage problems as they arise.

The London Array off Margate in Kent has been the world's biggest offshore wind farm, but the Walney Extension is now the largest and demonstrates the technological change driving wind generation. The London Array requires 175 Siemens Gamesa 3.6MW turbines for its 630MW capacity. The Walney Extension achieves 659MW with just 87 machines, 40 MHI Vestas V164s rated at 8.25MW and 47 Siemens Gamesa SWT-7.0-154 units. Despite having only 87 turbines to London Array's 175, Walney Extension has the larger footprint, covering 145km^2 of sea against 107km^2.

A Wood MacKenzie[lxxi] report has suggested global offshore wind power demand will increase almost six-fold over the coming decade as costs continue to fall and new markets open. The study predicts average LCOE in Europe will halve between 2018 and 2027 as competition intensifies, turbines increase in size and economies of scale improve. "*CAPEX (capital expenditure) and OPEX (operating expenditure) across Europe will drop, on average, by 36 per cent and 55 per cent respectively by 2027,*" said Shimeng Yang, report author.

This is reflected in price. Companies were not be able to bid in the auction at a strike price higher than £56 per megawatt hour for projects deliverable in 2023-24 and £53/MWh for wind farms that will be up and running in 2024-25, as specified in the government tender document. Guaranteed prices in the last auction in 2017 reached as low as £57.50/MWh, while in the first comparable auction in 2015 prices averaged £117/MWh. Delivery costs have halved in two years. Advances in the design and engineering of turbines have helped reduce costs, with turbines getting bigger and better, and the size of arrays increasing. More powerful machines mean fewer turbines to serve the same number of homes, cutting installation and maintenance costs dramatically.

While Britain may be a good place to site wind farms, the output of those farms is variable, and that imposes charges that the Grid, has to bear. These include the cost of switching off turbines when the wind is too strong and needing back-up power (baseload) when the wind isn't strong enough. Then there are the additional grid and transmission costs of running electricity along power lines from dispersed generation sites away from sources of demand. These expenses are presently passed on to all customers, rather than borne by the investors. The costs may be relatively trivial when renewables are a small proportion of capacity, but they will increase quickly as it goes up. According to a 2019 study by OECD-Nuclear Energy Agency, system costs rise from $7/MWh at 10 per cent penetration to $17.50 at 30 per cent and $30 at 50 per cent. Above that, the study suggests they can rise as high as $50 (£38)/MWh[lxxii]. A British study in 2017 by the UK Energy Research Centre, appears to produce lower numbers at those lower penetration levels, although direct comparisons between the two studies are not easy. (UKERC does not look at scenarios above 50 per cent.)[lxxiii]

It is therefore prudent to consider what costs this might embed in the system. These could be substantial: with 75GW of offshore wind, the UK would get more than half its power from renewables. Add £38/MWh to current auction price and you end up with a number not far short of £100/MWh.

Proponents of renewables say there are fixes for instance using technology such as AI-enabled appliances to limit the need for back-up, or, building more cross-border interconnectors to allow wind farms to export unwanted demand. Neither is certain. Renewable-rich Germany already faces restrictions on energy exports from neighbouring countries not wishing to accept surpluses on windy days. The logical way to constrain overbuilding would be to force investors to bear the costs of their own variability. If they are right about the technical fixes, they should be willing to take the risk. The energy economist Dieter Helm has already suggested a solution, making renewables bid to deliver so-called "firm power" to the grid (and thus buying in any nature-induced shortfall). If subsidy costs did rise, that would at least be a clear signal to the public of the costs the system would be bearing. It might also level the playing field with other technologies such as nuclear, where the technology doesn't require future

R&D breakthroughs. This illustrates the need for robust costing of competing power sources in determining a zero-carbon roadmap for power generation reflecting both capital costs and risk assessed production costs.

So, wind has some issues to address and needs to be evaluated on a comparable basis to other power sources. But, even in the US, the potential for Offshore wind is significant. Wind power already accounts for 7% of US electricity generation, but new Offshore wind is starting demonstrated by the Orsted wind farms offshore New Jersey, Rhode Island and Massachusetts.

Total Wind production

When onshore and offshore are aggregated the operational capacity is 21,545,120 MW, Energy produced 58,391,193 MWh/pa, Homes powered 15,424,277 and CO2 reduction per annum in tonnes 26,826,829.

Wind generation will grow as costs fall and the UK has a competitive advantage given its length of coastline. What is interesting is whether this increase in generation will come from both offshore and onshore or will onshore be choked by "landscape" issues (see Chapter 14) where regulatory issues slow further onshore wind developments?

It is worth posing the question here in terms of landscape as to whether turbines are more detrimental than supply pylons? Supply pylons are accepted within AONBs (indeed a pylon supply system runs by my wood and it is questionable whether this meets AONB criteria if wind turbines do not. Perhaps pylons accepted because they have always been there, and without them communities are not connected to the grid.

Hydro

In 2017, hydropower accounted for around 1.8% of Britain's total electricity supply and 18% of our renewable energy. It is the fourth largest generated renewable energy source. In Sweden, by comparison hydropower accounts for 40% of energy supply. Globally, it is the largest source of renewable energy, accounting for a huge 71% of total renewable electricity generated and 17% of the world's total electricity overall. The countries leading global generation are currently China, Brazil, Canada, USA and Russia all of whom utilise hydropower far more than the UK.

Hydro power generation has not grown significantly in the last decade, largely due to the limited potential for new large-scale hydropower capacity. In 2009, hydropower in the UK produced a total of 5.2TWh (terawatt hours) of electricity and in 2016 this was only slightly more at 5.4TWh, a 3.8% increase. In comparison, wind power has grown from 9.2TWh in 2009 to 37.5TWh in 2016, an increase of 308%. This slow growth is going to be difficult to improve without radical change in the industry. Hydro power generation has suffered from environmental opposition as it typically involves making major changes to the local environment, affecting communities and fishing in rivers. Damming a river can also affect wildlife that previously relied on that river and its surrounding habitat for food or protection.

There are two types of new hydropower projects planned in the UK. Large scale tidal schemes and small-scale micro generation (like the Whitby Esk scheme described in Chapter 7). The most ambitious is the Swansea Bay Tidal Lagoon project which would be the first of its kind in the world of this size. Plans are for the lagoon to be constructed off the coast of south Wales formed of hydro turbines built into a 9.5km 'U' shaped wall. The energy of the changing tides around Swansea would generate electricity as the seawater flows in and out, filling and emptying the lagoon as it passes through the turbines. The natural energy of the tides would generate 320 megawatts - enough electricity to power 155,000 homes.

The £1.3 billion project could be in operation by 2023 and could eventually provide roughly 10% of the UK's electricity cutting 236,000 tonnes of CO_2 a year. It could become the blueprint for up to five other tidal lagoons located around Britain's coast, greatly increasing hydropower capacity in the UK. Questions have been posed about the cost of the project, and again a robust total life of project costing is needed to review where the project ranks in the UK's zero carbon road map. In its favour, unlike other renewables, solar and wind, tidal power can be part of baseload given its regular nature.

On a smaller scale Scotland has already completed and begun operating the world's largest 'tidal stream project', 2 km off the north coast, named 'MeyGen'. MeyGen has a much smaller 6 MW capacity compared to the 320 MW that Swansea Lagoon would be able to produce. MeyGen is run by SIMEC Atlantis Energy which describes itself as a global sustainable energy company, and Its manufacturing is focused in the UK. Aside from MeyGen it has a number of projects around the UK including in Scotland, the Sound of Islay, Ness of Ducansby, Brough Ness and the Mull of Galloway.
Simec Atlantis describes the Inner Sound of the island of Islay on Scotland's west coast as an ideal location for a 10MW tidal

array to provide clean and sustainable power both to the island, home to some of Scotland's most famous whisky distilleries, as well as exporting power to the mainland national grid. The Sound of Islay is a 21km passage of water separating the islands of Islay and Jura on Scotland's west coast. At its narrowest point, where it is just 1.4km wide, current speeds exceed 5 knots, but is generally well protected from wave action. It is 50m to 60m deep at its deepest point, which extends south from Port Askaig for approximately 1.5km. Thanks to this environment there is potential for an up to 10MW site, utilising 24meter rotor diameter AR2000 turbines.

In Northern Ireland, Strangford Lough is a large sea loch in County Down on the east coast of Northern Ireland and the nearest town to the site is Strangford. The 30MW project made-up of 24meter rotor diameter AR2000 turbines. Strangford Lough is one of the best tidal resources in the world given its consistent flow in a protected location which is not exposed to open ocean swell. More than 15GWh of generation was dispatched to the grid by Siemens' Marine Current Turbines and the pioneering SeaGen machine which generated electricity and data, vital to demonstrating the low environmental impact tidal generation has on marine flora and fauna.

In England, Portland Bill in Dorset has been identified as a site for tidal stream energy exploitation as it combines high tidal stream velocities around the headland with a location closer to population centers than other proposed sites in England. A 30MW site to the south of the Isle of Portland on the Dorset Coast, south of Weymouth, this project would deploy 24meter rotor diameter AR2000 turbines. These smaller schemes all have a place in the portfolio of renewable energy and need to be assessed on a consistent basis. In general Scotland has a major role in growing hydroelectric capacity in the UK. According to Scottish Renewables, in 2016 there were 27 hydropower schemes with planning consent, and an additional projects 14 under construction. These projects have the potential to power over 42,000 homes in Scotland.

At the smaller scale, micro generation can also increase overall hydro generation using existing watermill sites and repurposing them as hydro generation. According to the government's Department for Business, Energy and Industrial Strategy, this could add approximately 1 to 2% of new capacity to Britain's hydropower generation, which although small, would still be of benefit to the UK's renewable energy supply. They are low cost, require no government support and cause minimal disturbance to the environments in which they are installed.

In the Chapter 7, I described the use of hydro as stored power *"In the UK, investment in pumped storage remains elusive because of a lack of long-term contracts and a regulatory framework that does not adequately value the grid stabilisation services provided by the technology"*. Clearly this needs to be addressed as part of the next issue, making the Grid function with a large variable renewable supply and dealing with system costs.

A Grid for zero Carbon

Perhaps the most important technological challenge is being able to adapt and update the Grid from the large scale centralised electricity generation of carbon power which has been the basis since its inception, to the diverse power sources which will comprise a zero carbon power mix. **National Grid** states *"In operating the system today in a safe and secure manner we typically need to schedule some conventional generation (e.g., gas and coals plants) so that we have the essential services necessary to ensure safe, secure and reliable system operation (e.g., inertia, frequency response etc.) as we cannot source what we need today entirely from renewable energy sources. This, at times, leads to some renewable generation that would otherwise be available being constrained off. This has a cost to consumers and increases the carbon intensity of the electricity system at that time.*

To enable operation of the electricity system at zero carbon, when there is the renewable generation available to support this, we need to fundamentally change how we plan, analyse and operate the electricity system and innovate in the development and deployment of new technologies, products and services."[lxxiv]

So, what does this mean? It is about better management of the energy produced better including domestic production and understanding and managing demand patterns so that electricity is used in periods when it is available by preferential pricing. It also means is that there will be greater emphasis on local generation and use (demand) being matched with production.

Examples include the "Energy Superhub" in Oxford, the world's first transmission-connected 50MW lithium ion and redox-flow hybrid battery systems as well as a network of 320 ground-source heat pumps. The electricity and energy from this facility will be used to heat and power around 300 social housing homes, with Cloud software and Artificial Intelligence (AI) set to be used to help the facility optimise demand and supply. It is estimated that each property powered by the hub will see a 25% reduction in its annual energy demand.

In Oxford, Scottish and Southern Electricity Networks will install around 90 small-scale low-carbon energy projects, which will be connected under a distribution System Operator approach to form a "local energy marketplace". The network will enable peer-to-peer energy trading among participants and aims to "unlock" flexibility across the City-region. Instead of selling to an energy company, small scale generators will trade electricity.

Battery storage is a major challenge. Renewables powered battery farms that store and feed the energy into the grid as its needed, struggle economically due to the price of the batteries and the huge difference in peak and off-peak transmission and distribution costs. Home storage devices like

Tesla's Powerwall are also struggling to be economic. Clearly addressing this issue is crucial. As an alternative it may be possible to use the storage capacity of electric car batteries as part of the grid to be drawn on at times of peak demand, thereby eliminating the need for extra generating capacity, or storage for excess power generated. The electric car would charge at different times, usually overnight. As electric cars become more widespread the amount of storage capacity will increase to a significant amount. This plan would need "super smart bi-directional chargers" that understand real-time energy prices and power demand, and allow customers to configure them, to optimise payback for their unused electrical power. There are already devices which divert renewable energy from export when price is low to part of the home grid where value can be created so in effect this new technology would build on existing technology.

The Grid will need to use large amounts of data to manage this generation at both a micro and macro level, but it will encourage small scale power generation being integrated into power supply in a way which it never has to date. The power outage in August 2019, demonstrates that managing the grid will not be simple. The Ofgem report analyses it as follows:

"At 4:52pm there was a lightning strike on a transmission circuit (the Eaton Socon – Wymondley Main). The protection systems operated and cleared the lightning in under 0.1 seconds. The line then returned to normal operation after c. 20 seconds. There was some loss of small embedded generation which was connected to the distribution system (c. 500MW) due to the lightning strike. All of this is normal and expected for a lightning strike on a transmission line. However, immediately following the lightning strike and within seconds of each other: • Hornsea off-shore windfarm reduced its energy supply to the grid • Little Barford gas power station reduced its energy supply to the grid The total generation lost from these two transmission connected generators was 1,378MW. This unexpected loss of generation meant that the frequency fell very

quickly and went outside the normal range of 50.5Hz – 49.5Hz. Our preliminary findings based on analysis to date are:

Two almost simultaneous unexpected power losses at Hornsea and Little Barford occurred independently of one another - but each associated with the lightning strike. As generation would not be expected to trip off or de-load in response to a lightning strike, this appears to represent an extremely rare and unexpected event. This was one of many lightning strikes that hit the electricity grid on the day, but this was the only one to have a significant impact; lightning strikes are routinely managed as part of normal system operations. The protection systems on the transmission system operated correctly to clear the lightning strike and the associated voltage disturbance was in line with what was expected."[lxxv]

Despite the focus on the Hornsea wind farm in the immediate coverage, the outage affected both carbon and wind farm sources. Renewables were not to blame per se, but the incident highlights the grid management issues.

Electricity networks.

Given the important new roles for electrification in both transport and heat, electricity demand will rise in most areas. Solutions that enhance system flexibility (e.g. smart charging of vehicles and hybrid heat pumps), will be important in ensuring that demand peaks are manageable and enabling maximum use of renewable generation. Many networks will need to be upgraded in a timely manner and future-proofed to limit costs and enable rapid uptake of electric vehicles and heat pumps. The cost of upgrading the distribution network capacity is relatively insensitive to the size of the capacity increase, as most of the cost is in civil works rather than equipment (e.g. larger cables). It is essential, therefore, that when grid capacity is increased, it is to a sufficient level to avoid having to upgrade the capacity again prior to 2050. A relatively large expansion in capacity is likely to have low regrets, 'future-proofing' the network to enable greater electrification if necessary and/or enabling demand to respond more readily to variations in low-carbon electricity supply. It is important that grid capacity constraints do not impede the growth of electric vehicles in the 2020s. It will therefore be important to make investments to upgrade electricity networks that anticipate the growth in demand. Transmission network capacity will need to keep pace with developments in generation (e.g. large-scale offshore wind) and inter-connectors, and, ensuring that peak demand can be met reliably in all areas on still days as well as on windy days. Thought needs to be given to who will pay for this.

Germany

The challenge for the UK is not unique. Other countries will have their own particular issues. The results of the German policy of Energiewende, the country's plan for transition to a low carbon economy have been successful to date with emissions down close to the 2020 target of 40% of 1990 levels. This reduction in emissions has been achieved in part however by the reduction in industry in trade exposed areas, in other words by exporting emissions. Steel production is down 10% since 2018 and manufacturing down 5% in the same period.

As nuclear plants are closed in Germany (following Green Party policy, seven have shut out of seventeen in 2011, with all to be closed by 2022), and renewables now comprising 47% of electric generation, the question is whether Germany can find a non-carbon source of baseload power to manage renewable volatility?

I must admit that I struggle with the German Grand Coalition on nuclear. Neighbours Sweden and France are heavily invested in nuclear and some part of the electricity used in Germany is nuclear through interconnector transmission, Germany may therefore effectively get rid of nuclear by using it from its neighbours! As renewable volatility increases with its growth to a higher proportion of generating capacity, it will be interesting to monitor whether Germany reconsiders nuclear and if it does not, what other solution it finds. Naomi Klein dismisses the connection between the German emission increase and the reduction in nuclear power without explaining what the non-carbon source of baseload power will be.[lxxvi]

Conclusion

The first issue for a power generation roadmap to zero carbon will be the removal of gas power generation. In the absence of CCS, gas will have to go the way of coal in power generation, and, be removed. Given the length of life of gas power stations, permitting new power stations after 2020 would work against the zero-carbon target. Gas has a dominant role in the current generation mix, so commitment to this change must be established in the next five years. If gas is not permitted as a fuel source for domestic heating after 2025 in new build properties, it would be illogical to permit new gas power stations after that date. With growing dependence on imported gas, this phase out of gas- powered electricity generation, will benefit the UK balance of payments.

The removal of gas from the power generation mix requires the establishment of multiple sources of baseload power manage renewable power generation volatility. To ensure the continuation of electric power supply through the transition to zero carbon electricity requires a robust risk assessment of how all the elements work together, and with the grid to ensure power delivery. Nuclear and hydro are the most developed base load producers with a zero-carbon footprint. The analysis of their cost should be vigorous for the life of investment power they deliver. Investment in these sectors will need to be structured, and new capacity development enabled by ensuring the planning system fast tracks these projects.

Other fluctuating source renewables such as wind and solar will assume a greater role, but this can only be maximised with both the baseload contribution of nuclear and hydro and a grid which manages production with demand. Again, the planning system has to change, to facilitate projects in the most suitable locations.

Electricity is currently the most expensive fuel for heating. As it becomes the dominant heating source that price issue will need to be addressed if we are not to see the development of electricity poverty. Electricity will become a very significant portion of the cost of living as it becomes dominant for power, transport and heating.

All these changes are enormous. While people believe that power generation can be decarbonised, it is less certain that they fully appreciate the amount of change to both power generation and consumer behaviour which will be required. Politicians need to explain this, and persuade citizens that these changes are necessary, then put in place a planning framework which allows them to be delivered swiftly, together with a finance plan which manages the cost of electricity to consumers.

10 BUSINESS & INDUSTRY

All the tables on UK emissions in this book are from data in 2017 UK GREENHOUSE GAS EMISSIONS, PROVISIONAL FIGURES Statistical Release: National Statistics 29 March 2018.

Business	1990	2017	Reduction (Increase)
Total	114.0	80.1	29.7%
Lubricant combustion in engines	0.3	0.0	87.0%
Refrigeration and air conditioning	0.0	11.6	-3237522.6%
Foams	0.0	0.4	100.0%
Firefighting	0.0	0.3	100.0%
Solvents	0.0	0.0	0.0%
One component foams	0.0	0.0	0.0%
Iron & steel - combustion and electricity	21.5	9.3	56.7%
Other industrial combustion & electricity	79.0	45.6	42.4%
Miscellaneous industrial	11.6	11.4	1.1%
Electronics, elecl insulation, etc	1.0	0.6	38.1%
Non energy use of fuels	0.0	0.2	100.0%
Accidental fires - business	0.0	0.0	83.3%
N_2O use as an anaesthetic	0.5	0.6	-15.4%

It's fashionable to criticise industry and business as the main culprits in terms of the slow pace of reducing emissions. The two tables above demonstrate that this is not the case. Industrial processes, as a sector, is the second-best performer in terms of reduction after land use in the UK. Business is the sixth best performer, but it is worth pointing out that the three worst performing sectors in emission reduction accounting for over 50% of UK emissions are transport, residential and agriculture. The interesting question is why there is so little political focus on these sectors by commentators?

Within business, the worst performing sector is refrigeration and air conditioning, both consumer sectors.

Industrial processes	1990	2017	Reduction (Increase)
Total	59.9	10.8	81.9%
Sinter production	3.6	1.3	63.3%
Cement production	7.3	4.4	39.6%
Lime production	1.5	1.1	28.0%
Soda ash production	0.2	0.1	39.5%
Glass production	0.4	0.4	9.3%
Fletton brick production	0.0	0.0	81.1%
Ammonia production	1.3	1.1	14.6%
Aluminium production	2.0	0.1	95.7%
Nitric acid production	3.9	0.0	99.0%
Adipic acid production	19.9	0.0	100.0%
Other - chemical industry	0.8	0.3	67.7%
Halocarbon production	14.4	0.2	98.8%
Magnesium cover gas	0.4	0.1	71.1%
Iron and steel production	2.1	1.2	41.7%
Titanium dioxide production	0.1	0.2	-73.0%
Bricks production	0.6	0.3	51.3%
Non ferrous metal processes	1.4	0.0	100.0%
Use of N_2O	0.0	0.0	-39.8%

A key challenge for the UK in terms of business and industrial processes is the membership of the EU Emission Trading System (EU ETS). Brexit will pose the question whether the UK should leave the EUETS? There is concern that if Britain leaves the EUETS, then UK holders of permits will sell their permits and the change in the balance between supply and demand will lead to a price fall in the EUETS market. The UK does have a robust pricing system for emissions described in Chapter 19 which has had a higher price than the EUETS for long periods of time. If the UK does leave the EUETS, then its pricing mechanisms for carbon will need review, management and a clear forecast price decided to achieve emission reduction targets.

The CCC comments on Industry and Business are interesting. They state, "*although energy intensity is falling, it is not clear that this reflects full implementation of cost-effective energy efficiency measures, as some of the reduction in energy intensity reflects shifts in output from more to less energy-intensive sector.*"

"*Manufacturing contributed 60% of industrial GHG emissions.*

– Combustion emissions, from burning fuel for the production of low- and high-grade heat, drying/separation, space heating and electricity generation for own use accounted for 85% of manufacturing emissions. – Process emissions from chemical reactions within industry (e.g. calcination of limestone in the production of cement) accounted for the remaining 15%. – The manufacturing subsectors with highest GHG emissions include iron and steel, construction, chemicals and cement and lime. Refining of petroleum products, fossil fuel production and fugitive emissions made up 40% of industrial emissions. Fossil fuel production and fugitive emissions accounted for two thirds of this, over a quarter of which were non-CO2 emissions. In addition to these direct emissions, industry consumed almost a third of UK grid electricity, implying indirect emissions of 23 MtCO2e, around 5% of UK GHG emissions. Industrial production and emissions are not evenly spread across the UK. For example, industry accounted for 30% of total Welsh emissions in 2016, with around half of these coming from the Port Talbot steelworks."

"Our analysis suggests that between 1992 and 2007 improvements in energy intensity and switching to lower-carbon fuels were the largest contributors to the reduction in direct CO_2 emissions in the manufacturing and refining sectors. Improvements in energy intensity averaged around 1.6% per year over this period and switching to fuels with lower direct emissions saved 0.6% per year. However, between 2007 and 2009, the majority of the fall in emissions occurred due to a contraction in manufacturing output, which disproportionately affected more carbon-intensive firms. Over the period 2009-2015 there was a rise in industrial output and the fall in direct CO_2 emissions can be attributed to a structural movement towards a less carbon-intensive mix of industrial output (accounting for 25% of the change), improvements in energy intensity (45%) and changes in fuel mix (30%)."

"The fifth carbon budget advice published in December 2015 updated our view on the scope for reducing direct emissions in industry to around 80 $MtCO_2e$ in 2030 from 105 $MtCO_2e$ in 2017.

Within this analysis we identified 13 Mt/year of abatement opportunities: Energy efficiency improvement. Improving the process of producing goods can save both emissions and energy, and thus reduce firms' costs. There are many forms of energy efficiency which are specific to each industrial sector including: energy and process management, best available and innovative technology, waste heat recovery and use, material efficiency and clustering. We identified around 5 MtCO$_2$e of cost-effective abatement potential by 2030. Bioenergy used for space and process heat. Sustainable biomass can be utilised as a fuel or feedstock replacing current fossil fuel sources. We identified around 4 MtCO$_2$e of costeffective abatement potential by 2030. Low-carbon electrification of space and process heat. As electricity from the grid continues to decarbonise to 2030 and beyond, there is potential to reduce the use of fossil fuels and therefore emissions through low-carbon electrification of space and process heat, primarily through use of heat pumps. We identified around 1 MtCO$_2$e of cost-effective abatement potential by 2030. Industrial carbon capture and storage (CCS). CCS can be applied to large industrial sites that have few alternative abatement options, such as iron and steel, refining, cement, chemicals and industrial combined heat and power (CHP). CCS could be feasible for deployment in a range of industrial sectors during the 2020s, reducing annual emissions by around 3 MtCO$_2$e by 2030, on a path to more significant implementation by 2050."

"However, there are significant risks that sufficient industry abatement will not be encouraged because (a) the proposals remain very high level and need to be turned into firm, clear and detailed policies and (b) some of the actual policies have issues relating to design, implementation, incentives and/or funding. There are risks for each of our key areas of abatement: energy efficiency, low-carbon heat and industrial CCS (Table 4.4). The most significant concerns are that: The new proposals for industrial CCS and 20% improvement in energy efficiency lack critical detail on timing and implementation and need urgently to be turned into firm policies. There are no clear proposals to support a switch to low-carbon fuels

for industrial process heat after 2021." [lxxvii]

What is notable about this analysis is the slow pace of reduction identified in the report and the concerns about industrial CCS and improvements in energy efficiency. Given target emissions of around 80 MtCO$_2$e in 2030, the need to increase the scale of CCS is dramatic given that *"CCS could be feasible for deployment in a range of industrial sectors during the 2020s, reducing annual emissions by around 3 MtCO$_2$e by 2030, on a path to more significant implementation by 2050".* Of the 25 MtCo2e proposed by 2030, CCS contributes 12%. The question glossed over here is how will the remaining 80 MtCo2e be reduced over the remaining twenty year period, between 2030 and 2050? If the plan is to remove 25MtCo2e in 10 years, the remaining 80Mt will need to be removed at twice the rate over the next twenty years.

The pace of change in commercial scale CCS will need to be dramatic if the 2050 target is to be met. What is perhaps more worrying is that the CCC doesn't appear to have a plan B. Of course, some of the reductions will occur if power generation is decarbonised which would remove 23 MtCo2e, but this still leaves a large gap in terms of emission reduction for which there do not appear to be concrete plans.

In the European context, Business Europe has made the following demands for EU policy:

"Trade exposed sectors need protection until a global carbon price exists – carbon, energy tax and electricity. All sectors – including households and buildings – must bear the cost of the transition to a low carbon economy. Industry alone cannot bear these costs. Member states will not achieve emission reduction targets at 2050 from Industry alone. ETS and non ETS emissions must be treated consistently. Different pricing mechanisms need to be justified in policy terms. A long-term framework is needed to provide a roadmap for a competitive Europe and long term investment decisions in the transition to a low carbon economy for all players. Building stock

has a 50 year + replacement cycle."

The CCC report doesn't address these questions directly and in part that is the danger of setting a unilateral target rather than participating in a multilateral target (which isn't available). All the comments by Business Europe are pertinent for the UK. Trade exposed sectors operating in global markets will need protection to avoid their competitive position being undermined. If this doesn't happen, it will likely lead to the export of those industries, together with their jobs, to countries with less onerous carbon reduction policies which will have no effect on the level of global emissions. Merely exporting emissions serves no purpose. In the CCC report, iron & steel and chemicals are very good examples of trade exposed sectors.

Conclusion

Industry has been the kicking boy of emission reductions for some time, but its contribution to UK emissions is less than either transport or power generation and only slightly greater than residential. There are policies and technologies identified by the CCC, which will reduce industrial emissions. But they will not eliminate emissions in this sector by 2050, unless there is a dramatic change in the application of CCS for industrial emissions and its scale.

The CCC comments are instructive: *Carbon capture (usage) and storage, which is crucial to the delivery of zero GHG emissions and strategically important to the UK economy, is yet to get started. While global progress has also been slow, there are now 43 large-scale projects operating or under development around the world, but none in the UK.*[lxxviii] Carbon capture and sequestration account for 0.1% of global emissions at present

In designing policy, government needs to find a balance between emission reduction and the competitive position of businesses competing globally, while the sharing of emission reduction burdens by countries is not equal. The UK used to have an aluminium smelter on Anglesey powered by the nuclear power station at Wylfa. Industrial and emission reduction strategy need to be joined up so that industry can survive decarbonisation by accessing non carbon power. Unfortunately, the Anglesey smelter did not survive when the nuclear power plant did not renew the electricity supply contract in 2009 and subsequently closed in 2011. Green policies which de-industrialise the UK are not the answer. They reduce the UK economy and employment and move emissions to other countries, but, leave global emissions unchanged. The UK may need a policy for domestic emissions and a separate policy for emissions by trade exposed sectors until an international agreement on emission reduction is in force.

11 TRANSPORT

All the tables on UK emissions in this book are from data in 2017 UK GREENHOUSE GAS EMISSIONS, PROVISIONAL FIGURES Statistical Release: National Statistics 29 March 2018.

Transport	1990	2017	Reduction (Increase)
Total	128.1	125.9	1.7%
Civil aviation (domestic, cruise)	1.0	1.1	-7.3%
Civil aviation (domestic, land/take off)	0.5	0.4	7.5%
Passenger cars	72.3	69.6	3.7%
Light duty vehicles	11.6	19.4	-67.1%
Buses	5.3	3.4	36.2%
HGVs	20.5	20.8	-1.4%
Mopeds & motorcycles	0.8	0.5	31.3%
Road vehicle LPG and biofuel use	0.0	0.3	-300.0%
Incidental lubricant combustion	0.2	0.2	-29.6%
Urea use in abatement technology	0.0	0.1	-100.0%
Railways	1.5	2.0	-36.0%
Railways - stationary combustion	0.5	0.0	99.6%
National navigation	7.6	5.3	29.9%
Incidental lubricant combustion	0.0	0.0	91.1%
Fishing vessels	0.9	0.6	30.9%
Military aircraft and shipping	5.4	1.6	70.6%
Aircraft support vehicles	0.2	0.6	-151.5%

Transport is 27% of UK emissions, and the largest sector in terms of emissions albeit the one with the worst record for reduction since 1990. Indeed, within transport, the only sub sectors which have reduced emissions are civil aviation (as opposed to international aviation), passenger cars, mopeds, buses, railways, shipping and military aircraft. Transport emissions are in large part determined by the choices we make, not government decisions. SUV cars are now 30% of cars in the EU and the UK, despite their greater emissions, we continue to choose to buy them. According to an IEA report (October 2019), in global terms, *"As a consequence, SUVs were* *the second-largest contributor to the increase in global CO$_2$ emissions since 2010 after the power sector, but ahead of heavy industry (including iron & steel, cement, aluminium), as well as trucks and aviation."*[lxxix] This is an indictment not of government, but our personal choices.

The reduction in emissions for road transport over the last 29 years is just 3.7%. In the period when energy supply removed 165 tonnes of emissions, transport managed just over 2 tonnes of emissions in a sector with roughly the same level of emissions. Yet for all the coverage from the motor industry about reduced emissions, one would expect there to be a more dramatic reduction. There isn't, because the cars we choose to buy are bigger, heavier and have bigger engines.

What we need to remember in this sector, is the importance of the EU in determining transport policy and standards (this will still apply when the UK is outside the EU due to the size of the EU car market). The German car industry has enormous lobbying power in Brussels, something I have witnessed. This is not surprising given the importance of the industry to German economic performance, but also because as someone recently described, *"the US has a problem with their love of guns, the Germans have one with their love of cars"*. Changes to motor transport within the EU will always be considered within the prism of the effect on the German economy. One has to look no further than the impact of diesel-gate to see that the EU will not challenge the German car industry in the face of German government opposition or obstruction. For the German car industry, the transition to a non-carbon car industry is probably as difficult as the transition of oil companies to energy companies. In both cases, one needs to view their conversion to a new greener vision with caution.

Cars: The current position

The scale of change required is enormous. The statistics on vehicles on the road demonstrate this. By 2018, non-petrol and diesel cars accounted for 6% of newly registered cars in the UK. This was an increase over the 1.4% in 2013. But the biggest shift in the period was from diesel to petrol with diesel falling from 49.8% in 2013 to 31.7% in 2018. While this fall was good for particulate levels it was not for CO2 as diesel cars are more efficient in terms of emissions. Interestingly, the UK has a lower share of new diesel than the EU average (2017).

In terms of actual vehicles, the number of cars on the road in 2018 was 31.5m, of which 18.5m were petrol and 12.4m diesel (DVLA). If these statistics broadly continue it would be necessary to remove 30.9m carbon cars and replace them with 30.9m non carbon / electric cars to achieve a net zero carbon position for the car sector. Labour promised to change 20m cars to electric by 2030, while current government policy is to ban the sale of new petrol and diesel cars from 2040. These policies don't remove carbon cars from the roads by the date, they stop the addition of carbon cars. To remove carbon cars would require both people buying electric vehicles and being banned from keeping carbon cars.

It is ironic that we live in an internal combustion world, as originally electric cars were more popular than those with internal combustion engines which were considered unreliable and dirty. From 1890 electric vehicles from different automakers were being manufactured across the U.S. New York City even had a fleet of more than 60 electric taxis. By 1900, electric cars were at their peak, accounting for around a third of all vehicles on the road. During the next 10 years, they continued to show strong sales. By the 1920s, the U.S. had a better system of roads connecting cities and towns, with the discovery of Texas crude oil, petrol became cheap and readily available for all Americans, and filling stations expanded across the country. In comparison, very few Americans outside cities had electricity at that time. Ultimately, electric vehicles all but disappeared by 1935. Of course, these electric cars wouldn't have been low carbon given the electricity supply mix based on carbon.

Current government policy is to ban the sale of carbon cars from 2040. The policy is silent on what happens to old carbon cars and when they will be removed from the roads.

Commercial Vehicles: The Current Position

Turning to commercial vehicles, in 1996, there were 2.2 million vans registered in Great Britain of which 60% were diesel. By 2016 there were 3.8 million vans, of which the vast majority (96%) were diesel powered. (DVLA). In addition, there were 493,600 heavy goods vehicles registered in Great Britain in 2016. Their average gross vehicle weight in 2016 was 22.1 tonnes, compared with 17.7 tonnes in 1996. In 2016, 22% had a gross vehicle weight of over 41 tonnes; hardly any fell into this category prior to 2001 when the general weight limit for articulated vehicles was increased from 41 to 44 tonnes. (DVLA). Since 1996 therefore the size of heavy goods vehicles has increased both absolutely and in the mix of the fleet. Bigger heavy goods vehicles equate to more emissions.

Over the last twenty years, vehicle stock has increased by 40%. The largest increase was for LGVs at 75%, followed by motorcycles at 64%. Growth in HGVs was 15%, but buses & coaches fell by 1%. At the end of 2017, the numbers of licensed cars and LGVs were at their highest ever levels. The numbers of motorbikes, HGVs and buses & coaches, on the other hand, remained below the peak levels, reached between 2004 and 2007. Again, more vehicles equate to more emissions assuming the same average mileage.

The freight business has responded to proposals for carbon reduction targets with strong opposition. There is a proposal to ban the sale of diesel lorries by 2040 in the UK. *"This proposal is simply impractical and doesn't take account of reality,"* said Rod McKenzie, policy director of the Road Haulage Association,[lxxx] which represents 6,000 lorry operators in the UK.

"Banning one fuel type before a replacement is competitive, or even

identified, is high risk and could undermine efforts to encourage replacement," said SMMT chief executive Mike Hawes. *"The industry is committed to a zero-emission future and is investing heavily in electrified and other technologies to get us there, but while industry can ultimately deliver the technology, it cannot dictate the pace of change nor the levels of market demand."* [lxxxi]

The government admitted that *"the pathway to achieving this is not as clear as for cars and vans"*. A government spokesman said: *"We are taking action now to incentivise freight companies to move to cleaner HGV fleets, including through investment in research and development for greener vehicles and by introducing higher charges for the dirtiest lorries using our roads. "Tackling the issue of pollution and investing in green technologies is a priority, which is why we have a £3.5bn plan to improve air quality and reduce harmful emissions."* Again, this policy stops adding carbon lorries, it does not remove them all.

Conversations with Swedish government officials illustrate the problem of freight as they recognise that decarbonising freight (and larger freight vehicles in particular) over long distances will be very difficult.

Current Options

Not only has the number of vehicles has increased, but the size of their engines has also increased, and these two factors have neutralised most of the benefits of more efficient engines. For this reason emissions in the sector have not reduced to any significant extent. The key other factor is personal choice, as we are choosing to buy or lease more bigger cars, especially SUVs despite the coverage on the need to reduce emissions.

Clearly, we need to remove hydrocarbon vehicles, this will not be an easy process and there are significant issues to overcome. There are ameliorating measures which could be taken immediately. In the first oil shock in the 1970s, the US introduced lower speed limits to reduce the use of petrol and this could be an option.

In the short term, a more technical option would be to increase the level of ethanol made from wheat or sugar beet that is blended into petrol from the current limit of 5% to 10%. According to the All Party Parliamentary Group for British Biofuel, *"Introducing E10 would assist in the UK achieving its GHG reduction targets – saving the equivalent emissions of taking 700,000 cars off the road – while also being delivered at a low carbon cost relative to other options."*[lxxxii]

They also outline the consequences if Ethanol is allowed to, *"decline and likely disappear forever"* as part of the fuel mix. *"The UK economy will likely soon lose a vital and valuable £1 billion bioethanol industry. Without the swift introduction of E10 - by 2020 at the latest - the British Bioethanol Industry will continue to decline and likely disappear forever resulting in the loss of thousands of jobs. If the British Bioethanol Industry is lost, the UK will likely become dependent on increasingly scarce and less sustainable biofuel from abroad including Used Cooking Oil (UCO) from China.*

If the British Bioethanol Industry is lost, British farmers will need to purchase an increasing volume of animal feed from less sustainable sources, in particular soya based feed from regions in South America, further exacerbating the issue of deforestation. British farmers will also lose an important domestic market for surplus feed wheat".[lxxxiii]

This illustrates that the options for decarbonisation have consequences for jobs, international trade, farming and deforestation even for something as humble as biofuel additives. It demonstrates that Green Deal advocates are oversimplifying the complexity of issues, as each of the decisions we take to work towards zero carbon has consequences, some of which are negative. We need to understand these consequences to make optimal decisions. Both of the initiatives described above, (speed reduction and ethanol) reduce emissions, but they are not options to achieve zero carbon. For that we have to consider electric cars.

Electric Cars: Electricity Demand

To move from 6% non-carbon cars to 100% non-carbon cars requires a huge increase of over 30m cars in the UK. This raises a number of new issues, which our economy does not, currently, have to deal with.

The IEA forecast that, *"Starting from a low base, less than 0.5% of the total car stock, this growth in electric vehicles means that nearly 7% of the car fleet will be electric by 2030".*[lxxxiv] This forecast suggests that government targets may be difficult to achieve unless the UK is the exception in take up of electric cars, remember that Labour promised to make 66% of the UK car fleet electric by 2030.

The major issue is extra electricity supply from non-carbon sources. If we assume that on average a car covers 15,000 km per annum and uses 10kw per 100 km, then the power use will be 1500 kw per annum per car. For 30m cars this requires an additional annual generation of 45 TWh in addition to current generation of 338 TWh. There will be additional generation capacity needed for LGVs and HGVs. We would need to have this additional non-carbon capacity on stream in the 2040s.

If we have the electricity supply for electric cars, the next issue is to how to charge them, and this has implications for the grid. A recent PWC report "Charging ahead – the need to upscale UK electric charging infrastructure" looked at charging capacity. The report shows:

"Homeowners are the largest share of vehicle drivers – 78% of them have access to off-street parking. Battery electric vehicles (BEV) drivers plug in to charge throughout the day at different locations, the most common group 35% charge at home (off-street) and typically between 5pm – 8pm. Many UK drivers have access to off-street parking meaning a lot will choose to charge their ve-

hicles at home. To cope with this extra demand for electricity, it is critical that residential power grids are reinforced and / or smart technologies are deployed." To give an example, my home has a solar installation and only uses electric power, to make this feasible it had to be upgraded from single phase to three phase supply. Availability of off street-parking is lower in cities, particularly London. In London, only 48% of vehicle drivers have off-street parking compared to the UK average of 72%. Other major UK cities have similar challenges, where levels of vehicle drivers with access to off-street parking range through 61% in Edinburgh, 61% in Cardiff and 65% in Manchester. As those who live in a city, are less likely to have access to off-street parking, access to public charging points will play an important role in supporting EV adoption rates."[lxxxv]

So, aside from the need for 45 TWh of generating capacity, that capacity will have to manage a demand for electricity occuring from 5 to 8pm which will impact the delivery requirement of electricity production. In cities, the public charging infrastructure will need to be extensive to cope with those drivers with no off-street parking. A possible solution could be induction charging which works by installing a pad on the underside of an electric car. Once that aligns with another pad hidden underneath the road surface, electricity is passed to the car via induction.

The change in the supply system from petrol/diesel to electricity is big. No longer will petrol need to be imported, refined and transported to petrol stations. The Electricity power supply will require an increase of greater than 10% to supply the power for electric cars, but the grid will also need to cope with both the charging needs and the timing of that charging for cars.

Electric cars: Power source

If we focus on the components of batteries which are the power source for electric cars, the key issue is the supply of cobalt. The graphic below shows 2017 production and global proven reserves. Energy Reporters reported on 22/11/2018 that *"A cobalt shortage could undermine attempts to bring electric cars to the market, suppliers are warning auto-manufacturers. The metal, a by-product of copper mining, is in demand for the lithium-ion batteries used in electric vehicles but shortages could delay the transition to green motoring as Cobalt will be in short supply from 2025 on, according to the Joint Research Centre, the scientific advisory at the European Commission.* [lxxxvi]

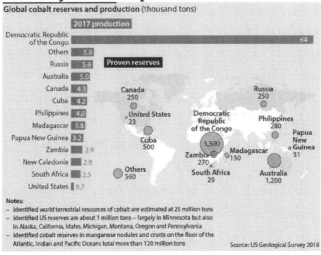

The problem is that a single electric vehicle requires between 6kg and 12kg of cobalt. This translates into the following figures, tonnes of cobalt needed to produce new electric vehicles to replace the existing non carbon stock. If one assumes 6kg per car (the lower end of estimates) and current global cobalt production of 94,000 tonnes (Cobalt Institute) the UK would require two years of global production to move to 100% electric cars. In addition, the EU would need nineteen years of global production. To convert the world's existing cars requires 600m tonnes! As EVs and plug in hybrid electric vehicles (PHEV) grow in popularity, an estimated 120,000 tonnes of cobalt will be required each year by 2030, as demand ramps up. It is difficult to see production keeping up with demand.

Aside from production issues, the pie chart of global cobalt reserves, shows how dominant DRC reserves are. Given the political volatility of that country this dependence is worrying to say the least.

Lithium and other minerals – the strategic challenge

Governments are taking the challenge of the resources for electric batteries very seriously. This concern arises because lithium is a major component in batteries. It is extracted in Australia and Chile with processing largely in China. This concentration of processing poses a strategic challenge for the West given the potential importance of electric batteries. As part of the Faraday challenge in the UK, a consortium including Cornish Lithium is looking at the production potential for Lithium in Cornwall.

Global demand for lithium is predicted to increase to 785,000 tonnes LCE by 2025, from 217,000 tonnes LCE in 2017. The mining industry needs to discover new sources of lithium to ensure supply can keep up with demand. Cornish Lithium believes that Cornwall potentially contains significant quantities of lithium in geothermal brines, making it a priority target for exploration. It is primarily focussed on extracting lithium from known occurrences in brine and in hard rock. Cornish Lithium is also evaluating the potential in Cornwall for other metals particularly those vital to modern technologies such as electric vehicles and power storage batteries. The recent discovery of lithium which can be extracted from waste dumps by the Rio Tinto group in California may indicate further sources.

The US, Canada and Australia are also working together to help the wider discovery of mineral resources used in low carbon technology and to ensure that these minerals are extracted within governance frameworks which support good environmental and social policies. Simon Moores (Benchmark Mineral Intelligence) was quoted in the FT 11 June 2019, *"whoever controls these supply chains controls industrial power in the 21st century".* [lxxxvii] China currently accounts for 80% of the world's rare earth production. The US Commerce Department report published a list of critical minerals which include:

"Aluminum (bauxite), antimony, arsenic, barite, beryllium, bismuth, cesium, chromium, cobalt, fluorspar, gallium, germanium, graphite (natural), hafnium, helium, indium, lithium, magnesium, manganese, niobium, platinum group metals, potash, the rare earth elements group, rhenium, rubidium, scandium, strontium, tantalum, tellurium, tin, titanium, tungsten, uranium, vanadium, and zirconium."

Imports account for more than 50% of domestic demand for twenty nine of them and 100% for fourteen of them. Despite Democrat promotion of the Green Deal (which is dependent on access to these minerals) the report drew immediate fire from them. They claimed that the new strategy would harm the environment and amounted to fresh concessions to multinational corporations. *"This administration has set shameful new records for industry giveaways, and this is one of the worst,"* said Raul Grijalva, Democratic chairman of the House of Representatives Natural Resources Committee.

Security of supply could be one the key challenges for western countries in their de-carbonisation strategy. The left will have to accept that the environmental concerns around extraction will apply globally and that extraction under western standards may be better than extraction in countries with lower standards whatever happens the minerals do need to be extracted if we are to switch to electric cars in the numbers described.

An Alternative Solid-State Batteries

New entrant Dyson proposed to develop Electric Vehicles based on "solid-state" design — the most talked-about of the new technologies. Unlike current lithium-ion batteries that use liquid electrolytes to move energy around, solid-state batteries use "dry" conductive material. Solid state batteries are lighter and they don't require liquid cooling. They should be longer lasting and fire-proof, but the big question is whether they will they be price competitive? They could potentially charge more quickly, but in terms of timing, these vehicles may be 5 plus years before they are scaleable.

There is a lot of interest in this technology; Dyson acquired Sakti3, Caterpillar has purchased a stake in Fisker, andVolkswagen has invested in QuantumScape. This may be wise as *"Ultimately, solid-state lithium batteries may not require cobalt at all, but so far their production processes and costs are unproven"* according to Green Car Reports[lxxxviii] who also report that Panasonic (major battery supplier to Tesla) has a strategic aim to reduce Cobalt annually. Dyson announced in October 2019 that the technology would work but that the cost was too high, so this challenge to Cobalt based batteries may not occur in the current cost climate.

Cobalt – the problems

Car producers have already tried to buy forward supplies of cobalt due to their fears over the shortages which will be created by increased demand. Both Volkswagen and GM have commented on this. VW first proposed this in 2017, perhaps based on the car industry belief that suppliers would do as they were told as usual in the motor industry. Instead, talks broke down with mining industry sources saying *"They are looking for prices below the market, they have a lot to learn about cobalt. We didn't get into the details of how much tonnage they would need."* In a new world, old industries will need to learn that the low carbon economy has different power dynamics.

The price of cobalt jumped sharply in 2017 and early 2018 and remains more than double its price at the end of 2016. Bloomberg estimates that by 2030, global demand for cobalt could be 47 times greater than it was in 2018. Ultimately, new sources of cobalt will be needed, especially in the late 2020s, when national and EU plans to switch to electric vehicles will start to have widespread effect. The Joint Research Centre report said the EU should act to promote production within the bloc and work closely with countries such as Australia and Canada, *"whose importance as cobalt producers is expected to increase."*[lxxxix] The EU should mine more of its own cobalt in addition to recycling. Finland is the only EU country where cobalt is mined, though Spain, Sweden, and some other EU countries also have reserves, according to the report. Mining in the EU would be more expensive than importing from the Democratic Republic of Congo but, in the context of improving battery technology to minimize cobalt.

To tackle potential cobalt shortage, car companies and their battery suppliers could reduce the amount of the metal they use, eliminate cobalt from batteries altogether, or find new sources, including recycling used batteries. Recycling costs are not currently economic however, costing €1 per kg to recover raw material worth a quarter of that. Recycling lithium costs five times as much as extracting material. Not surprisingly only 5% of lithium-ion batteries are recycled currently in Europe. This may change based on the impact of demand on cobalt prices which could have the effect of making recycling cost effective. In comparative terms, producing an electric vehicle contributes, on average, double the amount of energy compared to producing a combustion engine car. This is mainly because of its battery. The bigger the electric car and its range, the more battery cells are needed to power it, and consequently the more carbon is produced.

The DRC Problem

Cobalt production is dominated by the DRC. This poses real issues as the environmental benefits of cobalt in electric car batteries must be weighed against the costs of production which include (according to the World Economic Forum): *"Social challenges and human rights abuses such as hazardous work-*

ing conditions in poverty, exposure to pollution and other issues".
The recent tensions at a Glencore mine show the instability of
the situation. The company claimed that over 2,000 informal
miners were operating on its mining lease with over 40 killed
in a pit-wall collapse. The lack of a functioning state and the
rule of law mean that Glencore calls in the army to maintain
order. This is the country with the largest global contribution
to Cobalt production, in risk assessment terms this is a very
unstable base on which to build the enormous growth in cobalt demand and supply. These issues need to be factored into
the need for cobalt, if electric vehicles are to be based on lithium batteries.

Freight Vehicles

In cities we are all aware of electric delivery vans, which are
proliferating and addressing the pollution issues, in particular
particulates. There are positive steps with British Gas and SSE
pledging to replace their existing fleet of vans with all-elec-
tric models by 2030. British Gas will electrify its 12,500 vans,
the third largest fleet of vehicles in the UK, to transport its
15,000 engineers across the country to customer homes. SSE
has committed to switch its 3,500 vehicles, the UK's seventh
biggest fleet of cars, to electric models, and install charging
points for its 21,000 employees. Facilities management firm
Mitie plans to switch 20% of its 3,500-strong car and van fleet
to electric by 2020, and, will install 800 charging points.

But freight is a much bigger problem. Frevue works on this
area for the EC and its comments on Electric Freight Vehicles
(EHV) are interesting:

*"For a medium sized electric freight vehicle, weighing between
3.5 and 7.5 tonnes, a positive business case is possible although
still challenging. Specific circumstances, like the exemption from
paying the congestion charge for EFVs, have a very positive effect
on the business case for the EFV. For the large EFVs, the purchase
price for the individually retrofitted vehicle currently remains sig-*

nificantly higher than for conventional trucks. Though not impossible, it remains difficult to get to a positive business case. The impact of diesel and electricity prices will have a big impact on the level of cost advantage of EFVs over CFVs. Energy prices differ across Europe, due to taxes and rates set by government. Freight operators with a large fleet who pay low electricity rates are likely to be the first to transition to electric freight, as they can organise fast charging infrastructure internally. As all current large EFVs are converted from conventional lorries, there is a high initial cost that makes the total cost of ownership higher than that for a conventional equivalent unless the vehicle is driven between 650,000 and 1,000,000km. This means there is currently not a good business case for large EFVs."[xc]

"Charging infrastructure must be upscaled in line with the number of EFVs in use, meaning that timely upgrades in electricity grids and production are necessary. Increased sales of EFVs are needed to push the demand for this infrastructure."[xci]

So, this analysis identifies a number of issues. These range from the cost of electricity relative to carbon fuels, the need for purpose built EV freight vehicles and the need to provide the infrastructure to support the range of these vehicles by charging points. Again, the high cost of electricity compared to carbon fuels (an issue in heating) is significant – pricing electricity in an economy powered by electricity is a real challenge particularly in the transition period when switching from carbon to electricity is desired.

Another option is to adapt Trolleybus or Tram technology for Freight transport. *"Germany is trialling a new highway that uses overhead electrified cabling to recharge the batteries in hybrid vehicles as they drive, the Siemens eHighway is designed to work with a custom Scania hybrid truck developed by VW Group. Germany's pilot of the technology is currently operational on a six-mile stretch of autobahn near Frankfurt and is set to run until 2022, after which it could be expanded more broadly across the country. The eHighway works by delivering 670 volts of DC power to a truck's "pantographs" or conductor rods. The system only works at speeds of less than 56 mph, but while in use it means that the hybrid vehicle can run entirely on its electric motor while simultaneously charging its battery. At the end of the electrified segment of road the truck can continue to draw from its batteries, switching to its diesel engine when they're fully depleted."* [xcii] With the technology vehicles can drive at up to 56 mph / 90 kph. But electrifying the roads in this way has a very high price tag.

Perhaps another way to examine this issue is to ask why so much heavy freight is on the road? There are large numbers of shipping containers on flat bed lorries on the A13 using Harwich, and Felixstowe ports and other similar roads. Should consideration be given to using rail for long distance transfer of shipping containers within the UK, offloading to road freight for final delivery? This idea has been proposed in East London with containers railed into Liverpool Street station which are then distributed by electric vehicle within London. Electrifying road and rail freight would appear to be the only way, to decarbonise long distance road freight.

Trains – is Hydrogen the answer?

In a speech in February 2018 by then transport minister Jo Johnson, he stated that the government wants to phase out diesel trains on the UK rail network by 2040. He said that ending reliance on fossil fuels is a priority for the government, both to curb carbon emissions and to improve air quality. Making such a statement is the easy part. The question is how should this be taken forward: by electrifying the entire rail network, or introducing onboard energy storage with batteries or hydrogen? Or perhaps a combined battery/hydrogen solution would work best? A poll of industry experts resulted in 41 per cent of respondents opting for electrification of the whole rail network, and just under a quarter (23 per cent) choosing a combination of batteries and hydrogen. Of those opting for a single energy source, 15 per cent went for onboard storage with batteries, and 13 per cent elected for onboard energy storage with hydrogen. Some of the comments from poll participants were pretty trenchant. *"The vacuous comment from the Transport Minister on the intended deletion of diesel fuel demonstrate some serious weaknesses in his under-standing of traction economics, train performance and long-term security of supply issues. Has he ever had to sell transport services (freight and passenger in aggressive marketplaces with lots of al-ternatives?) I doubt it."* While some still advocated diesel, fuel cells were supported. *"Advanced fuel cells are the only option that could do the job without massive unaffordable infrastructure alterations."* Another *"Hydrogen is the obvious replacement. It re-quires no electrical catenary wires, so we don't have to make our Victorian tunnels taller. No icing, tension or breakage problems and no resistance losses. If hydrogen trains are 'untested', why are DB ordering a fleet of them for suburban use in Germany?"*

The Breeze project promises to rollout Hydrogen trains to replace diesel trains. These hydrogen-fuelled trains can run on existing track without the need for expensive overhead power cables required for electric operation. Given that only just over 40 per cent of the UK's rail network is currently elec-trified, and the vast majority of trains running on diesel, there are cost benefits to this solution. UK rail minister Andrew Jones said: *"Hydrogen train technology is an exciting innovation which has the potential to transform our railway, making journeys cleaner and greener by cutting CO2 emissions even further. We are working with industry to establish how hydrogen trains can play an important part in the future, delivering better services on rural and inter-urban routes."*

That ignores the problem with Hydrogen identified in Chap-ter 7. The cost of producing hydrogen *"means it is necessary to produce hydrogen fuel industrially and, in the commercial world, as much as 95% of all hydrogen is produced by burning fossil fuels. This leads to a quandary: for a hydrogen fuel-cell car to work, it's necessary burn oil, gas or coal to produce, store and use hydrogen in sufficient amounts to power a number of cars."* This same problem applies to Hydrogen for trains. The Rail Freight Association continues to advocate more efficient diesel trains, presumably because they don't see a current workable alternative.

The challenge for rail therefore is how to run trains on the 60% of the current network which is not electric and uses diesel trains. Hydrogen would provide cost savings over the capital cost of electrifying the network completely, but it is produced from carbon. Until this issue is addressed at a scalable level it is not the answer in a zero-carbon economy. The only solution is electrification with non-carbon electricity as the power source. Depending on the cost per km this is in the range of £7,392bn for costs of £1m per km to £20.697bn for costs of £2.8m per km (which is the currently achieved figure). Registering the comments above, electrification does have problems with installation in tunnels below a certain height. This could be addressed by battery use in tunnels charged on open track. Given the carbon source of hydrogen currently, it is difficult to see an alternative to electrification as that alternative would rely on technology which is not scalable to the needs of the railway system.

Taxation – the fly in the ointment

These technologies will all benefit from a competitive low cost of electricity, certainly that is required in the transitional phase, as it would be needed to encourage take up. This raises a large cost issue, however, for government. Where does the money come from to hold down electricity prices in a period when a decline in fuel duty coincides with the switch to electric cars. The government currently raises a significant amount of revenue from fuel duty. In 2019/2020 fuel duties are forecast to raise £28.4bn or 3.5% of government receipts. To put this in perspective, Corporation Tax is forecast to raise £55.5bn during the same period. So, decarbonisation will reduce government income as fuel duty drops with the fall in petrol and diesel consumption, unless it is replaced by another source of taxation.

How will the government make up this shortfall? There is the problem of what to do to raise revenue without choking off non carbon investment. The only obvious target is to tax electricity as this will be the dominant power source. Electricity is currently taxed at a reduced rate of VAT of 5%. If electricity is to be taxed more highly than now, how is the issue of fuel poverty to be addressed, given that power forms a higher percentage of the expenditure of the less affluent than the more affluent population. Will this therefore lead to different tax rates on electricity dependent on the final use? Will electricity to charge a vehicle be taxed more highly than domestic electricity thus replacing fuel duty?

This is a major fiscal issue for an economy which is decarbonising. The tension between encouraging the use of carbon free electricity and the need to replace fuel duty is a real conundrum. One can argue that if electricity for transport is taxed more highly this is no different than the fuel duty in equity terms. However, if electricity is taxed at different rates for different uses with domestic use lower and transport use higher how will the government remove the danger of tax avoidance? This would suggest the need for separate metering for domestic and transport use.

Conclusion

To reiterate the beginning of this chapter, transport represents 27% of UK emissions. It is the largest sector in terms of emissions, but the one with the worst record for reduction (along with aviation and maritime, the other transport sectors). The reduction in emissions for road transport over the last thirty years is just 3.7%. The UK is not alone, and other countries have struggled to reduce emissions in this sector.

In part this is about personal choice, again to quote the IEA report of October 2019: *"As passenger cars consume nearly one-quarter of global oil demand today, does this signal the approaching erosion of a pillar of global oil consumption? A more silent structural change may put this conclusion into question: consumers are buying ever larger and less fuel-efficient cars, known as sport utility vehicles (SUVs)....SUVs were the second-largest contributor to the increase in global CO_2 emissions since 2010 after the power sector, but ahead of heavy industry (including iron & steel, cement, aluminium), as well as trucks and aviation.*

While discussions today see significant focus on electric vehicles and fuel economy improvements, the analysis highlights the role of the average size of car fleet. Bigger and heavier cars, like SUVs, are harder to electrify and growth in their rising demand may slow down the development of clean and efficient car fleets."

These figures put the transition from fossil fuels to electric into perspective. We as consumers, are buying cars which emit more carbon by choice. We are increasingly buying cars which are harder to electrify again by choice. We are increasing global oil demand by our choice in buying and driving these cars. If we are to switch to electric cars, we will have to wean ourselves off the desire for SUVs. Each method of reduction poses serious issues. Electric vehicles with Lithium Ion batteries are dependent on cobalt which has serious supply issues with dependence on the DRC. Hydrogen looks to be a good solution but only if production from non-carbon sources can be achieved and in significant volumes. Solid State batteries don't have such supply issues, and while the technology can be made to work, costs are prohibitive. It may be a key technology in the future, but is not proven yet, forcing us to focus on Lithium Ion batteries.

For road freight and rail, the issue (if we dismiss hydrogen) is the need for electrification of the railways and major roads. Both will require significant investment and the cost for each is likely to be roughly the same per km. With UK motorways totalling 3497 km the cost would be between £3.5bn and £9.8bn. Railways would cost between the range of £7.4bn for costs of £1m per km to £20.7bn for costs of £2.8m per km. Together £10.9bn to £30.5bn. Electrification of major roads and motorways would obviate the need to divert freight onto the rail network.

The government will have to address the fiscal loss of road fuel duty implicit in decarbonisation and decide the revenue source to replace 3.5% of the revenue it currently provides in the UK, this suggests that electricity for driving may be subject to a similar tax and that different rates of tax (VAT,etc) will apply to electricity consumption for that purpose.

Finally, the government will need to control the price of electricity to encourage this transition, which is no easy feat.

12 PUBLIC SECTOR

All the tables on UK emissions in this book are from data in 2017 UK GREENHOUSE GAS EMISSIONS, PROVISIONAL FIGURES Statistical Release: National Statistics 29 March 2018

Public Sector	1990	2017	Reduction (Increase)
	13.5	7.8	42.1%

The public sector has shown a good decrease in emissions with the fifth highest reduction as a sector as a result of energy efficiency and rationalisation of the central government estate. The 2018 UK Greenhouse Gas Emissions, Provisional Figures Statistical Release: National Statistics report states that in common with residential, a significant proportion of these emissions arise from gas used for heating. Unfortunately, and strangely the Committee on Climate Change does not analyse emissions for the public sector in contrast to the report 2018 UK Greenhouse Gas Emissions, Provisional Figures Statistical Release: National Statistics, why is not clear? So, the position is similar to the analysis in Chapter 17 on Residential, the public sector needs to eliminate its dependence on Gas.

The report "The Clean Growth Strategy Leading the way to a low carbon future"[xciii] states *"While central government has shown what is possible, we now want the wider public sector to reap the benefits of this approach. The annual energy bill across all public sector buildings in England and Wales is estimated to be around £2 billion and this could be reduced significantly, releasing funds for front line services. The NHS is responsible for around a third of public sector carbon emissions and in 2015/16 around*

£570 million was spent by the NHS Trust on energy.

The public sector also has a key role to play in demonstrating best practice, promoting transparency over emissions reporting and catalysing markets in energy efficiency by implementing measures at scale.

To meet the UK's 2050 target, emissions from the buildings and activities of the public sector will need to be near zero. As with homes and commercial property, this means improving energy efficiency and energy management, and decarbonising the heating and cooling of buildings as far as possible.

In the 2015 Spending Review, the Government announced £295 million of new funding for public sector energy efficiency across the UK. In England, this increased funding is invested in the existing public sector energy efficiency loan scheme, which is available to the wider public and higher education sectors. The loan scheme administrator currently manages £210 million, and this will rise to some £385 million by 2020. This revolving loan scheme will continue to be recycled to at least 2025. Similar schemes run in Scotland and Wales received £40 million of the 2015 spending review award."

This is all laudable aspiration, but the public sector still makes up 2% of UK emissions (the NHS just under 1%) and it is difficult to find concrete plans or costings. The levels of finance look to be small given the scale of the challenge, and it is worth remembering that the reduction to date has largely been achieved by substituting gas for other carbon fuels. The removal of gas is a much larger challenge. If the solution proposed for residential is also appropriate here, then the scale of investment in heat pumps will be huge unless community schemes to use district heating are applied, particularly in NHS properties.

The scale of investment

To date, carbon reduction has been achieved by switching to lower carbon fuel. The next step is to move to renewable and this inevitably has a higher capital cost. The question is, how will government finance this change?

A good example is the installation at Kings Mill Hospital in Mansfield. A cooling system with a capacity of 5.4 MW at the new hospital is claimed to be the largest in Europe to reject heat to a lake, in this case a water reservoir providing 90% of cooling for the hospital. Installed by Skanska, the system can also provide up to 5 MW low-grade supplementary heat to the gas-fired boilers when cooling demand is low. A network of heat exchangers submerged in the neighbouring Kings Mill Reservoir is used to extract or reject heat through a closed-loop system.

The "NHS Energy Efficiency Fund Final Report – Summary February 2015" states *"If the NHS halves its built environment carbon emissions it could save 9% of NHS total emissions, some 2.25 Million tonnes of CO2 annually, deliver the cash savings directly back into healthcare and, therefore, trigger a step change in NHS organisational behaviour. Very crudely, simply factoring up the outcomes of the NHS EEF project to save 2.25 Million tonnes, some £330m of benefits may be available annually across the whole estate, £165m annually for a cut in emissions of only 25%."*[xciv]

This is a common feature of reports at national and local Health Trust level; what is consistent in these reports is the absence of any attempt to quantify the capital cost of these measures and how that is funded. Even if the assumption is that these actions will be cost effective with relatively short cost payback periods, a consistent approach to cost and pay-back is needed to ensure the most effective investments are made. The issue emerged in a dispute between Chancellor Hammond in 2019 and the Prime Minister. The Chancellor estimated the investment cost of zero carbon by 2050 at £1tn (including the public sector). The question is how this would be financed. To put this in perspective, the investment element of government pending in 2019-2020 is estimated by the

Office for Budget Responsibility at £47bn. To invest a further £1tn would double the current investment budget for over twenty years.

Conclusion

The public sector may only be 2% of UK emissions, but the plans to remove them are vague. How the investment for these plans will be decided is not clear, and the competition for funds between carbon reduction and improving and or increasing capacity will complicate matters. Until a clear investment methodology is determined, there must be considerable doubts that the public sector will meet a zero-carbon target by 2050, both absolutely and, in a cost effective manner.

13 AGRICULTURE

All the tables on UK emissions in this book are from data in 2017 UK GREENHOUSE GAS EMISSIONS, PROVISIONAL FIGURES Statistical Release: National Statistics 29 March 2018.

Agriculture			1990	2017	Reduction (Increase)
Total			54.0	45.6	15.5%
Stationary and mobile combustion			5.2	4.3	16.4%
Incidental lubricant combustion in engi			0.0	0.0	96.3%
Enteric fermentati	Cattle - enteric ferme		19.9	16.8	15.6%
	Sheep - enteric ferme		4.9	4.0	18.1%
	Goats - enteric ferme		0.0	0.0	-7.7%
	Horses - enteric ferm		0.3	0.4	-67.4%
	Pigs - enteric fermen		0.3	0.2	34.2%
	Deer - enteric fermen		0.0	0.0	34.1%
Wastes	Cattle - wastes		5.8	5.3	8.6%
	Sheep - wastes		0.2	0.1	17.6%
	Goats - wastes		0.0	0.0	-7.7%
	Horses - wastes		0.1	0.2	-60.8%
	Pigs - wastes		1.6	1.0	41.2%
	Poultry - wastes		0.5	0.4	5.1%
	Deer - wastes		0.0	0.0	34.1%
Other (agriculture	Liming		1.0	0.9	7.5%
	Direct soil emission		11.2	9.2	17.5%
	Field burning		0.2	0.0	100.0%
	Urea application		0.3	0.3	-5.0%
	Indirect soil emission		2.4	2.2	7.7%

Agriculture produces 10% of UK emissions. As a sector it will be difficult sector to reduce emissions, because agricultural emissions are not largely carbon; the main agricultural sources of greenhouse gas emissions are:

"Enteric fermentation (flatulence) by ruminant animals such as cattle, sheep and goats , which produce methane (CH_4) emissions; enteric fermentation is a natural part of the digestive process for many ruminants as anaerobic microbes decompose and ferment

food in the rumen, then they are absorbed by the ruminant; this digestion process is not 100 % efficient, so some of the food energy is lost in the form of methane; measures to mitigate enteric fermentation would not only reduce emissions, they may also raise animal productivity by increasing digestive efficiency; soil nitrification and denitrification, which produces nitrous oxide (N_2O) emissions; nitrification is the aerobic microbial oxidation of ammonium (NH_4) to nitrates (NO_3), whereas denitrification is the anaerobic microbial reduction of nitrates to nitrogen gas (N_2); manure decomposition, which produces methane and nitrous oxide emissions."[xcv]

The problem is there is no roadmap to eliminate agricultural emissions, in part because of the methane issue, and secondly because modern agriculture's efficiency (and food yield) is built on large scale mechanisation, like road freight, therefore it cannot easily transform to electric renewable power. Having said that, the UK sits below the EU average, and other countries have bigger problems. Those countries with agricultural emissions above 15% will have a very difficult task in achieving zero carbon. Ireland will only achieve zero carbon if the Irish agricultural sector is decimated.

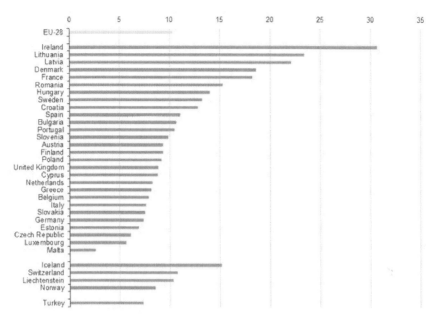

This poses an interesting question for a zero-carbon target; can it be achieved if we continue to eat meat or eat a smaller amount of meat? Perhaps a more distressing question for many is, can we have as many carnivorous pets as we do in a zero-carbon world? There has already been much comment about whether our diet compatible and sustainable with a zero-carbon economy? Again, in common with other issues, these are not government questions, they are decisions which we as individuals need to make. Should we all become vegans? Should our pets change to a largely non-meat diet too? The report, "Healthy Diets from Sustainable Food Systems" from the EAT-Lancet Commission summarises the position that diets will need to change dramatically to be sustainable in terms of food production. *"Food is the single strongest lever to optimize human health and environmental sustainability on Earth. However, food is currently threatening both people and planet. An immense challenge facing humanity is to provide a growing world population with healthy diets from sustainable food systems. While global food production of calories has generally kept pace with population growth, more than 820 million people still*

lack sufficient food, and many more consume either low-quality diets or too much food. Unhealthy diets now pose a greater risk to morbidity and mortality than unsafe sex, alcohol, drug and tobacco use combined. Global food production threatens climate stability and ecosystem resilience and constitutes the single largest driver of environmental degradation and transgression of planetary boundaries. Taken together the outcome is dire. A radical transformation of the global food system is urgently needed. Without action, the world risks failing to meet the UN Sustainable Development Goals (SDGs) and the Paris Agreement, and today's children will inherit a planet that has been severely degraded and where much of the population will increasingly suffer from malnutrition and preventable disease."

They advocate that "A planetary health plate should consist by volume of approximately half a plate of vegetables and fruits; the other half, displayed by contribution to calories, should consist of primarily whole grains, plant protein sources, unsaturated plant oils, and (optionally) modest amounts of animal sources of protein."[xcvi]

This would involve a dramatic reduction in the consumption of meat in developed countries. If you look at the menus of most restaurants and pubs, or and watch the cookery shows on TV, it is clear that the majority of dishes served are meat based. The reason for that this is what we choose, so, no government can do more than advise people to eat less meat, only we, as the consumer, can make that decision.

UK agriculture in context

Agriculture is responsible for 10% of the UK's carbon emissions, with livestock production responsible for an estimated 5% of total emissions. The most significant animal contributor to enteric fermentation and waste is cattle (including both meat and dairy production). Approximately 2.1 million cattle and 14 million sheep are slaughtered annually in the UK, supplying over 1.1 million tonnes of meat to the human food chain, with a farm gate value of over £3 billion.[xcvii]

A United Nations publication suggested global emissions from livestock made up around 14.5% of all carbon emissions. This was revised down from an earlier estimate of 18%.[xcviii] This is a global issue exacerbated by lifestyle choices that the beneficiaries of globalisation are making. As middle classes around the world grow from globalisation, their consumption of meat is increasing (even in "vegetarian" India). An EU report concluded that the emissions from livestock are estimated to be responsible for around 17% of all emissions in the EU[xcix], higher than the UK figure due to more efficient production systems in the UK.

In terms of alternatives it is arguable whether a significant proportion of UK farmland is primarily suitable for not growing grass. Without grazing ruminant animals (cattle and sheep) it is questionable whether this land could be used for food production on a large scale. Actively managed pastures are a good carbon sink, storing carbon which would otherwise be released into the atmosphere. A zero-carbon policy for farming poses some therefore massive questions for the both the farming sector and land use in the UK as well as the consumer. According to the National Farmers Union (NFU), the UK Low Carbon Transition Plan requires that by 2020 emissions from farming are at least 11% lower than the existing levels.

"This means that to meet the 11% reduction target for beef, an efficiency gain equivalent to 320g per day extra growth and 5 extra calves per 100 cows per year is needed – it is believed that this is technically achievable." "To meet the target for lamb, an efficiency gain equivalent to 20% per day extra growth and 7.5 extra lambs per 100 ewes per year is needed – and again this is believed to be technically achievable." Reducing GHG emissions and improving efficiency are compatible. "Steady improvements in production efficiency have taken place over the recent years, with 5% fewer

prime cattle and lambs required to produce each tonne of meat in 2008 than in 1998.

Research indicates that the three main areas of breeding, feeding and management offer opportunities to make the required reductions. The genetic potential for progress in beef and sheep breeds for improvements in feed efficiency is largely undeveloped, but modern breeding techniques will allow rapid progress." My experience in visiting farms in Wiltshire is that the technological changes in animal husbandry are producing significant improvements in the context of largely field feed animals. With this emphasis on field fed animals as a result, "UK beef and lamb production is not driving demand for imported soya and, therefore, not significantly contributing to deforestation in some parts of the world. The level of soya meal use in sheep and beef diets is very small in the UK."[c]

This is borne out by an analysis of soya imports. The total volume of soya consumed in the UK is estimated to be equivalent to 3.8 million tonnes of soybean representing 3.1 million tonnes of direct imports. The UK imports soya beans, meal and oil directly from producer countries and through intertrade with Europe. Approximately 90% of the EU's soya is used to feed livestock, so the majority of UK imports are soya meal. The UK imports of soya per year, breaks down to 2.26 million tonnes of Soy meal, 0.68 million tonnes Whole soy beans, and 0.16 million tonnes Soy oil. Only 400 hectares of soy beans, were actually grown in the UK. Of the Soy meal approximately 90%, is fed to pigs, poultry and farmed fish.[ci]

Due to the climate, the UK and Ireland are recognised as being more suited to grass production than other EU countries. As such a higher proportion of milk is produced from grass, and a lower proportion from concentrates or other cereal-based feeds. In late April, May and June in the UK, when the grass is at its most nutritious, grazing dairy cows can maintain their own body weight from grass and produce up to 25 litres of milk per day without concentrates. It is interesting to compare the conversion of soya into milk by cows compared to direct soya milk production. On the basis of these calculations, cow's milk comes out significantly better than expected with between 60 and 112 litres of milk produced for each kilo of soya meal fed to cows, compared to 7.5 litres of milk produced from each kilo of soya beans turned into soya milk. [cii]

This illustrates the complexity of policy decisions on achieving zero carbon. Growing soya beans may appear more beneficial than dairy production in direct carbon terms, but if Soya is grown at the expense of deforestation, the benefit is more difficult to ascertain. This is recognised in the following from the European Environment Agency. *"In a global food system, Europe's imports and their consumption have an environmental, social and economic impact beyond European borders. In 2013, Europe had net imports of around 27 million tonnes of soybeans and soybean products for oil production and animal feed. This means Europe is dependent on overseas land for its own livestock production most of which is in South America."*[ciii] Put more simply, when you order a burger is that indirectly leading to deforestation, if the cow it comes from is fed soy?

Meat consumption

Meat is more difficult. Aside from beef, global greenhouse gas emissions from pig and chicken supply chains are relatively low. Pig supply chains are estimated to produce 0.7 gigatonnes of CO_2 equivalent per annum, representing 9 percent of the livestock sector's emissions. Chickens are estimated to emit 0.6 gigatonnes of CO_2-equivalent, representing 8 percent of the livestock sector's emissions. The UK imports 25% of chickens consumed and 45% of pork consumed. The corresponding figures for lamb and beef are 30% and 35%. One can argue that meat emissions are understated as meat produced elsewhere and imported is not included in UK emissions figures.

Pets pose an even more difficult and emotional question. It is estimated that *"dogs and cats are responsible for a quarter of the greenhouse gas emissions caused by animal agriculture, according a 2017 US study, which adds up to a whopping 64 million tons of carbon-dioxide equivalent emitted in the production of their food in the US. But scientists remain divided about the role our pets play in global warming."*[civ]

I haven't found much on studies about pet food and emissions in the UK, but Reuters reported that *"Studies suggest pets consume about a fifth of the world's meat and fish, and a dog's carbon footprint is more than twice that of a 4x4 car"* and *"calculated the impact of our pets' diets on the climate as comparable to emissions from 13.6 million cars."*[cv] Again, this is a matter of choice for citizens, as no government can legislate on this. If price is used to discourage meat consumption, issues of social equity would arise as to whether the poor should bear a disproportionate share of the burden while the rich continue to eat meat? The same issue would apply to pet food; should only the rich have pets?

There is work to be done, on developing animal feed from sources that will not produce methane in the farm animal's guts. How acceptable this will be to consumers and animal rights groups is not yet clear.

How can farming cut its emissions?

Aside from the question of whether we should eat meat, what can farming do to reduce its emissions? The following examples from the Farm Cutting Carbon Toolkit[cvi] illustrate the issues the sector faces and some potential methods of reduction.

Caplor Farm Herefordshire

"Caplor Farm's main source of emissions in the past year were the

agro-chemicals, principally fertilisers, used on arable crops, which represented 61.5% of total emissions. Fuels accounted for 22% of emissions, showing the importance of steps to reduce fuel use on any farm. This would undoubtedly be higher were it not for the focus on reducing this. There were smaller emissions from live-stock (8.5%) and fertility, as well as a result of materials used on the farm. Hedges and field margins sequester significant amounts of carbon on the farm (around 8% of the total), and there could be scope to increase sequestration from soils.

Another change is the introduction of cover crops, grown between rotations, retaining vital nutrients in the ground and building Soil Organic Matter. For example, clover is often grown, which can fix nitrogen in soils as a natural fertiliser. The farm has used a variety of different sources of organic matter over the years totalling man-ner thousands of tons and is currently investigating an organic source of fertiliser in the form of a green manure or compost, and already uses chicken droppings instead of Ammonium Nitrate."

Cotswolds

"Nitrogen is an important chemical for farmers as it is a natural fertiliser for plants. However, too much nitrogen can cause prob-lems as it may end up being washed into our rivers where it can impact on our drinking and bathing waters and on our precious aquatic ecosystems. Loss of nitrates to ground waters is one of the main issues on the thin "brashy" soils over limestone of the Cotswold catchment. One possible solution is to grow winter cover crops, such as vetch, radish, rye and mustard, which naturally soak up nitrogen and improve soil structure.

Some of the crops had taken up a notable amount of nitrogen and produced large volumes of organic matter, perfect for returning to the soil as green manure to improve soil structure and water-re-taining capacity for the following crop. Reducing the amount of fertiliser needed adds to the economic benefits. Other benefits in-clude reducing erosion and loss of phosphates, increasing organic matter and improving soil structure."

Shimpling Park Farm Suffolk

"*Total carbon-equivalent (CO2e) emissions amounted to 1,150 tonnes. The main sources of emissions came from Fuels (33.5%) - mostly diesel use, and Fertility (54%) - including nitrous oxide emissions from crop residues and green manures. Fuels This mostly came from diesel use in tractors and combines (29%). There is also diesel used in road vehicles for the farm business. This is to expected in a mechanised arable system. Electricity on the farm amounted to 4% of total emission, mostly used for grain drying. It's also worth noting that a 50kW array of solar PV panels exports around electricity offsetting 16 tonnes of CO2, as well as providing some 'free' electricity to the farm.*

Fertility Nitrous oxide emissions from crop residues of arable crops (beans, peas, wheat and oats) contribute to a large percentage of total emissions at 29%. This is due to nitrogen in the crop residue being oxidised in the soil and being released as nitrous oxide. Leguminous green manures (red clover) contribute a further 17% of emissions through nitrous oxide released during nitrogen fixation. This appears to be a very negative attribute of green manures, however they can also contribute to a substantial increase in organic matter levels, which sequesters atmospheric carbon. In effect this at least 'balances out' the nitrous oxide emissions. Also worth mentioning is the 2.8% of emissions from the application of rock phosphate.

Carbon is sequestered in perennial biomass and soils on farms. On this farm 60% of carbon is sequestered in woodlands, whilst permanent field margins (21%) and hedges (18%) are the other main carbon sinks. The total carbon sequestered on the farm (454 tonnes of CO2) offsets 40% of all carbon emitted by the farm business."

The way forward

Some themes emerge from these examples, which are worth quoting at length.

Firstly, carbon sequestration in farming from woodland, field margins, and hedges can have a significant impact on net emissions. In addition, winter cover crops, such as vetch, radish, rye and mustard, which naturally soak up nitrogen, may reduce emissions of nitrous oxide. Government policies should be directed to supporting and maximising sequestration planting on farms, and the reduction of farming on marginal land.

Secondly, there is the need to reduce nitrous oxide emissions and the use of nitrogen fertilisers (the impact of which is demonstrated in the Cotswolds example). Could the UK government unilaterally act on this without affecting the competitive position of the farming sector?

Thirdly, diesel. The focus on electric engines for cars has not yet filtered through to the tractor market to date. An NFU survey found that 5% of respondents already have an electric car or van on farm, and two-thirds are aware that battery electric tractors and machinery is likely to become available in the next five to ten years.

While the expected lower running costs and enhanced safety of electric farm machinery are important attributes, and advantageous, significant farmer concerns identified by the survey include higher purchase cost, limited range, and recharging downtime. As with electric cars, charging infrastructure is an issue, but in a different way. With the current *maximum electricity load in kW available on farms, only 27% of respondents said they could accommodate 100-kilowatt or above power, i.e. rapid charging.* The change from diesel to electric will have an impact, but there are investment issues particularly with the price of batteries. Electric drive does offer advantages with some implements and attachments giving more precise handling. One example is precision seeding. John Deere's Exact Emerge system for single seed placing, uses electric motors to place seeds within 1cm accuracy at a forward speed of 20kph. However, there are questions as to whether an electric tractor will be able to function at 268hp and above (200Kw), and whether this will require hybrid technology.

Agriculture will reduce some emissions, but questions remain as to the rump of emissions which cannot be removed, and what offset mechanisms are available to achieve zero carbon. As is suggested in Chapter 14, sequestration may change agriculture to agroforestry. This appears to be the way forward, with on-site offsetting combined with a less carbon intensive farming. This will change the landscape and the way in which we farm; only time will tell if this is acceptable to people.

14 LAND USE & FORESTRY

All the tables on UK emissions in this book are from data in 2017 UK GREENHOUSE GAS EMISSIONS, PROVISIONAL FIGURES Statistical Release: National Statistics 29 March 2018.

Land Use and Forestry	1990	2017	Reduction (Increase)
	0.3	-9.9	1000.0%
Forest land remaining forest land	-14.5	-18.0	-24.5%
Biomass burning	0.0	0.0	20.4%
Land converted to forest land	-0.6	-0.2	65.5%
Drainage of organic soils	0.0	0.1	-13.7%
Direct N$_2$O emissions	0.2	0.1	51.8%
Biomass burning	0.0	0.0	96.2%
Cropland remaining cropland	2.9	5.8	-100.9%
Land converted to cropland	11.3	5.1	55.1%
Direct N$_2$O emissions	1.0	0.5	54.9%
Biomass burning	0.0	0.2	-485.2%
Grassland remaining grassland	-2.3	-5.1	-116.8%
Land converted to grassland	-5.0	-4.1	16.9%
Direct N$_2$O emissions	0.0	0.0	-56265.7%
Drainage of organic soils	0.2	0.2	0.0%
Wetlands remaining wetland	0.5	0.3	30.9%
Drainage of organic soils	0.0	0.0	92.9%
Land converted to wetland	0.0	0.0	-123.4%
Settlements remain settlements	1.6	2.3	-38.4%
Biomass burning	0.0	0.1	-175.1%
Land converted to settlements	5.3	4.1	23.7%
Direct N$_2$O emissions	0.6	0.5	11.3%
Harvested wood	-1.6	-2.0	-23.0%
Indirect N$_2$O emissions	0.4	0.2	39.3%

"The one who plants trees, knowing that he or she will never sit in their shade, has at least started to under-

stand the meaning of life." Ranbindranath Tagore

"The best time to plant a tree is 20 years ago, the second best, is now". Chinese proverb

The UK in the global context

A recent report from Climate Focus states:

"On average, an area of tree cover, the size of the United Kingdom was lost every year between 2014 and 2018. While hotspots of increasing tree cover loss have emerged in Africa in the last five years, Latin America still loses the most tree cover every year. In June 2019 alone, deforestation rates in the Brazilian Amazon increased by 88 percent compared to the same month last year. The expansion of agricultural commodities continues to be the largest driver of deforestation. Over ninety percent of global deforestation linked to agricultural commodities and urbanization occurred in the tropics."[cvii] This doesn't just apply to the Amazon, the Atlantic forest in Brazil is another area. Aside from Brazil, Honduras, Nigeria, Phillipines, Benin, Ghana and Indonesia have lost over a quarter of their trees. The recent fires in Australia have destroyed an area the size of England to the Severn, Crewe and the Wash.

It may be argued that in the light of this, what can the UK do? Like other aspects of decarbonisation, no country or region can stand alone in its actions, but this should not be used as an excuse to do nothing. Through this chapter and book, I am going to refer to tree planting generically as opposed to the business of forestry.

Can planting trees solve our Decarbonisation targets?

Many promote the use of tree planting as a solution for our decarbonisation targets based on the simple fact that over its life a tree will sequester carbon. Carbon Neutral an Australian organisation, , which describes itself as a Carbon solutions provider and re-forestation developer uses the following methodology, *"Carbon sequestration is measured on a per hectare basis. That may vary from 100 to 300 tonnes CO_2-e per hectare at year 30 depending on site and rainfall. Tree density also varies from 500 to 2000 stems per hectare. Measuring trees per tonne CO_2 is therefore highly variable. As a rule of thumb, we currently adopt 15 trees per tonne as a conservative estimate."*[cviii]

Green Energy Consulting claim that in the UK *"the amount of CO2 a tree will offset depends on many factors, such as the type of tree, where it is planted and the amount of room it has to grow. On average, one broad leaf tree will absorb in the region of 1 tonne of carbon dioxide during its full life-time (approximately 100 years)"*[cix]

This is not an exact science. These are rule of thumb calculations, and the amount will depend on the tree, its location geographically, the planting density and thinning policy over time. (Trees in the UK are planted at roughly two metre intervals under Forestry Commission guidance and the grant system. As the tree matures, this planting density mean that a number of trees will be removed (thinned). If one looks at a mature tree plantation, then the trees will be spaced about four metres apart for a fully mature group of trees. For the purposes of this chapter, I will use 1 tonne per tree.

The fundamental challenge with tree planting is where to plant? The land area needed to meet the CCC target (see below) is very large. The balance of land use between farming (and which type of farming), woodland, and forestry and other use needs to be identified otherwise tree planting targets will not be met. Another option is to integrate more trees into existing land use in a hybrid land use, e.g. agroforestry. The challenge of land use with an increasing UK population will pose issues given the negative effect of building additional homes and infrastructure, coupled with the food and energy use a growing population requires.

Spoiling the landscape

One of the issues with tree planting is how it sits in the landscape. To increase tree planting will require change to our landscape and people will need to accept and agree to this. Two examples illustrate this issue.

Ireland has been planting forests as part of its plan is to plant more trees. From having just 1% forest cover in 1900, Ireland now has 11%, covering 770,000 hectares. It has just committed to planting 8,000 more hectares each year to reach 18% coverage, but not without controversy and local objections are common. This is partly due to Ireland's need to compensate for the emissions from its dairy industry, vehicles and its dependence on fossil-burning power plants that make it one of Europe's worst countries in terms of the scale of its emissions. Ireland generates over 70% of its electricity from carbon (OECD). Greenhouse gases per capita of 12,763kg compares to the UK (9,172kg), Sweden (6,051 kg) and Netherlands (11,440kg).

Opposition to this policy is developing because of the way this policy is being implemented. Is planting *"dark, dank abominations that kill wildlife, block sunlight and isolate communities"*[cx] a good policy? A major part of the reason for the opposition to tree planting is the Sitka spruce, a coniferous evergreen that dominates Ireland's afforestation programme. Originally from North America, it grows quickly and tall – up to 100 metres – and flourishes in Ireland's damp, temperate climate. Raising a significant biosecurity risk as a dependency on near monoculture is a significant vulnerability to pests and disease.

About half of Ireland's trees are Sitka spruces. They supply wood for pulp, plywood, pallets, fencing, garden furniture and building materials, low quality single use items, where the carbon is recycled almost instantly, much of it exported to Britain. But they absorb carbon, which is important as Ireland tries to avert fines of hundreds of millions of euros for missing targets on emissions and renewable energy. Ireland's plan is to curb greenhouse gas emissions and set a path for net-zero carbon emissions by 2050. With emissions from agriculture set to rise, not fall, an important part of the strategy depends on planting 8,000 hectares of new forest each year, of which there will be a lot more Sitka spruces. The Guardian reported, John O'Reilly, the CEO of Green Belt, Ireland's biggest private forestry company, said Sitka grew three times faster in Ireland than Scandinavia, driving a sustainable sector that generated jobs, created essential building materials and benefited the environment. Resulting in low density timber, suitable only for low quality products. *"The faster it grows, the greater the quantity of carbon it will sequester from the atmosphere."*[cxi]

The issue with planting trees, therefore, is which type of trees and the balance between economic return and the impact on landscape. Forestry is an unwieldy industry that takes decades to change. It may be necessary to look at how markets for carbon might be constructed to enable the flow of finance across to landowners for carbon sequestration and storage rather than forestry per se.

The second issue is preserving "natural landscapes". In the UK, George Monbiot has identified an area where the preservation of the landscape hinders tree planting. His book "Feral"[cxii] make the case that the UK has fetishized upland landscapes free of trees, for a number of reasons, but primarily sheep. Monbiot focuses on the impact on a number of upland areas, but in particular, upland areas of central Wales where tree cover is sparse. The number of bodies which forbid the return of the landscape to its former state is overwhelming, representing group think for the status quo. The EU states that *'land abandonment in less advantageous areas would have negative environmental consequences'* (Common Agricultural Policy towards 2020)[cxiii]. On the contrary, low land prices in central Wales might make it a particularly attractive location to establish carbon sequestration woodland.

The Forestry Commission has published a map of Wales showing that no tree planting will be sanctioned in most of the upland areas. The NFU of Wales has stated *"reducing the number of sheep 'has a severe detrimental impact on upland biodiversity'"*. Its sister organisation, the NFU of Scotland *"fewer sheep…means under-grazing of traditional pastures, a loss of diversity, a return to bracken and brash and the potential for irreparable damage to Scotland's beautiful landscape"*. The polite response to this is it is mistaken!

Some challenge to this policy is emerging. Monbiot quotes *"I am told by a senior civil servant that an insurance company recently investigated the possibility of buying and reforesting Pumlumon, the largest mountain in the Cambrians, on whose slopes both the Severn and the Wye arise. It had worked out that this would be cheaper than paying out for carpets in Gloucestershire (flood damage). It abandoned the plan because of likely political difficulties."*[cxiv] The Countryside Council for Wales chairman is quoted *"He acknowledged that the idea of keeping the uplands open and treeless 'does need to be challenged'"*.[cxv]

The double benefit of carbon sequestration and reducing flood risk is a low cost policy change which addresses two major issues in times of increasing climate volatility. The UK has suffered from different patterns of rainfall since the millennium, and the frequency of flooding has increased. This has been the result of the increase in the amount of rain falling in short periods of time, combined with the speed of run off water from upland areas with low levels of vegetation (which as a result absorb less rain as it falls). The planting of trees on marginal land, particularly uplands, will absorb more water and slow the run off, addressing one cause of downstream flooding. Aside from the emissions benefit of tree planting, encouraging tree planting in areas to reduce run off would be a cheaper, more cost-effective form of flood defence, than infrastructure down stream without this upstream mitigation.

"Woodlands for Water, a joint initiative by the Forestry Commis-

sion and the Environment Agency, aims to promote the creation of new woodland where it can best help to reduce downstream flood risk and rural diffuse pollution."[cxvi]

Even lowland farming is affected. Monbiot highlights the effect of EU policy in this regard. *"They are laid down in a European code with the Orwellian title of 'Good Agricultural and Environmental Condition'. Among the compulsory standards it sets is 'avoiding the encroachment of unwanted vegetation on agricultural land'. What this means is that if farmers want their money, they must stop wild plants from returning."*[cxvii] *"The infamous 'fifty trees' guideline ensures that pastures containing more than fifty trees per hectare are not eligible for funding.... The government of Northern Ireland has been fined £64 million for ... giving subsidy money to farms whose traditional hedgerows are too wide"*[cxviii]. A strange world.

Slower run off water from uplands will also have the benefit of making the management of water for irrigation easier.

Tree Planting

You might find this map surprising. The South East has the highest densities of tree cover in England and Wales. What is also clear is that our upland areas, have some of the lowest.

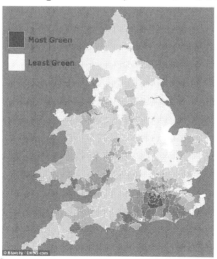

The **Climate Change** Committee supports a target to plant

three billion trees by 2050 in the UK together with planting 200,000 miles of hedgerows. It is important to put this in perspective. The proposal to plant three billion trees doubles the number of existing trees in the UK, and gives us thirty years to plant them! The CCC also called for a 40% increase in hedgerows, but it does not make clear if it means 40% more length, or simply 40% more biomass.

The area of woodland in the UK at 31 March 2019 is estimated to be 3.19 million hectares with 3bn trees (average density of 1000 trees per hectare). This represents 13% of the total land area in the UK, 10% in England, 15% in Wales, 19% in Scotland and 8% in Northern Ireland. (Forest Research) The additional tree planting of 3bn proposed by the CCC will presumably increase the land area to closer to 25% in the UK (still a far lower percentage than many European countries) if the same densities are used. To give a feel for what this means, 3.2 million hectares is equal to combined size of the historic counties of Yorkshire, Lincolnshire, Devon and Norfolk – the four largest counties in England. Put another way, this is twenty times the area within the M25 motorway of 1,572 square kilometres or It is 150% the area of Wales. Given devolution, the distribution of these trees between the four parts of the UK may prove to be be an interesting negotiation.

The UK is in the bottom five of the table in terms of forestry as a percentage of land area in Europe. The UK has had tree planting targets for some time but on a modest scale which are often not met. Thirteen thousand hectares of newly created woodland were reported in the UK in 2018-19.[cxix] More trees are not exclusively created by planting. Natural regeneration, which will often result in a scrubby habitat, in contrast to woodland (but beneficial for wildlife) can be a significant force. George Monbiot's rewilding (with a little human help) could create more trees. For further discussion see George Monbiot "Feral" and Isabella Tree "Wilding".

The table below[cxx] illustrates that current levels of planting are totally inadequate to achieve this new target. If we continue to plant at the current rate it will take 125 years to plant 3bn trees not 30. And it is important to remember that the current rate of 13,000 hectares also includes restocking, whereas the CCC target is for new tree planting net of those trees which are cut down, fall down or are affected by disease (like ash die back currently affecting ash trees).

Woodland Area,Planting and Restocking, 2012-2016 (000s ha)

Year	England	Wales	Scotland	N Ireland	UK
2012	6.3	2.8	14.7	1.3	25.1
2013	6.6	2.9	13	1.5	24
2014	7.8	3.2	16.2	1.5	28.7
2015	8.8	2	16.1	1.5	28.4
2016	4	1.9	12.4	0.8	19.1
2012-2016					125.3

I planted four hectares of broadleaf trees in 2012 in Wiltshire and have managed this wood since. This has taught me what is necessary to manage a tract of woodland and the work involved. Many who comment on forestry in terms of carbon seem to have little practical experience of the issues of woodland management. I have just reinstated a stretch of hedgerow on one of my boundaries, from this experience, planting the target of 200,000 miles of hedgerows will not be an easy task and there may be issues with finding the skilled individuals to do this. Watch any you tube video on planting a hedgerow and you will get a sense of what this is like. The Forestry Commission provides grants to encourage both planting and woodland management but the complexity of many of the documents will be impenetrable to many small woodland owners. **This approach will not be sustainable to achieve the required rate of tree planting.**

From the Forestry Commission website re grants

"You can apply for capital funding to establish new woodland, including planting trees and installing tree guards, fencing and gates. You could receive up to 80% of the standard costs for these items and a contribution of 40% of the cost of roads and tracks needed

to support the woodland's establishment (including agent fees and VAT, where applicable). Payments are capped at an average £6,800 per hectare across the area for planting and protection (not including forest roads and tracks)."

The problem here is that there are minimum areas to qualify for grants, and obviously the grant does not cover the cost of the land. While the grant appears generous, at required planting densities the amount per tree will barely cover the cost of the tree and the tree guard needed to protect the saplings from first rabbits and deer.

Given current levels of planting at existing support levels, what will incentivise the planting of four times as many hectares of woodland per year to meet the 3bn tree target? Which landowners, public and private are going to be prepared to do this, and where will the trees to be planted?

Current grant policy states that trees should be planted with tree guards. At an average cost of £1.50 for a 1.2 metre tube, 3 billion trees will cost £4.5 billion. In addition, these protect young trees from deer and encourage early growth of the tree.

Deer

Wild Deer eat and kill young trees. To meet the 3bn target for trees, the deer population of the UK will need to be managed and controlled.

"The UK is home to six species of deer – the red, roe, fallow, Sika, muntjac and Chinese water deer. Of the six species, only the red deer, Britain's largest land mammal, and the roe deer are indigenous. Meanwhile, while it may not be native to Britain, the fallow deer are usually seen as such since they have been in the country since the 11th Century. It has been around 150 years since the muntjac, Sika and Chinese water deer were introduced in the country. Among the six species, the red and the fallow deer are the most common in the UK."[cxxi]

Currently, Britain is experiencing a deer population explosion. It is estimated that there are already 2 million deer in the country. Since 1999, the number of deer has doubled in the UK. Deer are protected from being hunted and being treated as pests under the 1963 Deer Act. Records show that, population growth has occurred since the implementation of this legislation. Other government policies like the **push towards the production of overwintering crops, which provide deer with year-round food sources sustain deer. Warmer winters further reduce mortality.**

A high number of deer may lead to over-browsing of woodland, there is almost a 70% decrease in foliage of below two metres in areas with dense deer populations. *"The overabundance of deer is changing forests and putting other species at risk of extinction, **scientists say that deer cull is already necessary at this point.** Given the current deer population, around 50% to 60% of deer need to be killed to achieve the right or a favourable density."*[cxxii]

We may need to consider **mechanisms be implemented to restrict fecundity.** Yet another difficult choice to make, consider this in the light of the current reaction to the culling of badgers.

Tree health

The government publicises the threat to tree health. *"The damage to our trees, woods and forests from insect pests and organisms such as bacteria and fungi is significant. The rapid increase in movements of goods and people between countries has increased the risk of spreading pests and diseases. They can travel hidden in plants, plant products, packaging, wood, vehicles and holiday-makers' luggage - even in the soil carried on shoes."*[cxxiii]

Tree health is so crucial to successful planting. The UK has suffered a series of tree diseases over the last decade and most are associated with the fact that it does not produce enough trees to be planted, and significant proportion of new trees are imported from mainland Europe. The government lists eighteen tree pests on their website, and twenty two tree diseases.

In addition to imported trees, pests such as Asian Longhorn Beetle arrive in packaging. The outbreak in Kent that was successfully detected and eradicated (via scorched earth approach), was traced to pallets and crates carrying stone tiles from China.

The most publicised tree disease of recent years is ash dieback and it is worth quoting an article from the BBC. *"The outbreak of ash dieback disease is set to cost the UK in the region of £15bn, it has been estimated. Scientists expressed shock at the 'staggering' financial burden on taxpayers. The authors warn that the cost of tackling the fallout from ash dieback far exceeds the income from importing nursery trees. It was an imported nursery tree that initially brought the deadly disease to these shores. The disease, also known as chalara dieback of ash, was first reported in the UK in a nursery in 2012, and was recorded in the wider environment for the first time in 2013. "We estimate that the total may be £15bn"* explained lead author Dr Louise Hill, a researcher at Plant Sciences at the University of Oxford. *"That's a third more than the reported cost of the foot-and-mouth disease outbreak in 2001."*

Report co-author Dr Nick Atkinson[cxxiv], then senior adviser at the Woodland Trust, said: "What you have to look at is, essentially, the risk we are taking by trading across borders against the benefits, which is the financial gains coming from that market," he told BBC News. "The £15bn cost that we are now facing is the direct outcome of a trade that was worth a few million pounds. What we were drawing attention to is that there is this huge financial and economic impact of a tree disease epidemic." The authors, writing in the journal Current Biology, estimated that the total cost of ash dieback would be 50 times greater than the annual value of trade in live plants to and from Britain."[cxxv]

This is a direct consequence of the "freedom of movement" of plants within the EU. This vulnerability poses two questions for the proposed tree planting programme proposed. Should the UK restrict tree imports as seedlings to attempt to reduce the risk of diseases being brought into the country which could counteract the tree planting required? If this is the case (for which there is a very good case) then the tree nursery sector in the UK will need to increase dramatically to meet the increased demand from the fourfold increase in planting required to meet the 3bn tree target, and the subsequent need for trees going forward for restocking.

In Germany, there are concerns of a different nature, German forests which cover 11.4m hectares are threatened by heat, drought, storms, forest fires, beetle plagues and a fungi blight. It is estimated that 143,000 hectares have been destroyed. The concern is so great that the issue, known as *waldsterben*(dying forest) is a top priority.The Guardian reported that the agriculture minister, Julia Klöckner, has announced a forest summit, to agree on a multimillion-euro action plan. Klöckner has pledged €500m (£460m), to be paid out of the government's energy and climate fund, to finance it. *"Our forests are massively damaged,"* Klöckner said, visiting Moritzburg near Dresden, which has been badly hit, many of its trees brown and dying, mainly due to drought and beetle infestations. The association of German foresters (BDF) has said German forests are close to collapse. *"The forest is the best way to save the climate, but right now the forest itself is a victim of the climate catastrophe,"*.[cxxvi]

George Monbiot wrote in the Guardian on 15 August 2019 *"Ash dieback is just the start of the killer plagues threatening Britain's trees"* While it is hard to prevent some diseases spreading within the UK, it is possible to stop their import. Introduce a ban on the import of all live plants except those grown in sterile conditions. The problem with myriad pests and diseases is that they make achieving additional tree planting targets more difficult given the need to plant even more trees (and hope they survive). As an example, larch tree disease has infected approximately 9,000 hectares of larch trees in Wales, kills the trees once infected. This represents half the trees planted by area in the UK in 2016.

How robust will tree planting plans be in the light of these climatic and pest issues? It may be that the island status of the UK helps with such issues, but this will only be the case if pests are not imported. We may also have to countenance the planting of species more accustomed to current mediterranean temperatures. At a Forestry Commission seminar in Wiltshire (2016), the most likely forecast scenario of climate in Wiltshire in 2080 was the same as that of Northern Greece now. Forest Research's own genetics analysis, however, shows that locally sourced materials are most likely to survive change. Trees are highly adaptive, and the vast majority of variation, can be captured locally. The argument for mediterranean trees also simplifies climate change as simply an increase in mean annual temperature and reduction in precipitation. It is far more likely that stochastic[cxxvii] shocks such as a late frost or acute summer drought will be the major determinants of tree survival.

This leads us into the issue of the visual landscape versus the land use for trees needed to decarbonise.

Landscape

The British have a fetish about the landscape. Monbiot identifies two major issues that need to be challenged if the landscape is to change to accommodate forestry, sheep and the natural landscape, so we can be freed from what Monbiot calls the "*conservation prison*".

There are a plethora of NGOs and other organisations who see their primary objective as the preservation of the (current) landscape. The National Trust is a good example. The charity's mission statement is to "*work with others to conserve and renew the nation's most important landscapes*". However, this focus on conservation has meant that the charity's commitment to renewables has been questioned, due to its opposition to wind turbines. The irony is that our current natural landscape is a man-made with little reference to "natural" landscape. What is clear is that a large tree planting programme, which converts over 10% of the total UK land area to forestry and woodland will have a major effect on what our landscape looks like in the planted areas. One wonders if conservation NGOs be able to accept this? Of the total forest area in Britain at present, around 30% is publicly owned and 70% is in the private sector.[cxxviii] How can we double this area, and who will be the public or private sector actors that strive to achieve this and how will they be incentivised?

There are many examples of government bodies which maintain a *"conservation prison"* in their policy on land use. To quote from the "South Downs Integrated Landscape Character Assessment" *"thick deposits of loessic soil which formerly capped the chalk attracted Neolithic farmers, who farmed within clearings in the wildwood. Agricultural communities continued to clear the tree cover and farm the downland on an increasing scale until the Romano-British period, leaving extensive traces of their field systems and settlements across the character area. Consider opportunities for planting to soften the existing urban fringes. Planting should recognise and reveal the subtleties in the landscape and avoid a standardised approach. Woodland is usually confined to lower slopes while isolated woodland clumps are features of some ridgetops."*

This recognises that the current landscape is man-made not natural; the policy is aesthetic at the expense of the environmental challenge, and should *"reveal the subtleties in the landscape"* and should be *"confined to lower slopes while isolated woodland clumps are features of some ridgetops"*. Drive around much of England and you will see just this pattern imposed on the landscape. To increase the area of forestry and woodland to meet the target, however, will need a rethink of just such policies.

We should consider whether new planning consents should carry a requirement for a certain percentage of canopy, e.g. 25%. This would provide a greener, more pleasant experience for people, lock up carbon, and deliver valuable ecosystem services such as mitigating surface water flooding and providing summer shade (cooling urban heat islands). Such a policy is completely counter to plans to increase housing density in major cities like London.

Sheep are also a problem. The "Celebration of the Pastoral Heritage of Britain, Counting Sheep" by Philip Walling describes our affection for sheep all 23 million of them. No mention is made of the carbon footprint of these sheep. Mr Walling ends his introduction with this elegiac paean: *"This book is an attempt to give a flavour of the wonderful story of how we and our versatile, compliant companions made our landscape in the great endeavour of taming the wilderness. For man and his sheep stand in partnership outside wild nature, on the side of the civilised world, transforming its vegetation for human benefit."* It is difficult to reconcile this approach with the landscape needs of de carbonising, and surely it needs to be rethought fundamentally. This attitude to sheep and landscape is a major challenge to reforesting those areas of land which are low quality, and currently used for sheep rearing.

Again, to quote George Monbiot, this time from the Spectator[cxxix]: *"Deep vegetation on the hills absorbs rain when it falls and releases it gradually, delivering a steady supply of water to the lowlands. When grazing prevents trees and shrubs from growing, and when the small sharp hooves of sheep compact the soil, rain flashes off the hills, causing floods downstream. When the floods abate, water levels fall rapidly. Upland grazing, in other words, contributes to a cycle of flood and drought. This restricts the productivity of more fertile lands downstream, both drowning them and depriving them of irrigation water. Given the remarkably low output in the upland areas of Britain, it is within the range of possibility that hill farming creates a net loss of food."*

In Wales *"according to the 2010 figures, the average subsidy for sheep farms on the hills is £53,000. Average net farm income is £33,000. The contribution the farmer makes to his income by keeping animals, in other words, is minus £20,000."* "Farmers *argue that keeping sheep in the hills makes an essential contribution to Britain's food supply. But does it? Just over three quarters of the area of Wales is devoted to livestock farming, largely to produce meat. But according to the UK's National Ecosystem Assessment, Wales imports by value seven times as much meat as it exports."*

Such comments have incensed Welsh farmers, but the points which Monbiot makes have to be seen in the context of the need not to rewild as he advocates, but to reforest. Like the South Downs, should we be reforesting upland areas given the benefits of better water release in a period of more extreme weather changes and higher rainfall in the UK?

Finally, The Climate Change Committee states: *"Afforestation targets for 20,000 hectares/year across the UK nations (due to increase to 27,000 by 2025), are not being delivered, with less than 10,000 hectares planted on average over the last five years. The voluntary approach that has been pursued so far for agriculture is not delivering reductions in emissions."*[cxxx]

This poses some interesting questions. Why do the figures differ from those of Forest Research quoted above? The implication is that as the *"voluntary approach that has been pursued so far for agriculture is not delivering reductions in emissions"*, presumably some form of government direction is required. The question is what?

Conclusion

Tree planting can reduce carbon emissions by the simplest form of carbon sequestration. Other plants will do this but generally, new woodland is the most efficient method. The UK has to date not achieved its existing tree planting targets and the current levels of planting will not achieve the additional 3bn trees which the CCC support by 2050. Clearly the current policy is not working. The challenges to this target, come from a number of different fronts, and government policies will need to change and work in a coherent way to achieve this target.

Landscape

This will need to include a change in the land use policies for marginal and lower value land to be used for forestry and tree planting. This will require National Parks, Local Authorities and NGOs to recognise that the need for tree planting is more important than whatever vision of landscape they maintain. Upland tree planting will also help reduce the impact of flooding downstream, by absorbing water in the upstream sections of rivers and their feeder streams.

Tree Health

It is obvious that planting trees to meet a target is pointless if they die from tree diseases, particularly those imported from overseas such as ash dieback. The recent policy change to restrict imports of oak where there is potential infection is to be welcomed, but a reliance on restrictions of this kind means that the UK needs to develop a tree nursery sector to produce the trees needed to achieve such ambitious tree planting targets and a sustainable sector thereafter. This does not exist at the scale required at present.

Deer

The current Deer population size will need to be managed and a review of the protection under the 1963 Deer Act needs to be undertaken urgently. Nothing short of a realistic cull is required.

Finance

The current grant system does not incentivise the planting of trees to meet current targets and will not achieve the CCC targets without review. The carbon sequestration benefit produced needs to be included in a way that is easy to quantify and access. A different regulatory regime should apply to small woods between one and ten hectares in size compared to larger woods. This should have a lighter touch and complying with the grant application requirements should be easier than at present and should not require professional support. Support should continue for tree planting. Other areas of focus should include hedgerow planting and reinstatement, fencing and access tracks for timber extraction and facilities to store and process wood fuel (as a feedstock for biomass). Planting trees on marginal land is one of the most cost-efficient ways to reduce carbon emissions.

Government policy needs to recognise that there is a role for both large areas of tree planting and small woods. There are many people who would like to plant a wood, but the current regulatory regime does not encourage this. There should be a policy framework to encourage the planting of small woods. Small is beautiful.

Planning

All small woods face the same challenges as large woods in terms of planning regulation. Many owners or those seeking to create small woods experience difficulties with the planning system.[cxxxi] These include the gaining of permission for sheds or barns to store equipment and works that improve access to the wood both to the highway and within the wood. These are necessary to improve the creation of, and the active management of small woods.

The definition of "forestry" for planning purposes has not been reviewed since the Town and Country Planning Act (1948). Forestry should be treated in the same way as agricultural land for planning purposes. Currently, the cost of applying for permission for even simple changes is significant, and often requires professional support. Restrictions, such as those imposed by the Forestry Commission in Wales indicating that no tree planting will be sanctioned in most of the upland areas, have to change.

15 WASTE MANAGEMENT

All the tables on UK emissions in this book are from data in 2017 UK GREENHOUSE GAS EMISSIONS, PROVISIONAL FIGURES Statistical Release: National Statistics 29 March 2018.

Waste management	1990	2017	Reduction (Increase)
Total	66.6	20.3	69.5%
Landfill	60.2	14.1	76.6%
Waste-water handling	5.0	4.1	17.0%
Waste Incineration	1.4	0.3	79.3%
Composting - non-household	0.0	1.1	100.0%
Anaerobic digestion	0.0	0.2	100.0%
Mechanical biological treatment	0.0	0.6	100.0%

Waste management has been another success story in emission reductions. It accounts for 4% of UK emissions. Success in reducing emissions has been primarily due to reductions in emissions from landfill and waste incineration. Waste - water handling has been less of a success story.

What is interesting is that the success to date and the plans for the future depend on two factors, firstly, a fiscal cost to reduce landfill (Landfill Tax) and consequent on that cost the encouragement of recycling on the one hand, and secondly, the active participation of individuals in the measures which have and will reduce emissions. The government action (Landfill Tax) only works because we sort our rubbish. This wouldn't have been achieved if local authorities weren't able (with the cooperation of their residents) to collect sorted waste. Certain areas are better (rural) at this than others (metropolitan) which may point to some problems with emission reduction in other sectors generically. This is both our issue and theirs'.

Landfill Tax

A key element in the success of landfill tax has been the simplicity of the design of the tax. It was the first tax in the UK with explicit environmental purpose, and was a stand-alone instrument, with no overt links to other policies. It was also a domestic measure. Another important element was the consultation exercise with industry conducted ahead of the introduction of the tax. A key outcome of this consultation was the banding of the tax into inert and non-inert wastes and the change from a value to a weight-based tax. As someone involved in consultation on environmental taxes in the UK, landfill tax has been the most successful due to its simplicity and the lack of overlap with other measures. As a domestic measure, it does not involve trade exposed sectors, and therefore should act as a model for other domestic measures.

Waste management companies were surveyed after its introduction with the conclusion that the low level of the tax was one of several barriers to higher effectiveness. This led to an increase in the level of the tax in 1998/99, as well as the introduction of the duty escalator. There are currently no planned reforms to the tax, but with the benefit of hindsight, the tax could have been more effective with the introduction of a third band for stabilised waste (outputs from mechanical biological treatment plants) extending the tax to other residual waste disposal, e.g. incineration.

The tax is paid by landfill operators, who pass on the costs as gate fees to Local Authorities and businesses who wish to dump waste, thus creating an incentive for them to reduce the waste sent to landfill. The standard rate has increased from its initial rate of £7 per tonne to a current level of £82.60 per tonne (90 euro). One of the key issues with environmental taxation is whether the tax is part of general taxation or hypothecated for a specific purpose. Around 10% of the total revenue from the landfill tax has been channelled to the Landfill Communities Fund between 1996 and 2015.

It was estimated that the tax would raise GBP 500 million per year. Actual revenue receipts were around GBP 400 million in 1997/98 peaking at around GBP 1.2 billion in 2013/14, and falling to around GBP 900 million in 2015/16 (all figures HMRC). The recent fall is due to the reduction in the amount of waste landfilled. This illustrates that green taxes should not be viewed as long term revenue raisers for governments but as price signals to change behaviour.

Further refinements to the tax could include a lower rate for stabilised wastes. The rationale is that these wastes, because they are biologically stabilised, would generate significantly less greenhouse gases when landfilled than untreated mixed wastes. Such a lower rate would have decreased the cost of non-thermal treatment options, thereby increasing the capture of material for recycling, and leading to associated benefits. The tax could become a 'waste tax'. This would increase the cost of other treatment operations, particularly incineration, improving the business case for reuse and recycling.

The report "Landfill Tax in the United Kingdom" by Tim Elliott for the Institute for European Environmental Policy [cxxxii] states that *"The UK's landfill tax is highly replicable and there are numerous landfill taxes currently in place across the EU. The UK's landfill tax is one of the simpler among these in terms of structure, with just two bandings. However, the process of gradually announcing increases in the rate could be cut short. A realistic level required to stimulate change should be set and announced well in advance, for example €50/t, with an annual escalator set in advance to increase the rate gradually. The rationale for the tax therefore is clearly defined as resulting in changes in the management of waste within the sector, rather than simply internalising the environmental impacts from landfilling itself."*

In Europe, the rates for Landfill Tax vary from 3 euro (Lithuania) to 100 euro (Belgium), the UK is therefore at the top of the range in terms of its Landfill Tax. Twenty three EU Member States have a tax (Austria, Belgium, Bulgaria, Czech Republic, Denmark, Spain, Greece, Estonia, Finland, France, Hungary, Ireland, Italy, Lithuania, Luxembourg, Latvia, Netherlands, Poland, Portugal, Romania, Sweden, Slovenia, Slovakia, UK), as well as Norway and Switzerland. Four EU Member States do not have a landfill tax (Cyprus, Germany, Croatia, Malta).

Emissions

Emissions from waste were 19.9 MtCO2e in 2016, an increase of 0.9 MtCO2e from 2015. Waste accounts for almost 4% of total UK greenhouse gases (GHGs). Greenhouse gas emissions mainly comprise methane emissions from the decomposition of biodegradable waste in landfill sites, with the remainder (10%) from treatment of waste water and incineration of waste. Methane is emitted when biodegradable wastes – most importantly food and paper/card – decompose anaerobically (i.e. in the absence of oxygen). Emissions have fallen by 64% since 1990 due largely to reduced emissions from landfill sites. A key driver in this has been the EU landfill directive which requires significant reductions in landfilling of biodegradable municipal waste (to 75% of that produced in 1995 by 2010, to 50% by 2013, and to 35% by 2020). Will the UK continue to follow these targets when it leaves the EU?

By contrast, the aerobic process of composting does not produce methane because methane-producing microbes are not active in the presence of oxygen. Composting is one method to reduce methane emissions from organic waste currently stockpiled or sent to landfill. Composting practices that minimise anaerobic conditions and maximise aerobic conditions will be the most effective at reducing greenhouse gas emissions.

There are a number of schemes, which encourage waste reduction in the food sector. WRAP's Love Food Hate Waste Programme, introduced in 2007, encourages voluntary reductions in food waste. Food waste generated by English households has fallen by over one million tonnes between 2007 and 2010. The Courtauld Commitment, a responsibility deal in the grocery retail sector, prevented 0.7 million tonnes of food waste between 2005 and 2009 and aims to further reduce household food and drink waste by 4% between 2009 and 2012.

The effect of landfill tax has been the diversion of waste towards recycling and other treatments. Partly incentivised by this, local authorities have supported the sorting of waste through providing for recycling (and in some cases separate food waste) collection, composting, and investment in waste treatment facilities. Methane capture and anaerobic digestion has been improved by a combination of permit conditions and financial incentives for capturing methane from landfill and anaerobic digestion (under the Renewables Obligation, Feed-in Tariffs, Renewable Heat Incentive and Renewable Transport Fuel Obligation). This has driven investment to significantly increase capture of methane at landfill sites primarily to power heat. The increase in 2016 was due to a decline in the level of methane captured at landfill as methane flared decreased. However, landfill emissions are currently above the path for cost-effective emissions reductions to 2030. Biodegradable waste sent to landfill and methane captured are both off-track.

England lags behind both Scotland and Wales. Key indicators such as the amount of recycled waste and separate food waste collection show slower progress in England than the rest of Great Britain. This is indicative of Scotland and Wales having more ambitious targets in place, backed by policies to achieve this. However, this is also partially explained by the devolved authorities receiving the landfill tax receipts to fund programmes, unlike in England.

There is still no legal requirement on English local authorities to introduce separate food waste collections, which means that food waste collected separately remains a very small proportion of total waste collected, only 1.6% in 2016. Around two-thirds of English local authorities offer food waste collections, although a third of this is mixed in with garden waste. This is lower than in Scotland and Wales where more ambitious action has resulted in much higher collection rates; over 80% of households in Scotland have access to food waste collection. This equates to around 1.95m households, up from just over 0.5m households in 2013. All local authorities in Wales collect separate food waste. Aside from actions in Scotland and Wales, there may be lessons to learn from other countries. A combination of regulation and innovative measures has, for example, led to a transformation of food waste awareness and collection in South Korea. The Government has acknowledged that more needs to be done to encourage local authorities to increase food waste collection and make citizens aware of their responsibility to reduce food waste entering landfill.

Once again, the metropolitan areas are behind the rest of the country (an irony which occurs many times, given the perception that metropolitans are greener than the hinterland!). To quote the "Bag it or bin it? Managing London's domestic food waste" February 2015 from the London Assembly Environment Committee:

"Food waste is a huge environmental problem. The UK alone creates seven million tonnes of household food and drink waste, sending that waste to landfill is especially harmful to the environment. There is political consensus that reducing the amount of landfilled bio-waste is a key policy priority. In London, the Mayor recognises that processing food waste will play an important role in boosting the city's recycling and composting rates. Sending less of London's food waste to landfill is becoming an urgent priority

for practical reasons too, the Greater London area contains very little landfill capacity, and sites outside its boundaries accepting its municipal waste are expected to be full by 2025. Recent attention has rightly been focused on how much of the food we buy gets eaten. Supermarkets have been criticised, in particular, for the way that their buying and selling practices contribute to food waste. This report concentrates on what happens to the food we do throw away. The London Assembly's Environment Committee has looked at how well London is performing in collecting and processing food waste, and our report explores the potential strategies that will make recycling food waste more cost-effective, easier for residents and local authorities, and better managed. In recent years, London has greatly reduced the amount of domestic waste it sends to landfill, but food waste still accounts for around 20 per cent of its household waste. London also does not stand out nationally for its success in recycling — while recycling rates vary widely across the capital, there is particularly low participation in inner London. More London boroughs are collecting food and green waste than in the past. However, London urgently needs to introduce or extend food waste recycling in its high-density housing stock."

"London as a whole, does not stand out nationally for its success in recycling. Since 2008, the amount of London's local authority-controlled waste sent to landfill has declined significantly, but the city, on average, still has one of the lowest household recycling rates among English regions, at 34 per cent. Moreover, London's overall recycling rates have virtually levelled over the last three years with almost half of London boroughs recycling less in 2013/14 than the previous year. Rates for inner London, at 16 per cent, are exceptionally low. The next poorest performer nationally – the West Midlands – has a total recycling rate of 31 per cent, nearly double that of inner London."

"London urgently needs to introduce or extend food waste recycling in its high-density housing stock. Most boroughs offer kerbside collections. 17 of the 33 London boroughs also offer collections from multi-storey flats or estates, but coverage is much lower here: only

ten have an extended service to more than half of all flats. 16 boroughs do not collect food waste from flats at all; two of these have confirmed that they are introducing a collection service to some flats or estates. The densely populated inner London boroughs, with high proportions of flats, tend not to have separate collections for food waste. Overall, half of London's households still lack access to separate food or organic waste collections."[cxxxiii]

In Manchester, *"Food waste is currently the largest recyclable element of the waste stream that remains within the residual bin. We aim to inspire residents to think about how much food they waste and encourage them to recycle all of their left-over food."* And Manchester's leaflets state that *"Cooked and uncooked food **can** be recycled in your food and garden bin at home. Please note that food waste **can't** be recycled at any of the 20 Recycling Centres across Greater Manchester. This is because the Recycling Centres are not licensed to accept segregated food waste."*

The key issue therefore in reducing emissions from waste that goes to landfill is food waste, but the main contributors to that food waste in landfill are metropolitan. When asked if food waste collections would be acceptable, the main concerns of city dwellers were smell and vermin. Unless metropolitan citizens are prepared to take this step, achieving zero emissions in this area won't be achieved. Again this isn't a government problem, it's our problem.

There is potential to reduce food waste further. The amount of food waste from households deemed to be avoidable or under the revised definition 'edible', reached 5m tonnes in 2015 according to estimates from the Waste Reduction Action Programme (WRAP). Voluntary initiatives to reduce food waste include the 'Love food hate waste' campaign which provides advice and tips to consumers, while 'Courtauld 2025' is targeting a 20% reduction in waste across the food supply chain from producer to consumer.

There is significant potential to divert biodegradable waste away from landfill and towards recycling, composting, anaerobic digestion (AD), mechanical biological treatment (MBT) and incineration with energy recovery. This will require investment, but the technology is there as the chapter on technology demonstrates. The question is where will the finance for this come from?

Methane capture at modern landfill sites is over 80%, and can reach as high as 90%. However, non-capture leads to flaring. These sites will play a bigger role as legacy emissions from older (and less efficient) landfill sites decline. Faltering progress in 2016 may reflect more widely on the loss of momentum in waste management with evidence showing that recycling rates have plateaued, which is most apparent in England:

There has been a small increase in UK household recycling rates to 44.6% in 2016 from 40.2% in 2010. At this pace, meeting the EU target for the UK to recycle at least 50% of household waste by 2020 will definitely not be achieved. Splitting this by country, reveals similarly low rates in England. In contrast, a concerted policy drive in Wales, including 100 WRAP (2018) Household Food Waste report, restated data for 2007-2015 to show improvement. The Committee on Climate Change has proposed the introduction of statutory targets and better separate waste collections. Wales has boosted recycling rates from 44% to 56.7% during the same period. Wales is, as a result, on course to meet its statutory target to recycle 70% of waste by 2025.

Waste water management

Waste water emissions total 4.1MT.

The Environment Agency report "Transforming wastewater treatment to reduce carbon emissions" paints a bleak picture.

"Without intervention, increased wastewater treatment under the Water Framework Directive (WFD) is likely to increase carbon dioxide (CO_2) emissions by over 110,000 tonnes per year from operational energy use and emissions associated with the additional

processes required. This is a small increase with respect to the water industry's carbon footprint of five million tonnes, but the increase more than doubles the operational and capital emissions of individual works that require additional processes."

"The Shadow Cost of Carbon (SPC) now also feeds into cost-benefit analysis. However, compared to the very significant capital costs of schemes, the SPC may not offset the increased capital costs of a least-carbon solution and no case will be made for the investment."

"Increased treatment under the WFD has been estimated by this study to increase carbon emissions by over 110,000 tonnes a year due to operational energy use associated with the wastewater treatment processes. This may be considered a small increase with respect to the water industry's carbon footprint, but, is significant with respect to the wastewater function studied."

"Widespread use of enhanced anaerobic digestion with CHP, and of energy optimised activated sludge, could see savings of over 102,000 tonnes CO2 a year assuming 50 per cent optimisation in the industry. There are significant uncertainties associated with this modelling. The wastewater function of the water industry is likely to require not only major investment to meet the initial requirements of the WFD, but also significant investment to offset the carbon impacts of the WFD."[cxxxiv]

There appears to be no cost-effective way to reduce emissions in waste water management as the capital costs are so high, and therefore even with the support of a high carbon price there would not be a return on capital. Such capital costs would be funded by increasing water bills. Waste water management is 0.9% of the UK emissions. If there is no economic way to reduce these emissions, then zero carbon for the UK can only be achieved with some form of greater offsetting, such as planting more trees.

Conclusion

Great steps have been taken in reducing emissions from waste management. The reductions in landfill emissions is the result of a simple policy framework, which was worked out in consultation with the Industry. However, the remaining emissions pose difficult problems in reducing them as some are achievable, but some more intractable. For landfill, the remaining emissions relating to food waste do not require government will alone, but demand citizen acceptance and participation as well.

The position for waste water management is more problematical as there does not appear to be a cost effective solution. Waste management may be an area which stops the UK achieving zero emissions unless the residual emissions are capable of being offset. Firstly, the Government needs to put in place new policies. Specifically, this requires. Mandating a landfill ban of most bio-degradable material no later than 2025, in particular banning five waste streams – namely, food, paper/card, wood, textiles and garden waste from going to landfill. Secondly, managing emissions from legacy sites more effectively. Thirdly, providing landfill tax receipts to English local authorities to invest in recycling (as is the position in Wales and Scotland. Above all, the Government needs to educate citizens on their role in reducing these emissions, waste produces more emissions than cement and iron and steel together. Our choices can reduce most waste emissions.

16 RESIDENTIAL

All the tables on UK emissions in this book are from data in 2017 UK GREENHOUSE GAS EMISSIONS, PROVISIONAL FIGURES Statistical Release: National Statistics 29 March 2018.

Residential	1990	2017	Reduction (Increase)
Total	80.1	66.9	16.4%
Residential combustion	80.0	65.2	18.5%
Use of non aerosol consumer products	0.0	0.0	27.0%
Accidental fires	0.0	0.0	51.0%
Aerosols and metered dose inhalers	0.0	1.6	100.0%
Composting	0.0	0.1	-186.7%

Residential is 15% of UK emissions. It has a bigger share than agriculture and is only just smaller than business, but for all the column inches on business needing to reduce emissions there is very little coverage of residential emissions, our emissions.

Housing is a big problem with de-carbonisation. In part this is because the stock of housing only changes relatively slowly, at present only 1% of the housing stock changes each year. As a result, to remove residential emissions we need to either retrofit existing housing or accelerate the change in housing stock. The second option looks to be unlikely, in no small part due to the love of the old in UK residential housing stock and restrictions on change imposed by the planning system in terms of conservation areas and listed buildings.

If this does happen and planning regimes do permit change in future, we might speculate about the cost of potentially retrofitting energy saving features on to the bulk of the UK's twenty seven million homes. In 2008, the then science minister Paul Drayson, launched a pilot scheme to establish what was needed to cut housing emissions by 80 per cent. It spent up to £150,000 per dwelling, and the project managed in some, but not all cases, to hit the reduction target. With that cost as a starting point and assuming economies of scale and "learning by doing this", could reduce by three-quarters to, say, £37,500. Multiply that by twenty seven million and you are at £1 trillion. This is the figure Chancellor of the Exchequer Mr Hammond quoted for the cost of reducing emissions, but this £1 trillion is for residential which is 15% of the emission total. Recent claims that zero carbon homes would only lead to small price increases are not born out by the costs of each element required.

UK

In the UK, energy used for heating homes has increased by two-fifths since 1970, but less energy is used now for water heating and cooking than it was 40 years ago. More energy is now used for lights and appliances in homes than it was in 1970. In part this is because we heat our homes to a higher temperature than in 1970, and have increasingly sophisticated lights and appliances than we did in 1970.

The primary source of central heating in the UK is gas. In part this explained by the relative price of different fuels for central heating. A major challenge in eliminating Gas as the dominant fuel source will be to reduce its price advantage over electricity. Currently in costs per KWhth, Electric is roughly four times the cost of gas. This is a key issue skirted over in many public pronouncements. Citizens will only change fuel source if the cost is broadly similar so, why would they pay four times as much to use electricity? A zero-carbon world is primarily an electric world the cost of electricity needs to be managed for consumers to accept it. At present, this is not the case. The question is how can the relative cost of electricity be reduced for heating given the investment costs of increasing electricity supply?

The table shows the enormous role that gas currently plays in domestic power use.

| UK Domestic power use | | |
| Million tonnes oil equivalent | | |
	Domestic	% of Total
Coal	0.6	1%
Gas	25.5	63%
Oil	2.5	6%
Electricity	9.1	23%
Bioenergy	2.5	6%
Total	40.2	
Domestic as %		
of Total emissions	28%	

As is the case for Power Generation (Chapter 9), the UK needs to wean itself off gas as the source of domestic heating and reverse a trend which started in the 1970s with the discovery and advent of North Sea gas. Eighty six percent of UK properties use gas as the fuel for their central heating system. This poses two issues in the pursuit of zero carbon. First, the extra electricity power generation needed to replace twenty eight million tonnes oil equivalent of carbon fuels used for domestic power. And second the period over which this change will happen. A gas central heating boiler will have a life of approximately fifteen years (longer with careful use) so one can realistically assert that all the current boilers will no longer be in service after 2040.

The UK government has announced, in 2019, that gas boilers will not be permissible in new build properties from 2025. This announcement seeks to exclude new build from being connected to the gas grid, so no gas appliances of any sort will be permitted (gas hobs, etc). The proposal does not extend to existing property, but if the UK is to reduce gas consumption then the likelihood is that existing housing stock will be required to replace gas boilers with non-carbon power from a date in the near future, to be consistent with new build.

Otherwise, residential emissions will not fall.

The government announcement indicated that new build properties will need to install air source heat pumps as the heating source from 2025. A recent survey showed that heating engineers believe this will be the norm. This is a major change At present plumbers must undergo an extra year of training to be able to install an air source heat pump system and many do not. To make the switch from gas to air source heat pumps will require a major retraining programme.

The challenge for government will be funding this change. Estimates of cost are difficult, but the installed cost of air source heat pumps for twenty five million dwellings will be between £200bn and £400bn. Currently roughly 75% of this is funded through the renewable heat incentive (RHI). A new replacement gas boiler is going to cost between £3,000 to £4000 installed. An air source heat pump, however, will cost £6000 - £8000 installed or £12000 - £14000 for larger properties (Energy Saving Trust advice) but the real cost is not likely to be great when the RHI is factored in. So why were only 22,000 installed in the UK in 2017 (BSRIA).[cxxxv]

Planning

The UK preserves its built environment through a number of measures, the most widespread of which are Conservation Areas and Listed buildings. It is surprising how widespread they are. Calculating the number of dwellings in conservation areas is difficult. The Chartered Institute of Public Finance and Accountancy (CIPFA) provide an estimate of 390,182 hectares of land within conservation areas. There is however no data on the number of homes within these conservation areas. Catherine Bottrill has produced a paper "Homes in Historic Conservation Areas in Great Britain: Calculating the Proportion of Residential Dwellings in Conservation Areas "(Catherine Bottrill Researcher, Environmental Change Institute August 2005)

She concludes *"There were approximately 25 million residential dwellings in Great Britain in 2000 (the year of the CIPFA estimate). It is estimated that 1/5 of the housing stock was built pre1919 – 5 million dwellings. The approximately 1.2 million residential dwellings estimated to be in Conservation Areas comprise 4.8 percent of Great Britain's total housing stock and 24 percent of the historic housing stock."*

For Listed Buildings, *"The general principles"* in designating Listed Buildings are *"that all buildings built before 1700 which survive in anything like their original condition are likely to be listed, as are most buildings built between 1700 and 1850. Particularly careful selection is required for buildings from the period after 1945. Buildings less than 30 years old are not normally considered to be of special architectural or historic interest because they have yet to stand the test of time."* Historic England.

But Historic England also state on their website that *"Surprisingly the total number of listed buildings is not known, as one single entry on the National Heritage List for England (NHLE) can sometimes cover a number of individual units, such as a row of terraced houses. However, we estimate that there are around 500,000 listed buildings on the NHLE."*

The total number of dwellings in the UK in 2017 (combining the figures for England, Wales, Scotland and N Ireland) was twenty eight million, six hundred thousand. Dwellings in conservation areas make up about 4%, and listed building dwellings about 1%. That 5% are currently subject to various levels of restriction and the question is whether the planning regime will change to permit measures to reduce emissions for dwellings in conservation areas or those which are Listed Buildings. As an example, some planning authorities currently will allow the installation of double-glazed conservation units in listed buildings, and some do not. On this basis, an air source heat pump may not to be approved in a listed building.

My personal experience of planning has been that one has to

argue with a planning authority very hard to get permission for solar panels on Listed Buildings (they are as, Gloucester Cathedral Grade 1 listed has them). Indeed guidance often states that it is unlikely that solar panels will be allowed on listed buildings (this is incorrect). Equally there are restrictive covenants imposed by organisations such as the Duchy of Cornwall which are more draconian than the rules for conservation areas. In fact, solar panels are permitted if certain criteria, particularly visual, are met. I am not arguing here that we should trash our building heritage, but in much the same way that we have to reconsider our view of the "natural landscape", we need to find a sensible balance between conservation and reducing emissions.

EU

The position in the EU is similar according to Eurostat. In 2017, the residential sector, represented 27.2 % of final energy consumption in the EU. In 2017, natural gas accounted for 36 % of the EU final energy consumption in households, electricity for 24 %, renewables for 18 % and petroleum products for 11 %. The main use of energy by households in the EU in 2017 was for heating their homes (64 % of final energy consumption in the residential sector), with renewables accounting for almost a quarter of EU households space heating consumption.

Renewable power in the residential context

Domestic renewable power does offer the opportunity to manage, in part, the fuel costs of a dwelling and improvements in battery storage to store renewable energy, will enhance this.

Solar

The Solar Trade Association analysis shows that the UK has now reached one million solar homes in installed systems, if both solar PV and solar thermal are included. Statistics from DECC show that there are now 800,000 homes with solar PV electricity panels or tiles. The solar trade body also estimates that there are 250,000 homes that have solar thermal hot water heating panels. Together the two technologies are installed on 1,050,000 homes.

To date much of this investment has been supported by feed in tariffs (guaranteed payments for electricity production by solar PV). This is no longer the case (see Chapter 9). Costs have fallen dramatically by over a third since 2015. Tthe economics of installation are now compromised by the low price paid by energy companies for energy exported by domestic producers, and the difficulties in using the power as it is generated. The advent of battery storage systems will provide a means for this power to be used for domestic power more comprehensively.

Wind

According to the Energy Saving Trust, more than 4,000 domestic wind turbines were registered in the UK between 2010 and 2017, dramatically less than the Solar PV take up. Current economics mean that this is therefore unlikely to be a major area of growth.

Geothermal

Geothermal power has long been considered as a possible power source in the UK with equal application for heating. Geothermal energy plants are normally located in regions where there is volcanic activity, such as in Iceland and New Zealand. The first electricity to be generated from geothermal was at Larderello in northern Italy in 1904. There are now geothermal energy plants in twenty four countries throughout the world and there are deep geothermal energy systems currently being developed and tested in France, Australia, Japan, Germany, the USA and Switzerland as well as the UK. In Iceland, which has abundant geothermal energy resources, geothermal energy is used to provide the majority of the electricity and heating demands of the country.

Although the UK is not actively volcanic, there is still substantial geothermal energy at shallow depths, but it is exploited in different ways. The upper 10–15 m of the ground is heated by solar radiation and acts a heat store. The heat can be utilised by ground source heat pumps that can substantially reduce heating bills and reduce the associated carbon footprint. At a depth of about 15 metres, ground temperatures are not influenced by seasonal air temperature changes and remain stable all year around at about the mean annual air temperature (9–13 °C in the UK). The ground at this depth is cooler than the air in summer and warmer than the air in winter. This temperature difference is exploited by ground source heat pumps that are used for heating and/or cooling of homes and office buildings. There are different types of systems which can be broadly grouped into closed-loop systems and open-loop systems.

With increasing depth, the ground temperatures are also affected by the heat conducted upwards from the Earth's core and mantle, known as geothermal heat flow. When this is combined with the thermal conductivities of rocks this allows the prediction of subsurface temperatures. The UK's geothermal gradient, the rate at which the Earth's temperature increases with depth, has an average value of 26°C per km. Some rocks contain free flowing water (groundwater), and so at depth this water will be warm and can be extracted for use in district heating schemes or for industrial uses such as heating houses.

There are also regions in the UK where the rocks at depth are hotter than expected. This occurs in granitic areas because some granite generates internal heat through the radioactive decay of the naturally occurring elements potassium, uranium and thorium. Granites have very little free flowing water, but it is possible to engineer the fracture system such that water can be made to flow from one borehole to another through the granite. The extracted hot water is then at a sufficiently high temperature to drive an electricity generating turbine.

Parts of Cornwall have geothermal gradients that are significantly higher than the UK average due to the presence of granite and have potential for geothermal power generation. These systems are known as engineered geothermal systems (EGS) and are described below. I worked on advising a project in the early 1990s based at Cambourne School of Mines to try to realise this. Technically the project was successful, but the costs were too high for implementation.[cxxxvi]

The distribution of best resources is complimentary to the distribution of Mine Water discussed below. Given that this is a known technology applied commercially elsewhere, it should form part of the government's road map to zero carbon. It would also bring investment to rural areas whose economies would benefit.

Renewable Heat from Mine Water

Ironically, the UK's carbon legacy from coal may provide a source of renewable residential heating for a number of areas, in the UK. One of coal industry's underground legacies is the many galleries which remain underground, through which run an estimated 2bn cubic metres of water, heated by surrounding rocks to 12-16 degrees Celsius. Mine water has been regarded as a problem given its constituent parts (high in iron and pollutants) provide a potential threat to drinking water and rivers. Its management by the publicly funded Coal Authority cost £18m in 2018. This liability could be reduced by changing the management of this underground water and using this as a source of renewable heat

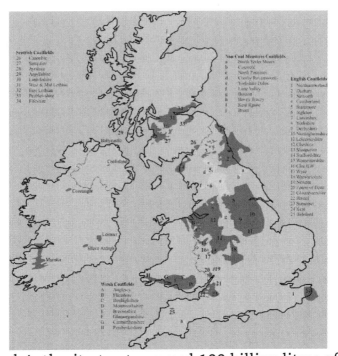

The Coal Authority treats around 100 billion litres of mine water every year. Much of this water is warm, ranging between around 12 and 20°C, with little to no seasonal variation in temperature. This makes it an ideal source of low carbon heating or cooling for heat networks using water source heat pumps. It is working in partnership with others to use this heat to provide a low carbon renewable energy solution. Where the UK can benefit is that legacy underground mining is often close to towns and villages so that the heat loss over distance is negligible, as the map from the Northern Mine Research Society shows.

Like offshore wind power, this resource from the UK's coal mining legacy, could provide a relatively cheap form of geothermal heating. It won't benefit London, but it could give "left behind" areas of the UK an economic and environmental boost.

Conclusion

Domestic emissions have fallen but are still a significant part of the total. The UK's love of Gas fired central heating is the predominant challenge in eliminating emissions. The current comparable price of electricity for domestic heating makes electricity as a source of heating an unattractive alternative, unless used in air source and ground source heat pumps. The cost of electricity is a key challenge in this sector, but also in general as the UK moves to an electric economy to reduce carbon emissions.

The government's policy is to encourage the installation of air source heat pumps or ground source heat pumps is a major change, and it will be interesting to see what level of resistance to this emerges particularly on cost grounds. The cost is significant as retrofitting is potentially both expensive and disruptive for some of the existing housing stock.

Geothermal energy and mine water would appear to provide a relatively cheap form of domestic heating in specific locations. Investment in project trials should be fast tracked to assess this technology and the number of dwellings which can be heated in this way. The potential area which could benefit from this technology is significant.

It is likely that domestic emissions may prove to be one of the most difficult emissions to reduce. While government regulation can make changes, these changes affect peoples' homes. Again, this represents about twenty seven million households making decisions and approving the guidance which governments provides and the financial support it provides. This is another example of Us not Them.

17 AVIATION AND SHIPPING EMISSIONS

Aviation and Shipping emissions are the dirty secret of emission reduction. These emissions are not included in the national emissions which form the basis of emission reduction targets and policies for national governments. So, justifiably you might therefore ask why when they are not included in the summary of UK emissions in the summary of UK emissions in Chapter 8. The answer is that the UNFCCC does not include it in the emissions reporting that countries are required to make.

Taken together, aviation and shipping accounted for 7.6% of the UK's total emissions in 2015; transport, including shipping and aviation, but also land journeys, accounted for 30%. Transport is the biggest sector in terms of removing emissions, and the one with the worst record.

The 2015 COP21 Paris talks ended with an agreement, which is regarded by many as encouraging and setting the ground for positive progress in coming years. International aviation and shipping, however, were omitted altogether from the final text. The two sectors account for around 8% of global CO2 emissions, so their exclusion is significant. Without regulation, or targets for emissions, estimates suggest aviation and shipping could account for as much as one third of global emissions by 2050, as demand for air travel increases, while emissions from other sectors such as energy generation are curbed. As the total amount of emissions is restrained, the proportion from aviation and shipping increase as a proportion if there is no restraint for them.

Aviation

The spectacular fudge at COP21 is fascinating in terms of how aviation managed through lobbying to neuter a fairly weak proposed action on aviation emissions. It is not surprising, therefore, that the press release from ICAO (the International Civil Aviation Organization) says how delighted it is at the outcome of the COP21, and how now: *"Every State and every global industrial sector must now redouble their efforts toward achieving substantial progress on emissions reduction if the COP21 legacy is to be achieved, and the civil aviation community is no exception."* Somehow the exclusion of aviation from the Paris agreement is interpreted by ICAO as *"a vote of confidence in the progress ICAO and the aviation community have achieved thus far."*

Progress to date is interesting. Within the EU, greenhouse gas emissions from international aviation have more than doubled since 1990. CO_2 emissions have increased by about 80% between 1990 and 2014. They are forecast to grow by a further 45% between 2014 and 2035. The number of flights has increased by 80% between 1990 and 2014. They are forecast to grow by a further 45% between 2014 and 2035. A similar pattern is seen for tonnes of air cargo which are up about 30% from 2005 to 2014, but although the number of all-cargo flights has declined by 4% over the same period. In the light of this, one would expect that the reduction of aviation emissions would be a priority issue for the EU, that does not appear to be the case.

The main aircraft engine emission pollutants are carbon dioxide (CO_2), nitrogen oxides (NOX), sulphur oxides (SOX), unburned hydrocarbons (HC), carbon monoxide (CO), particulate matter (PM) and soot.

Aircraft CO_2 emissions increased from 88 to 156 million

tonnes (+77%) between 1990 and 2005 according to the data reported by EU28 and European Free Trade Area (EFTA) members states to the United Nations Framework Convention on Climate Change (UNFCCC). According to data from the IMPACT emissions model[cxxxvii], CO_2 emissions increased by 5% between 2005 and 2014. The only good news is that the increase in emissions is less than the increase in passenger kilometres flown over the same period (2005 to 2014). This was due to an improvement in fuel efficiency, driven by the introduction of new aircraft, removal of older aircraft, and improvements in operational practice. The average fuel burn per passenger kilometre flown for passenger aircraft, excluding business aviation, went down by 19% over this same period. That is the end of the good news, however, as projections indicate that future technology improvements are unlikely to balance the effect of future growth in traffic. Under the base traffic forecast and advanced technology improvement rate, CO_2 emissions increases by 44% from 144 Mt in 2005 to 207 Mt in 2035.

In 2012, aviation represented 13% of all EU transport CO_2 emissions, and 3% of the total EU CO_2 emissions. It was also estimated that European aviation represented 22% of global aviation's CO_2 emissions. Similarly, aviation now comprises 14% of all EU transport nitrogen oxide (NOX) emissions, and 7% of the total EU NOX emissions. In absolute terms, NOX emissions from aviation have doubled since 1990, and their relative share has quadrupled, as other economic sectors have achieved significant reductions. NOX emissions are forecast to grow by a further 43% between 2014 and 2035. All of this should mean aviation emissions should be a priority for the EU and European countries, but the actual story is somewhat different.

What action has been taken?

Carbon dioxide emissions from aviation have been included in the EU Emission Trading Scheme (EUETS) since January

2012. However, a 'stop the clock' provision currently excludes flights to and from non-European Economic Area countries from the scope of the ETS in order to enable a global agreement on aviation emissions. Given developments within the International Civil Aviation Organisation (ICAO), the EU decided to continue with a reduced scope of aviation within the ETS during the period from 2013 to 2016. Only flights between airports located in the European Economic Area are presently included within the EUETS. Flights to and from outermost regions of the EU are covered only if they occur in the same outermost region.

The EU is relying on a global agreement on aviation emissions. Given the history of progress to date this doesn't bode well in terms of action. In 2008, the global stakeholder associations of the aviation industry (Airports Council International, Civil Air Navigation Services Organization, International Air Transport Association and International Coordinating Council of Aerospace Industries Association), under the umbrella of the Air Transport Action Group, committed to addressing the global challenge of climate change and adopted a set of ambitious targets to mitigate CO_2 emissions from air transport. These included an average improvement in fuel efficiency of 1.5% per year from 2009 to 2020, a cap on net aviation CO_2 emissions from 2020 (carbon-neutral growth), a reduction in net aviation CO_2 emissions of 50% by 2050, relative to 2005 levels.

What this "reduction" ignores is that if aviation emissions are stabilised at 2020 levels in a situation where other emissions are reducing to zero by 2050, then aviation becomes an increasing proportion of global emissions. One wonders why would this be acceptable, and furthermore why the base line is the base line for aviation emissions 2020, when it is 1990 for other emissions?

The ATAG goes on to say "*Hydrocarbon fuel is the only option for aviation…for now. At this stage, the only option to power commer-*

cial aircraft sustainably in the coming decades is by using hydro-carbon fuels. Encouraging progress has been made in recent years in the development of electric aircraft, with a number of small-scale prototypes, having already been flown. It is expected that in a few decades, short-range commercial aircraft will be technically feasible. Hydrogen can be burned in a turbine engine for aviation. However, there are significant technical challenges in designing a hydrogen-powered aircraft for commercial aviation and in produc-ing enough hydrogen in a sustainable way to supply the industry's needs worldwide."

To achieve these targets, all stakeholders agreed to closely work together along a four-pillar strategy of improved tech-nology, including the deployment of sustainable low-carbon fuels, more efficient aircraft operations and infrastructure im-provements. This included modernising air traffic manage-ment systems and a single global market-based measure, to fill the remaining emissions gap. While all of this holds together, the targets are less onerous than other sectors in national plans and one might wonder why.

These targets are to be monitored through state action plans, which are a voluntary planning and reporting tool for states to communicate information on their activities addressing CO_2 emissions from international civil aviation to ICAO. The level of detail in the information contained in them will ultimately enable ICAO to compile global progress towards meeting the goals set. The operative word here is voluntary, as only two thirds of countries have produced them.

Sustainable Aviation Fuels

Much is made of the contribution of sustainable aviation fuels. The ICAO states *"Sustainable alternative fuels reduce avi-ation GHG emissions through savings which are achieved in the production phase of renewable, biological material (feedstock), and in the process of conversion into fuels. Emissions reductions are not achieved in the actual combustion phase. This is due to strict fuel specifications which require sustainable alternative aviation fuels to have 'drop-in'" ie to be compatible with current jet engines."* And again *"Sustainable Aviation Fuels can play a major role in reducing international aviation emissions. ICAO work to foster the deployment of SAF will continue, in support of the ICAO goal of limiting or reducing the impact of aviation greenhouse gas emissions on the global climate." "By 2017, over 100,000 commercial flights had used a blend of alternative fuels, 4 airports were deploying alternative fuels on a regular basis, and at least 8 additional alternative fuel purchase agreements had been announced. The success of these initiatives proves that the SAF industry is evolving fast, making it a viable option for the aviation industry to address its environmental sustainability."* This all sounds very positive, its meant to, but the numbers are insignificant in the context of global aviation. There were 36.7 million flight departures in 2017. Alternative fuels account for 0.27% of the flights.

The European Aviation Safety Agency states: *"The price of bio-based aviation fuel relative to fossil-based kerosene is one of the major barriers to its greater market penetration. While a typical price for fossil-based aviation fuel would be €600/tonne, the price of bio-based aviation fuel produced from used cooking oil can be in the range of €950-€1,015/tonne. In addition, feedstocks that comply with sustainability requirements, such as used cooking oil and tallow used in the HEFA process, are in demand by the road fuel sector for biodiesel and green diesel production. It is expected that this competition between road and aviation will further increase in the coming years. However, despite the presence of these initiatives, the current consumption in Europe is very low when compared to the potential production capacity."*

Potential emissions savings from using biofuels may be as large as 80%, but, depend highly on the feedstock type and production processes. For biofuels originating from agricultural crops, the issue is the potential emissions generated by the direct or indirect land use conversion induced by the cultivation of the crops. From this point of view and the possible risks of competition with food production, alternative fuels produced from wastes are of special interest.

The conclusion from this is that *"Hydrocarbon fuel is the only option for aviation"* and aviation is subject to looser rules than other sectors (unlike cement which is cast as a bad carbon industry). The programme to reduce emissions is voluntary, and is self-monitored by the industry which is uncomfortable. Why are regulators so relaxed that they impose a slacker standard on aviation? Could it possibly have something to do with the fact that multilateral bodies are inevitably big consumers of aviation? Or whether the 27 member EU, could function without aviation?

Aviation is an important part of our global economy as the sector states (ATAG)[cxxxviii] *"Aviation provides the only rapid worldwide transportation network, is indispensable for tourism and facilitates world trade. Air transport improves quality of life in countless ways. Air transport moves roughly 3.8 billion passengers annually. The air transport industry generates a total of 63 million jobs globally. Air transport is responsible for transporting 35% of world trade by value. 54% of international tourists travel to their destination by air. Aviation's global economic impact is estimated at USD 2.7 trillion (including direct, indirect, induced and tourism catalytic). If the aviation industry were a country, it would rank 21st in the world in terms of GDP."* But other sectors are an important part of our global economy. Why should aviation be treated differently, why, given its scale, is international air travel outside emission trading schemes?

Again from ATAG[cxxxix] *"At the 39th ICAO Assembly, in 2016, Member States agreed on a global market based measure (MBM) which, together with other mitigation measures such as operational improvements, aircraft technology and the use of sustain-*

able aviation fuels, will help achieve international aviation's aspirational goal of carbon neutral growth from 2020. This MBM will be implemented in the form of the Carbon Offsetting and Reduction Scheme for International Aviation (CORSIA). 2 In line with Assembly Resolution A39-3, the average level of CO2 emissions from international aviation covered by the scheme between 2019 and 2020 represents the basis for carbon neutral growth from 2020, against which emissions in future years must be compared." Why is it that "CORSIA aims to stabilize net CO2 emissions from international civil aviation at 2020 levels" when the other sectors are required to reduce to 1990 levels?

Is Offsetting acceptable in a zero carbon world?

CORSIA is all about offsetting. *"There are many ways to achieve CO2 reductions that can be used as offsets, many of which bring other social, environmental or economic benefits relevant to sustainable development. Such offsets can be sourced from various types of project activities, including, for example, wind energy, clean cook stoves, methane capture, forestry and other emissions-reducing or avoidance projects." "It is forecast that CORSIA will mitigate around 2.5 billion tonnes of CO2 between 2021 and 2035, which is an annual average of 164 million tonnes of CO2. This is equivalent to the annual CO2 emissions from the Netherlands, all sectors included."*[cxl] This doesn't offset the emissions of global aviation.

Carbon Watch has commented *"To cover growth in emissions from international flights, a global mechanism has been established: the Carbon Offsetting and Reduction Scheme for International Aviation (CORSIA), which will start in 2021 and only cover increase in emissions from then on, i.e. it will not tackle emissions up to prior levels. Due to its very weak climate goal and the objective of compensating emissions through offsets rather than actually reducing emissions, this mechanism is completely out of step with the temperature goals adopted to avoid catastrophic climate change."*

CORSIA policy of offsetting stretches logic. If the objective is to reduce emissions to zero per se, then offsetting, unless it reduces emissions below zero (like tree planting), doesn't work as the project in which the aviation industry invests which offsets is already included in the trajectory towards zero carbon. Those emission reductions are already included in the zero target. This is classic case of double counting, it can be justified when the target is to reduce emissions. However, when the target changes to zero, then offsetting doesn't work to reduce emissions because the target is already zero. Offsetting in a zero-carbon target world, is a financing mechanism that doesn't of itself reduce emissions, the financing is helpful but it is financing, it is not reducing aviation emissions.

Aviation emissions rise because people are flying more. The only way to reduce aviation emissions (aside from sustainable fuel, which appears uneconomic) is to reduce the number of flights and the numbers of people flying. **The current "methods" of reducing Aviation emissions are not the answer. The way to reduce Aviation emissions is that we have to take responsibility for this. We have to fly less.**

UK

In 2015, aviation (domestic and international) accounted for 6.5% of total greenhouse gas emissions in the UK (UK aviation forecasts), with the majority coming from international flights. The Committee for Climate Change comments are weak on this subject: *"Only domestic flights are covered by carbon budgets as set by the Committee on Climate Change (CCC). The CCC does however assume that the UK share of international emissions is included in the overall target under the Climate Change Act, to reduce emissions by at least 80% by 2050. In the context of future UK policy and infrastructure investment decisions, the Committee has previously said that an appropriate long-term assumption for government planning is*

for aviation emissions to be around 2005 levels in 2050 (imply-
ing around a 60% increase in demand over the same period). The
Government is planning to publish a new Aviation Strategy in the
first half of 2019, including their long-term approach to climate
change. The Committee will set out an assessment of what this
strategy should involve around Spring 2019. This will include con-
sideration of the potential to reduce aviation emissions over the
period to 2050 and beyond, and the overall policy approach the
Government should pursue (including whether the ICAO CORSIA
scheme is an appropriate mechanism for formally including inter-
national aviation emissions within carbon budgets)."

Once again this begs the question, why aviation is being given such an easy ride? Courtesy of a UK Freedom of Information (FOI) request[cxli], the distribution of the population flying in the UK has been revealed, and it demonstrates that a small proportion of the population is responsible for most aviation emissions. In 2018, 48% of the population didn't fly. Of the 52% who did, 1% of the population accounted for 18% of flights, 10% of the population accounted for 52% of flights, 20% of the population for 70% of flights. This distribution pattern is not surprising, but shocking. To put this another way, 1% of the UK population is responsible for over 1% of UK emissions just by flying (18% of 6.5%)! The likelihood is that this 1% has a strong correlation to wealth. Given these figures charging a realistic price for emissions on anyone tak-ing more than two return trips by air a year might make good policy sense, particularly when the tax treatment of aviation is reviewed.

Pricing mechanisms

Airlines are not subject to a fuel tax on flights within, to or from the EU. *"Under the 2003 Energy Taxation Directive (ETD) most fuels and energy products in the EU are subject to tax. How-ever, Article 14 of that Directive permits member states to continue to exempt from taxation aviation fuel for domestic, intra and extra-EU flights. These exemptions first arose in bilateral air services agreements when aviation was expanding post-WWII. It was common practice – encouraged by industry and nonbinding resolutions by the UN's aviation agency, ICAO – to include mutual fuel tax exemptions in these agreements and this approach was widely adopted in Europe. The ETD exemption is not mandatory, and EU member states are free to tax aviation fuel for domestic aviation or, through bilateral agreements with other member states, fuel used for flights between them. To date no EU member states have availed of this provision except the Netherlands for domestic aviation. Norway and Switzerland have taxed domestic aviation fuel for many years."* Not only is aviation not subject to fuel tax, but it is zero rated for VAT. The comparison with car taxes is illustrative of the advantage which the tax regime gives aviation, it doesn't pay tax on fuel, but <u>you</u> do at the petrol pump. Similarly it doesn't pay vat, but <u>you</u> do. No wonder some air fares are cheaper than rail. The tax system is effectively subsidising them by not taxing aviation. *"Taxing aviation kerosene sold in Europe [by duty on all departing flights to all destinations of €0.33/litre] would cut aviation emissions by 11% (16.4 million tonnes of CO2) and have no net impact on jobs or the economy as a whole while raising almost €27 billion in revenues every year, a leaked report for the European Commission shows."* **Airport Watch**

Belgium and The Netherlands have recently proposed a European tax on commercial aviation. In a note shared with their European colleagues, the Belgian delegation proposed, *"A fair and correct pricing of air transport is recommended with regards to its impact on the environment. There is currently no taxation on kerosene or VAT tickets. More environmentally-friendly modes of transport such as railways are more taxed than air transport".*

Carbon Watch has suggested *"There are several options to implement a tax on aviation, ranging from taxes on fuel to ticket taxes, or per flight taxes. Independently from national measures taken, a deeper and more transparent dialogue among the Member States or clearer guidelines directly from the European Commission are required to better harmonize a possible European aviation tax."* **The UK has the highest charges in the EU for passenger duty on domestic and international flights of 40 euro. Only 5 other EU countries impose a charge above 10 euro, most do not charge.**[cxlii] **If Europe is serious about reducing Aviation emissions why is this the case?**

Shipping

Shipping activities also lead to significant emissions of greenhouse gases and air pollutants, noise and water pollution. Carbon dioxide emissions from global shipping could be 17% of all carbon dioxide emissions by 2050 if no further action is taken. While emissions of some pollutants from road transport have gone down in general (although not carbon dioxide), emissions from aviation and shipping continue to rise. By 2050, global aviation and shipping are together expected to contribute almost 40% of global carbon dioxide emissions unless further mitigation actions are taken.[cxliii]

In the UK, *"In its advice to Government on the fifth carbon budget the Committee recommended that international shipping emissions now be included within carbon budgets. The IMO agreement on a 2050 target for international shipping is consistent with the Committee's 2050 planning assumption, and the basis upon which the fifth carbon budget was set. It therefore reinforces the case that there is no longer any reason to exclude these emissions from carbon budgets. The Committee continues to recommend that Government should now include these emissions within carbon budgets." The Committee on Climate Change."*[cxliv]

The EU statement on marine emissions is *"After considerable efforts over recent years, the IMO agreed in April 2018 on an initial greenhouse gas emissions reduction strategy. In line with the internationally agreed temperature goals under the Paris Agreement, the strategy includes objectives to a) reduce total annual GHG emis-*

sions from shipping by at least 50% by 2050 compared to 2008 level and b) pursue efforts to phase them out as soon as possible in this century."[cxlv]

This all looks very familiar. Like aviation, marine emissions are to be reduced by only 50% instead of the reduction levels required for other sectors. The base year is 2008, better than aviation in 2020 but far worse than the 1990 date which applies for other sectors. It is also a date in the middle of the last recession. Again, like aviation, as emissions from other sectors reduce the proportion of global emissions from Shipping will increase, because of emission reduction rules decided by our governments and the EU. Shipping emissions represent around 13% of the overall EU greenhouse gas emissions from the transport sector (2015).

In 2013, the EC set out *"a strategy towards reducing GHG emissions from the shipping industry.The strategy consists of **3 consecutive steps**. **Monitoring, reporting and verification** of CO_2 emissions from large ships using EU ports. **Greenhouse gas reduction targets** for the maritime transport sector. **Further measures**, including market-based measures, in the medium to long term. The contribution of the shipping sector to emission reductions consistent with the temperature goals of the Paris Agreement remains an important issue in the EU. The recent amendment to the EU Emissions Trading System (ETS) Directive, emphasises the need to act on shipping emissions as well as all other sectors of the economy. The Directive also states that the Commission should regularly review IMO action and calls for action to address shipping emissions from the IMO or the EU to start from 2023, including preparatory work and stakeholder consultation."* It's a cut and paste of the Aviation process and has the same weaknesses.

Again, the Committee on Climate Change states "The overarching aim of the strategy is to peak GHG emissions from international shipping as soon as possible, and to reduce them by at least 50% by 2050 compared to 2008 levels."[cxlvi] There

is no criticism of this proposal. This despite the recommendation that Government should now include these emissions
within carbon budgets. The tone is one of acceptance. So how
could emissions be cut? "Following the 2008 financial crisis,
cargo ships slowed down to deal with lower trade volumes
and cut costs. A 12% reduction in at-sea average speed, known
as "slow steaming," *led to an average reduction of 27% in daily
fuel consumption and thus fewer greenhouse-gas emissions."* [cxlvii]
Clearly, slower ships would make a significant difference as
would the change from bunker oil to lighter fuels.

Finally, 40% of world shipping by volume is the transport of
Oil, LNG and Coal, i.e. carbon. As the transport of carbon declines, so will the size of Global shipping. If you exclude the
shipping of carbon, then emissions would fall by 40%. The
target above of 70% by 2050 is even weaker unless it is predicated on the continued shipping of carbon products at the
same level as today.

Conclusion

Aviation and shipping have been very successful in isolating
themselves from the emission reduction targets which other
sectors will have applied to them. It is difficult to see why
and how their lobbying has been so successful. The targets
agreed, reducing emissions compared to levels in 2020 and
2008, is totally inconsistent with other emission reduction
targets. While domestic enterprises will bear the full brunt
of emission reduction, these two sectors will not, benefitting
international trade over local enterprises. Importing goods
will not bear the same cost of carbon as domestic production.
It seems that support for the transportation sectors of globalisation is more important than a consistent approach to emission reduction affecting all sectors of the economy.

We have seen that the proportion of the population flying the
most is very small; 10% of the UK population take over 50%

of flights and many define themselves by the locations they fly to (just look at social media). In so doing they are defining themselves by the amount of carbon emissions they are responsible for.

Surely (and hopefully) this will be challenged be challenged and revised in the future. Aviation is in fiscal terms, a tax haven with low duties and no VAT. In any other sector this would be attacked on the basis that proper levels of taxation would pay for better public services. Aviation and maritime's carbon burden should be adjusted to reflect the tax and emission reduction burden other sectors bear.

PART 3

ACHIEVING NET ZERO

18 WHAT CAN I DO?

What does an ordinary person do, given that we are faced with a situation where most people, according to opinion polls, in the UK want action on climate change. What as individuals, can we do to achieve zero carbon by 2050?

The Personal is Political – and Environmental

Politics

The first and biggest act that individuals can take is to ensure that their elected representatives (MPs and Councillors) recognise that reducing carbon is the biggest issue we face. Those politicians urgently need to reach political consensus on policies to reduce carbon. Only political consensus will create the long-term policies needed to make changes that can be sustained and seen through. Political engagement is hard work when you have a job, family and commitments, but politicians do respond to voters if the voter message is clear. Make your message clear, not aspirational, but practical.

Aside from politics, what else can we do? Every decision we make has a carbon element; we all have carbon budgets, and some are much larger than others. The biggest issues for individuals in terms of the amount of their own emissions are residential heating, transport, air travel, food and thus agriculture, and food waste.

Our Homes

The first issue is our homes as 63% of domestic power use in the UK is from gas, mainly from gas central heating which is used in roughly 80% of homes. We need to change our heating source away from gas to renewable power. What this means is replacing your gas boiler, when it comes to the end of its life, with domestic renewables like air or ground source heat pumps and solar pv.

A challenge for government will be helping to fund this. A new replacement gas boiler costs between £3,000 to £4000 to install. An air source heat pump costs £6000 - £8000 installed so the real cost is the difference of £2000 - £5000, depending on the size of the property. In some cases, it may be higher than that in some cases.

The uptake of solar pv has been disappointing, particularly in metropolitan areas. More of us need to install this, as it is a simple proven technology which works.

Our Cars

The second issue is our transport. We need to replace our petrol and diesel cars with electric vehicles. This depends on a national network of charging points for people to change to electric cars (this is a key issue for our politicians, we need to lobby our politicians to do this) for people to commit to electric vehicles. The installation of charging points is already, however, happening along motorways at service stations and locally by local councils. If your council is tardy in installing charging points, demand more. Each time we change our cars, we make a personal carbon budget decision. If you are unwilling to change to electric yet, the alternative is to change first to a smaller carbon engine, then a hybrid, and finally an electric car. Making a decision to increase the size of a carbon car engine when you change your car is irresponsible if you truly believe in reducing your carbon target.

Our Travel

Aside from our car, remember, other travel determines our carbon budget. The key thing here is the amount we fly, and how we fly. In 2015, aviation (domestic and international) accounted for 6.5% of total greenhouse gas emissions in the UK, with the majority coming from international flights.

In Chapter 17, I described who flies. *"52% of the population fly, of these, 1% of the population accounted for 18% of flights, 10% of the population accounted for 52% of flights, 20% of the population for 70% of flights. This distribution pattern is not surprising, but shocking. To put this another way, 1% of the UK population is responsible for over 1% of UK emissions just by flying (18% of 6.5%)! The likelihood is that this 1% has a strong correlation to wealth."*

The class you fly also has an impact. A return flight London New York costs 0.67 metric tons carbon in economy, 2.42 metric tons carbon in business and 3.33 metric tons carbon in first. In contrast, a return flight to Madrid from London costs 265 kg of carbon, while taking the train costs only 43 kg.

The flight shaming movement in Sweden seeks to correct our love of flying by putting in perspective the environmental cost. Perhaps we also all just need to get to know our own countries better. It is clear from my research that the 52% who fly owe it to the 48% who don't fly, to fly less. What is even clearer is that the main burden in flight reduction should fall on the 20%, the 10% and particularly the 1% who take 18% of flights. Perhaps next time someone you know boasts about their latest long-haul adventure, you should remind them of the carbon cost. Flying is often discretionary, so reducing flying is a simple way to reduce emissions.

Our Food

5% of the UK's emissions come from farm animals, meaning meat and dairy. While we are not as bad as other countries in this respect (Ireland is the worst offender in Europe see Chapter 13) this is a real issue if we want to move to zero carbon.

The government isn't going to ban meat and dairy, as there are no votes doing so. This is therefore about our choices and moving towards a less heavy meat diet. This is our choice.

Food waste remains a problem. Chapter 15 described this problem and who deals with it it better (again it is metropolitan areas that are the laggards). The most successful areas in dealing with this show that emissions from food waste emission levels can be reduced dramatically. All of us need to either compost or agree to food waste collection, so that our emissions from food waste can be reduced.

Plant a wood or some trees

We can't all afford to plant a wood, but there are things we can do to improve carbon sequestration by planting which is the easiest way we can reduce emissions. Increasing the amount of planting and not concreting over our front or back gardens are small actions which cumulatively have an effect. Planting trees and hedges does have an effect and even if you don't have the land, you can help woodland groups who do to plant.

For the more affluent, planting a wood is a good thing to do, and not that difficult. Our leaders and influencers, our captains of industry should all be doing this and perhaps foregoing their expensive long haul holidays might help them do this and spend the money on this. And if you are a member of the National Trust or other conservation body, you should be demanding that they use their land holdings to plant more trees and help them do this. The National Trust owns 610,000 acres. Even planted on only half this land it would be able to plant 305 million trees (10% of the CCC target), start lobbying them to do this, and other organisations should follow suit. If you are a National Trust member, start lobbying them to do this, pushing this agenda. The recent promise to plant 20 million trees is not enough given the land owned.

You can also lobby your local authority to permit more tree planting and join local groups which plant trees.

Planning

Our planning system needs to be re-orientated so that carbon reduction is the key driver in its decision-making process, whether they relate to domestic renewable installations or new woods. The planning framework must change to to reduce carbon, both in national regulations and how they are interpreted locally.

Our Carbon budgets

Each of us has a carbon footprint defined by our emissions per head. However, this is a passive way to describe how we live.

I think it is better to think of our personal carbon budget, the amount of carbon we "spend", as this is about how each of us live and the individual decisions which we make. We need to think about what our carbon budget should be now and how we spend it. Each decision we make has a carbon cost (bottled water vs tap water is one of the easiest to see as it is a totally discretionary choice). There are some easy decisions like this which reduce carbon, but each decision we make affects that carbon budget as regards our choices homes, cars, and food. Only thinking about your individual situation and decisions will reduce carbon.

We might all ask ourselves, who is overspending on their carbon budget compared to the UK average of 7.7 tonnes? Three return business flights to New York uses up most of those average UK emissions, and that doesn't take account of other emissions spent Next time you see a celebrity jetting off somewhere to save the planet, think of their carbon budget and the sincerity of their comments on climate change versus actions. As in all things, actions speak louder than words. The car brands with the highest average levels of emissions are, Aston Martin, Porsche, Land Rover, Subaru, Infinity, Lexus, Jaguar, SsangYong and Jeep, all at 200g per km or above. Think about your choices, and those of others, and ask yourself (if you are wealthy enough) is it responsible to buy or lease these brands?

Next time your gas boiler needs replacing, consider an air or ground source heat pump before replacing like for like.

Life is about choices. We all need to think about our carbon budgets and how the choices we make determines how large those personal budgets are.

19 LIVING STANDARDS VS LIFESTYLE

The change to a zero-carbon economy is about long term living standards, and the sustainability of the planet we inhabit. Economists have focussed on living standards in terms of economic policy and the elevation of GDP as the key indicator of progress at the expense of a measure which incorporates the sustainable and environmental impacts of growth. If we produce large numbers of extra unsustainable goods, this increases GDP. If we use energy this increases GDP. Neither make sense if sustainability is included in our measure of economic wellbeing. Since the fall of Communism, the unfettered pursuit of GDP has held sway, for illustration of this one only has to look at China. There is a huge question as to whether this is sustainable in, both the transition to zero carbon, but also in a zero-carbon world.

The transition to zero-carbon will need to be managed in social terms. There are considerable challenges in regard to living standards, in particular for the poorer members of society given that fuel costs are a higher proportion of costs for the poor than wealthier. Finding a way to decrease carbon without reduce living standards for the poor will be difficult, but it is an issue which must be addressed and solved.

Globalisation

The start of globalisation broadly coincides with the fall of communism in 1989, and it is easy to forget how large area of the world was under of Soviet influence. The ability of western capital to access these countries, and lower production costs available was a key driver for globalisation and is described very well in Naomi Klein's "No Logo". The expansion of global trade was the result. If you want a rough guide to the state of global trade in the current model of globalisation, just count the number of ships anchored off Singapore from one of the hotels there. Check where the goods you buy are made to see the change which has happened in the last thirty years.

Zero carbon will slowly end the globalisation of power (with the proviso that carbon capture could sustain some form of global trade, but at a smaller level) as power becomes proportionally more electric and relies on local generation. Local produce may become more attractive in a number of ways. Indeed, if different countries reduce emissions at different paces, western governments may use tariffs, etc to support more expensive local produce against global products whose carbon footprint continues to be high (See Chapter 20). Here we must ask whether the countries which take the lead in decarbonising should introduce policies which benefit goods made in low carbon countries, and penalise goods made in high carbon economies? This is permitted by GATT rules where the objective is environmental protection, but it is obviously a complex area.

There are many relevant questions to pose. Should the UK import flowers, fruit and vegetables out of season by air freight from Africa and elsewhere out of season? Why do we transport bottled water? Lastly, is our unfettered free choice to consume acceptable, and should it be constrained to reduce emissions.

Globalisation means global companies, global teams and global travel. Global conferences which mean more aviation. The growth of multilateral organisations has inevitably led to more air travel. Whatever the subject or discipline, the need for this global networking is assumed to be needed and the travel that goes with it. Are short term secondments involving weekly air travel sustainable? As someone who flew too much, when working for a big company, had a global team, attended global conferences and attended multilateral organisations I recognise what drives this and my personal contribution to this. We will all have to learn to fly less.

Carbon Cost

Every purchasing decision we make for goods and services has a carbon cost. Some businesses are carbon businesses due to their need to involve carbon transport in their business model.

The travel business is a good example. Not only do airlines have a carbon business model, but those hotels, restaurants, and services which are used by customers who fly are carbon businesses too. DisneyWorld and DisneyLand are carbon businesses. Sport is also a carbon business, like other experience businesses when customers and participants fly to international sporting events. The food industry is a carbon business when it encourages the use of ingredients and products transported over large distances, the drinks Industry is the same.

To extend this further, think about Instagram. The pursuit of the perfect photo of an experience or place is actually a carbon business, as it encourages travel to achieve those images, and one could make the same comment about facebook to a lesser extent. Equally what is the carbon footprint of the music industry or the fashion industry?

The list goes on and on. Again, this is an "Us not Them" issue, because we all make these purchasing decisions and the more affluent you are the more of these decisions you make relating to such companies. If we are to reduce emissions to zero, then all of us are going to have to think about the carbon cost of our decisions, about our personal carbon budgets.

Metropolitan Life

Many of us live in a metropolitan world. We have become more metropolitan with globalisation and indeed the commonality between metropolitan areas is sometimes greater than between it and the rest of the country it inhabits. In 2016, an estimated 54.5 per cent of the world's population lived in urban settlements. By 2030, urban areas are projected to house 60 per cent of people globally. One in every three people will live in cities with at least half a million inhabitants. (UN)

The question this poses, is can we move to a zero-carbon economy and continue this level of urbanisation? As the section on power generation describes, UK urban areas have, to date, not invested in renewable power, either in terms of solar "farms" or wind turbines but also in terms of residential investment in renewables. One can argue that these metropolitan areas are enjoying a free ride on the hinterland of their countries in terms of the efforts to decarbonise. Is this fair and or sustainable and how will this play out politically as the pressure to ramp up renewables grows? Of course, renewable investment requires an interest in land whether for a solar panel, a wind turbine or a plant for biofuel, etc. and land is at a premium in urban areas. This still doesn't explain the poor comparative level of investment. Just drive round urban and rural areas and compare the number of solar panels on the roofs.

An article in The Guardian[cxlviii] about the ambitions of Copenhagen shows that cities can move towards zero carbon "*A green, smart, carbon-neutral city*" declared the cover of the climate action plan, before detailing the scale of the challenge: "*100 new wind turbines; a 20% reduction in both heat and commercial electricity consumption; 75% of all journeys to be by bike, on foot, or by public transport; the biogasification of all organic waste; 60,000 sq metres of new solar panels; and 100% of the city's heating requirements to be met by renewables.*" "*CO2 emissions have been reduced by 42% since 2005, and while challenges around mobility and energy consumption remain (new technologies such as better batteries and carbon capture are being implemented).*"

It is interesting to note that at a national level, Danish emissions have dropped 20% since 1990 (lower than the EU average) and per head emissions are around 9 tonnes per head (the EU average). Comparatively UK emissions have fallen 36% and 8 tonnes per head. One wonders if this is a case of greenwash in trumpeting the plan in Copenhagen?

This reminds us of the Camden Peoples Assembly "*After all, aircraft do not take off in Camden, there are no large power plants, and container ships do not pass through*" completely misrepresents the impact of urbanisation on emissions, (Chapter 8).

What will all this mean for the future development of cities, and can they grow in a sustainable way. While many cities talk about their zero carbon policies, do these really encompass all the emissions created by that city in terms of all the goods and services which they consume? Will UK cities be willing to build biogasification plants, wind turbines within their jurisdiction and increase the amount of solar panels dramatically?

Media

Most people's views on climate change and the changes in reducing carbon come from the media, be it press, tv or social media. The media is very good at reporting disaster stories, but their coverage of climate change and the challenges of de carbonising is poor, to say the least. This is hardly surprising in the world of twenty four hour news, stories come and go in rapid succession and most of the news coverage of climate change is about a piece of the story, not about the overall picture. The piece from the FT quoted in the Introduction is a noble exception.

There also seems little or no recognition that the advertisers from whom they raise money are sometimes selling carbon goods and services. The Guardian is a fine example of the current level of mixed messages we are receiving, lots of criticism of the lack of government action, but also lots of promotion of long-haul destinations and flying. The advertising industry uses the media to promote goods and services, but there is little critical analysis in the media of this influencing and the carbon costs which it promotes. The media also promotes the role of celebrity, and if you are a small campaign group, they want your story to be endorsed by one. The growth of "celebrity" has fuelled and endorsed greater consumption of goods and services in general and carbon goods and services as a huge part of that.

Influencers

The impact of celebrity culture over the last twenty years has been significant. The growth of celebrity has coincided with globalisation which is no coincidence. The question is can celebrity culture continue in a zero-carbon world? What defines a celebrity if not forms of conspicuous consumption; they jet off for trips to the sun to show off their bodies and lifestyle, they arrange transatlantic baby showers, and so on. Gatherings of celebrity influencers are flown in to somewhere nice, justified by their purchase of offsetting credits. But as the Chapter 17 shows, however if the target is zero-carbon then offsetting doesn't have a role as those credits are already utilised in achieving zero carbon.

Celebrity works because it is can be imitated and aspired to, by ordinary folk. Celebrity is underpinned by global brands. A list celebrities are paid to endorse and market. Are such global brands really sustainable in a zero-carbon world? If air transport becomes rationed by price, will global celebrity be less acceptable or attainable by those who it is directed at? If air transport becomes largely for the rich, will it be resented rather than admired. Perhaps we may see local, sustainable celebrity come back into being as it once was.

Tourism

The House of Commons Environmental Audit Committee estimates that while tourism is 10% of global GDP, air travel accounts for 5% of global emissions. Tourism has mushroomed in the era of globalisation with a new wave of asian tourists being the latest addition. Top destinations are swamped by this (see the coverage of Venice, Amsterdam and other cities). This type of tourism comes with a large carbon footprint.

As I have stressed numerous times, to achieve zero carbon, we will all need to fly less (see Chapter 17 on Aviation). If we do, what will be the impact on the global tourism business. Will tourism revert to a more local experience with a lower carbon impact. If it does, there then will be a distributional impact on where tourism occurs even if the size of the market remains the same.

What will be the effect on the market for second homes in other countries which depend currently on the infrastructure of tourism to make them accessible? Again, there may be distribution impacts. One wonders what would happen, for example to the economies of Southern Spain or Florida.

Migration

Globalisation has seen a large increase in migration for employment which is apparent in any major city. This migration comes at a carbon price, however, as migrants (not unreasonably) make trips to see family who may be dotted around the world. How will this work in a zero-carbon world? If the price of air travel increases (to ration it), will migration change and revert to the model which applied before cheap air travel in the 1980s. Students by and large studied in their own country twenty years ago. Now studying abroad is a more common. Again, this impacts aviation emissions.

Meat?

Browse through almost any restaurant menu, pub or fast food choices and the predominant offering will be meat. Then think about pets and about how many people you know whose diet is largely meat. In 2012 there were estimated to be 525 million dogs in the world, now the estimate is 900 million. That's an awful lot of meat. As developing country living standards rise, so does the consumption of meat globally. The countries which are the ten biggest meat consumers range from the US at 97 kg per capita to New Zealand at 67.5kg. The EU consumes 69.2kg per capita.[cxlix]

Developing countries will (unless something changes) trend towards western meat consumption levels with the possible exception of India whose vegetarian population is estimated between 20 and 40% (though there are questions as to how real this is level of vegetarianism is). In a zero-emission world, how does meat fit in? And what do we do about it?

Lifestyle or Living Standard

A lot of these issues are about lifestyle, and the question is how will lifestyle change as carbon consumption reduces? Businesses which have built themselves on globalisation and carbon will need to adjust as the changes required for zero carbon kick in. I cannot stress enough that this is about "Us not Them" as we will all need to decide the type of lifestyle we want, and how compatible that is with zero carbon. All the issues mentioned above potentially blow a hole in your carbon budget, so what will we do.

20 PRICING EMISSIONS

Many commentators advocate pricing emissions as the panacea to drive a reduction in emissions. My experience working in this field, has been that many clever ideas are put forward which rely on widespread adoption to be effective. To date, few other than the national or state schemes and the EU Emission Trading System (EUETS), have been established.

I first became involved in the use of pricing mechanisms in 2005 when I reviewed the taxation of Emission Trading Permits within the EUETS. What quickly emerged was a multitude of tax treatments ranging from tax deduction through deduction over time to being outside the tax net altogether (Portugal) which allowed the prospect of tax arbitrage for multinational groups acquiring permits in country A (obtaining a tax deduction) and using them in country B with an asymmetrical tax treatment. What followed was a paper setting out a consistent tax treatment within the EUETS. To be honest, most countries seemed uninterested.

This illustrates a key dilemma regarding pricing mechanisms (of which plenty have been proposed), which is how can they be applied consistently cross border. The first fundamental question for any carbon pricing mechanism is "will it cut global emissions" or will it merely move those emissions geographically with no overall global reduction. For this reason business has been concerned that any proposals do not lead to carbon leakage. The OECD report quoted at length below summarises this as follows:

"Most studies indicate that there will be some loss of production by domestic industry if carbon emissions are made costly at home

but not abroad. This argument is mainly based on the assumption that the industries complying with the domestic policies to reduce GHGs emissions will move their production to non-complying countries, reducing the employment opportunities and the economic output within the acting country."[cl]

Countries which take the lead in pricing emissions need to judge their policies against the risk of reducing employment opportunities and economic output in their country which by acting first. This will not apply to purely domestic emissions (hence the success of the UK Landfill Tax), but it will be a significant risk in an international context.

Emission Trading Markets

Using instruments through trading markets was the front runner at an early stage, largely driven by the EUETS. The benefit with a trading system is the market sets the price of the emission in real time and it changes daily (unlike a tax), providing a price set in a currency for the trading system (in the EUETS the euro) or country. In theory this appears to be a robust pricing mechanism. Unfortunately, in practice the pricing of permits was eroded by the willingness of the EU to issue permits in great numbers.

Sandbag[cli] (an NGO which monitors the EU ETS) has charted the volatility of the carbon price and the way that it fell to below 5 EUR in 2013 after an issue of additional permits. What is interesting is to compare these price levels (which would not persuade many producers to reduce emissions) with price mechanisms developed by member states in the EU. Volatility at these carbon price levels does not encourage investment to reduce emissions if the price going forward is not clearly signalled. However, it does provide many opportunities for investors (not the emitters themselves) to game the market

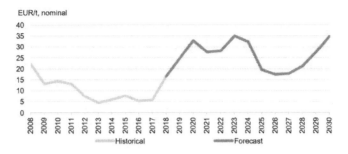

This chart from Powering past Coal Alliance[clii] shows the change after 2017 and the forecast.

What is clear from the chart is the spike in 2017 up to a price of 15+ euro and the forecast hockey stick in the period to 2020. But then significant volatility sets in again.

The Powering past Coal Alliance analysis is: "*There has been a strong inverse correlation between the cumulative oversupply, or total number of allowances in circulation (TNAC), and the price of carbon, since the financial crisis. This relationship somewhat broke down in 2018 as the price of carbon has gone up despite continued oversupply. The reason for the recovery is that a large number of speculators have entered the market on the expectation there will be scarcity in the future. The market's oversupply is due to its inflexible design. The cap was calculated using verified emissions in the first trading phase (2005-07). The 2008-09 financial crisis led to a drop in economic activity and its associated emissions in Europe, however, and there was no measure in place to reduce supply in case of an unexpected drop in emissions.*

In early 2018, the EU completed a carbon market reform, changing the future framework of the EU ETS. The reform is seen as quite ambitious, and the market responded by pushing the price to levels not seen since 2008. The biggest reason for optimism is that member state auction supply is being curbed by the market stability reserve (MSR), which started operating in January 2019. The MSR will remove allowances from auctions if the TNAC is above 833Mt and reintroduce them to auction if it falls below 400Mt, finally bringing flexibility to the supply of carbon allowances. The reform has doubled the MSR intake rate to 24% from 12% of the TNAC in the first five years (2019-23) of its operation. The change means that the mechanism will be able to quickly balance the market, bring scarcity to the market and push emissions reductions in the power sector.

The MSR will remove 1,117Mt EUAs from auctions in the first three years of its operation alone, according to BNEF modelling. The market will be short on an annual basis from the year it becomes operational, quickly eroding the oversupply that has built up. This should push the European carbon price above 30 euros per metric ton by 2020 and keep it between 28 and 35 euros in the following four years."[cliii]

This means that the design of the EUETS was not adjusted when the financial crisis reduced economic activity and emissions, so a surplus of emission trading credits arose. The design, including flexibility to respond appropriately to changing economic activity is crucial to the robustness of the system used. Given the inability of the EU countries to agree on a policy transition to zero emissions in 2050, it will be interesting to monitor how the EUETS performs over the next decade and how successful the system is in both maintaining and increasing the price. The decision for the 2024-2028 period will be key in showing the direction of travel.

Carbon Tax

Many people advocate a carbon tax as the best mechanism. A number of European countries have used it to establish a price higher than the EUETS, and a price that they can control. As of 2018, at least 27 countries and subnational units have implemented carbon taxes.[cliv]

The primary difference between using an emission trading market and carbon tax is the frequency of the adjustment of the price, and the ability of third parties to affect both the operation of the market and the future pricing of the market. Carbon Tax is a much blunter instrument; you cannot change a tax on a daily basis, as the market does in the EUETS. A national tax is priced in local currency so the price is subject to the vagaries of the exchange rate in international terms and again can't be adjusted rapidly or frequently to adjust to these changes. The national nature means that, if the exchange rate falls then the cost of the carbon tax decreases in international terms for foreign investors, and the cost will increase if the exchange rate goes up. Consequently, as an instrument, a carbon tax may be more appropriate for domestic business rather than international businesses.

UK

In 2013, Parliament enacted a carbon price floor under the system for certain sectors including electricity, a policy that essentially functions as a carbon tax. The Carbon Price Support was introduced at a rate of £16 (€18.05) per tonne of carbon dioxide-equivalent (tCO_2e). It was set to increase to £30 (€33.85) by 2020. However, the government decided to cap the Carbon Price Support at £18.08 (€20.40) until 2021.

The total carbon price that power sector emitters face is comprised of the Carbon Price Support plus the price of EU ETS permits, which currently stands at approximately £16.80 (€19). The total carbon price therefore amounts to approximately £35 tCO_2e – £11 higher than the Treasury's stated target price. This is also significantly higher than the EU price of carbon.

Some argue that Carbon Price Support has significantly reduced UK emissions from electricity generation as companies have switched from coal to gas; the presence of an alternative meant that coal generators did have to absorb much of the tax, making them uncompetitive.

If the UK leaves the EU ETS it will reduce the price of UK carbon emissions by removing the current value of ETS permits (£16.80/tCO_2e). The price will then become the price of the Carbon Price Support (£18.08/tCO_2e). This presents two related questions: will this be high enough to keep coal off the system, and if not, how will the UK government change their carbon pricing instruments?

Sweden

Sweden has for some time been the leader in carbon taxes which is not surprising given that the carbon tax was introduced in 1991 at a rate corresponding to SEK 250 (EUR 24) per tonne fossil carbon dioxide emitted. The Swedish government makes much of the fact that Sweden has cut emissions while seeing a significant rise in GDP as their graphic illustrates.[clv]

The tax, *"has gradually been increased to SEK 1 180 (EUR 114) in 2019 (currency conversion based on an exchange rate of SEK 10.33 per EUR). By increasing the tax level gradually and in a stepwise manner, households and businesses have been given time to adapt, which has improved the political feasibility of tax increases. A lower tax rate has historically been applied to industry outside the EU Emissions Trading System (EU ETS), while industry covered by the system is entirely exempt from carbon tax. As of 2018, however, the industry rate outside the EU ETS is the same as the general rate."*[clvi] The next graphic (again Swedish government)

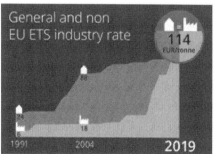

shows the increase in the carbon tax over time[clvii]. Having worked with Swedish representatives on Business Europe myself, their concern was to ensure that no business sector was competitively disadvantaged by the carbon tax vis a vis imports from countries with no carbon pricing in the same sector. Equally, they argued that if a sector was covered by the EUETS exemptions on competition grounds, then that sector should be exempt from the Swedish carbon tax for the same reason.

It is important to remember that Sweden has a largely decarbonised electricity sector. 80% of electricity generation is from nuclear and hydroelectric power with investment in wind building. Sweden's carbon tax primarily targets motor and heating fuels. A gradual increase in carbon tax rates provided the time to adjust and (reputedly) minimize political opposition. However, government funds are available to subsidize municipal and industrial initiatives. One example was using more bioenergy. That could involve switching heating systems from coal and oil to burning waste from forests.

France

The position in France is complicated. The carbon tax is added onto the Internal Consumption Tax on Energy Products, applicable to companies that produce, import, and or store fossil fuel. Typically, those companies pass on these taxes to consumers, by increasing the price of the fuel they sell. The carbon tax appears high at €39/tCO2 e (US$48/tCO2 e) in 2018, €56/tCO2 e (US$69/tCO2 e) in 2020 and €100/tCO2 e (US$124/tCO2 e) in 2030. The new trajectory for the next four years involves an annual increase of €10.4 (US$13) from €44.6/tCO2 e (US$55/tCO2 e) in 2018 to €86.2/tCO2e (US$107/tCO2e) in 2022.

The electricity sector in France is dominated by nuclear power, which accounted for 72.3% of total production in 2016, while renewables and fossil fuels accounted for 17.8% and 8.6% respectively. France has the largest share of nuclear electricity in the world. France's electrical grid is part of the Synchronous Grid of Continental Europe and is among the world's biggest net exporters of electricity. The French nuclear power sector is almost entirely owned by the French government and the degree of the government subsidy is difficult to ascertain because of a lack of transparency.[clviii]

As a result, carbon tax is charged on a very small proportion of electricity production, on motor fuels and direct use of fossil fuels in industry and heating. It is interesting that despite this, the Gilets Jaune protests arose when the price rise related to a small proportion of fuel. The high headline rate is not comparable with other states due to the dominance of nuclear power. France is also among the world's biggest net exporters of electricity, so *"nuclear free"* Germany imports nuclear generated electricity from France.

International competition: Interaction of emission trading and carbon tax

Business has argued through the process of establishing pricing for carbon, that any policy which exposes a European industry to a carbon cost when its international competitors do not bear it, would only have the effect of undermining European industry and exporting the carbon to that industry in countries which do not price carbon. As a result, exemptions for internationally exposed sectors have been sought in the EUETS and in country regimes. The European Greens have objected to this:

"Firstly, why should a carbon tax only apply to non-ETS sectors? There is no reason that two are mutually exclusive - they can in fact complement each other. There is also the fact that in the post-2012 ETS only firms in the power sector would have to pay for all their emissions permits. Other sectors have been - to a greater or lesser extent - exempted. This means that the ETS alone will fail to ensure the polluter pays for emissions from these sectors. To the contrary, it is likely to mean windfall profits undermining the integrity of the system."[clix]

Unfortunately, this rather purist view ignores the effect of global competition, and the likelihood that the emissions would just move to countries outside carbon pricing when that pricing reached a level which affected competition. It would also choke off any new investment in the sectors affected within the EU unless powered by renewable power. The only new Steel plant in Europe this century planned in Austria will be powered by renewable power.[clx]

The OECD report "Taxing Energy Use 2019"[clxi] shows how limited carbon pricing is globally, 85% of energy related CO2 emissions take place outside the road sector. Taxes only price 18% of these emissions. The price signal is at least EUR 30 per tonne for a mere 3% of non-road emissions". Which emphasises the exposure of internationally exposed sectors to global competition.

Border Carbon Adjustments

Another response to the issue of exporting carbon due to the impact of carbon pricing on trade exposed businesses, has been the advocacy of border adjustments on the import of goods from a country which doesn't impose carbon pricing into a country which does. If the UK increased its cost of carbon, therefore it would impose border adjustments on goods produced in a country which did not price carbon equally. Border Adjustments, also known as Border Tax Adjustments or Border Tax Assessments, are import fees levied by carbon-taxing countries on goods manufactured in non-carbon-taxing countries.

The 2013 report, "Changing Climate for Carbon Taxes: Who's afraid of the WTO?",[clxii] by former WTO appellate officer Jennifer Hillman, concludes that *both the letter and spirit of WTO trade rules permit countries with carbon taxes to adopt "non-discriminatory harmonizing tariffs." "These would protect energy-intensive trade-exposed industries by eliminating the competitive advantage enjoyed by exports from countries that don't tax carbon emissions. These tariffs would also create incentives for non-carbon taxing countries to adopt carbon taxes, since harmonizing tariffs represents revenue that the exporting country could garner by imposing its own carbon tax."[clxiii]*

The OECD paper "Border Carbon Adjustment and International Trade A Literature Review"[clxiv] by Madison Condon and Ada Ignaciuk states that: "*Most studies indicate that there will be some loss of production by domestic industry if carbon emissions are made costly at home but not abroad. This argument is mainly based on the assumption that the industries complying with the domestic policies to reduce GHGs emissions will move their production to non-complying countries, reducing the employment opportunities and the economic output within the acting country.*

Beyond the issues of comparability with existing legislation, there are also issues of determining the set of goods and sectors to be covered. First, such a determination involves deciding which goods are at risk. The main argument for a broad coverage of goods and sectors is the potential reduction of leakage. But including more sectors may impose larger transaction costs and additional methodological burden.

An additional argument often made against the use of BCAs is their complexity and their potentially high cost of implementation. Most of the existing literature assumes that BCAs would take the form of taxes on GHGs used in the production of a product, levied at the border. A tax would be levied on imports from countries without equivalent domestic climate-change-mitigation regulations. Products exported to these countries could benefit from a tax exemption, or a rebate. While an export rebate would limit the loss of competitiveness to domestic firms, it might actually work against decreasing global GHG emissions because it would weaken the incentive for domestic exporters to make their own production processes less carbon intensive.

Evaluating the amount of emissions attributed to the product. Presumably, the issue of calculating the amount of emissions imputed to exports produced within a country would have already been resolved under the domestic carbon tax or cap-and-trade system. EU production installations, for example, have an obligation to monitor and declare their emissions. Trouble arises when determining the carbon intensity of imports coming from foreign installations that do not monitor, and may not already know, their GHG emissions. One option that has been proposed would be to impose the same monitoring and reporting requirements on importers.

WTO rules would favour a carbon assessment and tax on a "product-specific" basis, "allowing an importer to demonstrate the actual carbon footprint of a specific batch of imports." The downsides of such an approach are obvious. For one, the administrative burden of monitoring and reporting could be quite high for the exporting country. In addition, certifying the accuracy of the data would be a monumental undertaking, requiring much international co-ordination and bureaucracy. There is also the potential for disputes if the parties could not agree on the appropriate measurement method, as is in the case of current disagreements over the life-cycle carbon emissions of biofuels.

How to distinguish between acting and non-acting countries. The Kyoto Protocol itself holds that compliance cannot be evaluated until the end of the emissions-reduction commitment period. By what means would domestic policy makers determine, in real-time, the extent to which foreign regulations are limiting emissions in order to evaluate the appropriate level of carbon levy to level on imports? Countries are currently employing a wide range of carbon-reduction policies including energy-efficiency standards and afforestation programmes. Evaluating the equivalency of these programmes against a carbon trading scheme would be a complicated

economic feat, leaving ample room for subjectivity."[clxv]

This OECD paper describes the concerns that business in Europe has had about trade exposed industries since the inception of the EUETS generally, where carbon pricing is not applied globally and therefore carbon leakage is the result. In addition, there are practical problems which Border Carbon Adjustments produce in terms of definition, enforcement, and international arbitration. The complexities of customs legislation and practice demonstrate that this would not be a straightforward way to deal with carbon leakage. The length of time to agree a methodology on a multilateral basis would be long, particularly as those countries with low carbon pricing would have no interest in the process until it stopped their exports. Compared to current "trade wars" this would be a major issue for international trade.

Offsetting

Some see offsetting as a form of carbon pricing. Airlines offer passengers the opportunity to pay to offset the carbon from their flight with the money used to invest in projects to reduce emissions, usually tree planting. There have been questions as to whether offsetting reduces emissions or merely assuages guilty consciences. Is the price of carbon used correct? Easy Jet announced an offsetting scheme which will cost the airline £25m per annum. The deal for offsetting costs is £3 per tonne, in contrast to that of the UK Carbon Support price of £18 per tonne. Is this £3 per tonne a realistic price? Furthermore, where is the money spent and is it effective?

We need to ask if offsetting about reducing emissions or is it just a financing mechanism to fund projects to reduce emissions. If the target is zero emissions, offsetting becomes redundant as the emission reduction is required anyway. Helping to achieve the target doesn't reduce emissions, but becomes a purely financing mechanism, it is no different to a bank loan to a project to reduce emissions. (See Chapter 16)

Conclusion

The OECD report "Taxing Energy Use 2019"[clxvi] shows that the world is very bad at pricing carbon emissions. This is not surprising given the length of time which the EU has taken to make the EUETS effective. There are many recommendations by academics and multilateral organisations like the OECD and World Bank on how to do this. What is really needed is not clever, complex ideas, but simple and effective measures.

Domestic emissions can be dealt with by either regulation (the use of coal in the UK power generation) or by pricing (UK Landfill tax is a good example). Carbon tax is a blunt instrument, but it has been successful in changing UK power generation, though also in the domestic context. Carbon markets, however, are more complex, and the question is, given this, are they more useful than a carbon tax? I would suggest that is questionable.

Emissions involving international trade are considerably more complex. To quote the OECD report again: *"Most stud-*

ies indicate that there will be some loss of production by domestic industry if carbon emissions are made costly at home but not abroad. This argument is mainly based on the assumption that the industries complying with the domestic policies to reduce GHGs emissions will move their production to non-complying countries, reducing the employment opportunities and the economic output within the acting country."

It makes no sense to introduce measures that move production to non-complying countries, reducing employment opportunities and economic output within the country which is acting on carbon. Such measures would also stifle investment in that country as well.

There is no sense in measures which move emissions around the world and have no effect on total global emissions. Trade exposed sectors need to be protected from this, until other parts of the world put in place emission pricing. Border adjustments may appear a solution; but their complexity should not be underestimated or the length of time it would take to introduce them, and the complexity of dispute resolution mechanisms.

Countries can use pricing to reduce domestic market emissions, but there is, at present, no easy fix for emissions from goods for international trade. In this stalemate, there will be more calls for border adjustments. If they are adopted, non-carbon globalisation will be challenged given the effect on international trade.

21 ACHIEVING ZERO EMISSIONS

Is it achievable by 2050?

What I hope is clear from the analysis of the UK, is that removing all emission by 2050 is both difficult in some sectors and ultimately not practicable in others given the technology which will be available and operational at a scalable level by 2050.

UK emissions by size of sector and Our emissions from these.

In broad terms we should be able to remove most emissions from Energy Supply, roughly half of Business/ Industrial Process, half of Transport, half of Residential, improve the sequestration of Land Use and roughly half of Waste Management. This equates to approximately 60% of emissions. Removing the other emissions will be tougher to achieve, although CCS may transform this for some sectors if it is scalable. This does not, of course, include Aviation and Maritime emissions. Our emissions, the ones depending on our decisions are roughly 50% of the total.

Anyone who promises to remove all emissions in the UK by 2025 or 2030 is misleading the public. It is just not possible given where we currently are, the technology we have, and the scale of investment required. Extinction Rebellion are wrong; their analysis of the problem is good, but their solution is not achievable in the timescale they promote and it is a false promise. This is not just about decarbonising electricity, but about decarbonising the economy and our individual lives.

As the analysis in the UK chapters shows, zero emissions would require (given current technology) a large number of choices, which many individuals would find difficult to accept like removing meat from our diet.

The Green Party in the European Parliament states : *"THE GOAL: Step up EU's climate ambition, by raising the EU 2030 climate target to at least 65% greenhouse gas emissions reduction, and implementing a Green New Deal to become a net-zero emission and 100% renewables-based economy well before 2050."* [clxvii] How 65% will be achieved by 2030 is the question; I think it is clear, that this is not a realistic objective, even though it is a reasonable position to aspire to. The statement to "become a net-zero emission and 100% renewables-based economy well before 2050" is totally unrealistic. As Chapter 9 on power generation shows, the volatility of renewable power production needs a form of baseload power which the Green policy document does not provide. It is interesting that The Green Party in the UK provide no target to remove 100% of emissions as well before 2050.

The Labour Party talks about bringing forward the aim to remove emissions by 2050 in time. Again, this is not achievable and misleading the public as to what can be done. Labour's document on Emission reduction "The Green Transformation: Labour's Environment Policy" contains many aspirations but few hard commitments. The section on agriculture makes no reference to the emissions of farm animals and meat. It proposes *"Create a National Transformation Fund that will invest £250 billion over ten years to help place our economy on a low carbon, sustainable footing."* The words *"to help place our economy on a low carbon footing"* is not a hard commitment and not one which will achieve *"bringing forward the aim to remove emissions by 2050 in time"*. Given the scale of investment needed which I've described in this book, £ two hundred and fifty billion sounds a large amount, but it only covers the lower range estimate for changing domestic gas heating to renewable power. Labour's 2019 manifesto promises were even higher, as if we were in a bidding war, in one not based on reality in terms of timescale or money.

In earlier chapters I have discussed a few of the big issues we face. Changing thirty million cars from carbon to non-carbon sources, converting freight transport to electric power looks very challenging without "electric roads", removing gas from the power generation mix, building enough wind turbines to increase renewables to close to 80%, replacing old and adding new nuclear power plants, removing gas from domestic heating where it has a current share of 63%, removing the gas central heating which heats 80% of homes, removing emissions from agriculture and stopping flying.

Each of these changes, taken individually, would be a major shift and a logistical challenge. Combined they involve a degree of change in a very short period of time that would potentially be chaotic. There is undoubtedly a consensus and acceptance that we need to act in the UK, but we first need to agree a timetable which is achievable and the priorities needed to achieve it.

Generals are often said to fight the last war, and much effort has been expended on the promotion of the dangers of climate change and the battle with climate deniers, (see Chapter 2 "This Changes Everything" – Naomi Klein). Little time has been spent on the need for change in emissions and finding the methods to achieve it. That is now the crucial issue.

How

I have framed the road to zero carbon as "Our Choice". There are plenty of examples in this book of where the solution lies not in the hands of government and regulation, but in the choices which we, as citizens, make. We live in a democracy and government cannot impose decisions like making people eat less meat. For a significant proportion of the emissions, it is individual choices which will have to change.

Perhaps the easiest decision is reducing the amount we fly. We need to see flying not as glamorous, but in terms of spending carbon. Governments can level the playing field by making Aviation pay the real cost of its carbon footprint. Taxes on aviation fuel should be at the same level as those on fuel for ground transportation. The UK government, the EU and European nations need to act, and act quickly, rather than rely on aviation industry bodies to take the initiative. But we, as individuals, also have to decide that we need to fly less to reduce emissions.

One of the simplest and cheapest ways to reduce emissions is energy efficiency. But how many of us turn off appliances when we can? Energy efficiency is about millions of little decisions which together add up to a large reduction in emissions. Energy efficiency costs nothing financially to achieve, and indeed saves us, the consumer money.

Domestic renewable power needs to be more widespread. The UK has approximately 800,000 homes with solar PV out of a total of 25 million, just over 3%. While solar PV installations on most dwellings provide part of the annual power usage of a dwelling (as they are usually up to 4 kW in size), each installation makes a difference. The question is why have so few people made this investment, and in particular why is the take up in metropolitan areas so low? Given the end of Feed in Tariffs, the government needs to consider how it can encourage more solar installations. The low take-up of solar PV is worrying as an indicator of what the take up of air source and ground source heat pumps might be going forward. As a non-carbon replacement for gas central heating they are the only option we have at present.

Commercial renewable power is another puzzling area. While some businesses have invested, most have not. There are significant opportunities that need to be grasped. Why for example does Network Rail not install solar PV on station roofs? Leeds station is currently being refurbished with a transparent roof, so why weren't solar panels considered with the power fed into the track network? The same can asked of TfL for its above ground estate, why can't solar be installed along rail tracks. Given that solar farms are economic in the UK, why aren't these bodies and others installing solar. The TFL Energy Strategy states its emission reduction strategy of *"Deploying solar across TfL estate and beyond (buildings/land/*

garages) ". There are good examples like Blackfriars Station, which became the world's largest solar-powered bridge providing 50% of the station's energy needs, and solar installations at Whitechapel and at Old Oak, but this is slow progress. Network Rail's claims *"We have launched a range of energy, cost and carbon reduction initiatives across Network Rail. For example, we are working hard to recover energy costs and encourage energy reduction throughout our managed stations. We're also aiming to reduce our carbon emissions by 11.2% over our current control period – a five-year time frame in which we plan and budget our activities."* There is more in the vision statement about reducing waste, however, than in investing in renewables. Why don't local authorities and central government also invest in renewables given their low cost of financing and their large property portfolios?

In waste management, we need to be more aware of the importance of sorting food waste so that it can be processed to avoid emissions, not leave it in landfill creating methane. This requires embracing separate food waste collection, particularly in urban areas which currently fall far behind rural areas.

In the Chapter 19 on Lifestyle I have commented on how the decisions we make about purchasing goods and services all have carbon consequences, some positive, some negative. Each of us therefore has the opportunity to reduce emissions in the decisions that we make. There are many little changes which we can make in our decisions in terms of both carbon and sustainability. This will not be easy, as the saga of recycling plastic coffee cups for coffee chains has demonstrated.

How Much

In Chapter 16, I quoted the following 2008 cost estimate: *"In 2008, the then science minister Paul Drayson launched a pilot scheme to establish what was needed simply to cut housing emissions by 80 per cent. It spent up to £150,000 per dwelling, and the project managed in some but not all cases to hit the reduction target.*

With that cost as a starting point and assume that economies of scale and "learning by doing" could reduce it by three-quarters — to, say, £37,500. Multiply that by 27m and you are at £1tn. This is the figure which Chancellor of the Exchequer Mr Hammond quoted for the cost of reducing emissions, but this is the figure for residential which is 15% of the emission total."

Any estimate of the size of the bill is difficult given the number of unknowns. Based on numbers in this book, it is quite easy to arrive at a conservative price tag of at least £1tn. This isn't based on massive spreadsheets, but the estimates described, and it is a ballpark number. It doesn't include the cost of retrofitting air source heat pumps to flats only the plain vanilla cost of a ground floor installation. It doesn't include anything for agriculture, for the cost of land needed to plant 3 bn trees, for waste management and aviation and maritime. It does include £250bn for new generating capacity, a smart grid and battery storage, which is a conservative estimate.

Current government capital expenditure is about £90bn per annum, so £1tn is an extra £30bn each year for the next thirty years.

What is achievable now?

There are some relatively easy choices that can be made to decrease emissions by significant amounts. The technology exists to do this in certain areas and should be fast tracked. Lex in the Financial Times has recently argued that solar pv is a better choice than forestry to reduce emissions. This is debatable when one includes the whole life cycle of both investments, but the question posed by Lex misses the point in that as we don't have a solution for all emissions, the policy we should be following, is to use all the different ways we have (at scalable size) to reduce emissions. It's not about choosing between options, it is about using everything we have. Our only real option is the technology we have which works now, the technology which works but which needs to be improved, and the technology we have which requires commercial scalable development.

Current Scalable Technology

Land Use change to sequester carbon, like energy efficiency, is the low hanging fruit of emission reduction and given problems with removing some emissions, current technology and cost (i.e. the water industry), the most obvious one to embrace. The scale of the challenge is significant in terms of increasing the area of forestry. The UK is at the bottom of the table in terms of forestry as a percentage of land area in Europe. Only Iceland, Netherlands and Ireland have a lower percentage, aside from Denmark, Belgium and Hungary, most European countries have above 30% with Sweden (69%) and Finland (72%) having the largest area.

As the chapter on Land Use shows, the CCC objective of planting 3bn trees would double the current percentage of land area to roughly 25% (which would still be low by European levels). This would change the landscape dramatically and need an enlarged forestry industry to achieve. Government, local planning authorities, and landscape and nature and conservation ngos would all need to agree this new approach. To achieve these numbers, the programme would have to start immediately given the current rate of tree planting. The financial support for this programme would also require swift decision making. The cost of the land on which to plant the trees is also an issue.

Solar PV: 800,000 dwellings have solar pv and there are 426 solar farms (2015) but solar provides only 3.4% of electricity generation. In European terms, the UK is 8th highest in terms of watts generated per capita. The CCC forecasts are that solar will more than double by 2030, but to do this requires *"auctions for low-carbon power beyond the Spring 2019 Contracts-for-Difference auction, sufficient to reach an emissions intensity below 100 gCO2/kWh by 2030, including a route to market for the* *cheapest forms of low-carbon generation (i.e. onshore wind and solar). This should include a long-term view of future auctions to give investor confidence, help support effective supply chains, and keep costs to a minimum."*

At a residential and commercial level, government policy to encourage investment in solar pv needs to be made clear. It also needs to be clear that it will be maintained as policy which fluctuates will not create the investment climate to support the growth in solar pv.

Offshore Wind Power has been the success story of UK renewables. The UK benefits from having a long coastline, and a large area of relatively shallow sea-beds, together combined with short distances from offshore windfarm landing points to major areas of consumption. Britain currently has the largest installed offshore wind capacity in the world. Unlike other sources of power, Offshore Wind has established a cost structure and scale of installation which allows it to compete with other fuel sources. As a result, there will be more investment and technological advances on offshore installations. The big issue, however, is managing the volatility of supply.

Heat Pumps:The CCC promotes Heat Pumps (both air source and ground source) as the key technology to replace gas as a heating source with a renewable. The issue with Heat Pumps is the cost of retrofitting them into current buildings rather than new build.

Green Match, a renewable installer calculates, a cost for four to six kW of £7,000 to £11,000 and in some cases for larger dwellings £14,000. Households equipped with an air source heat pump may be eligible to receive the Renewable Heat Incentive, a **UK Government grant** aimed at encouraging not only householders but also businesses and communities to use renewable heat technologies. This information is for ground floor installation, retrofitting flats will be more problematic and costly. These figures are likely to be realistic (rather than excessive) as Green Match is promoting air source heat pumps. Per million homes this produces costs of between £7 billion and £14 billion. The Renewable Heat Incentive recovers the capital cost over the seven-year period, in broad terms. There are fuel cost savings as well, but the capital cost has to be financed by the homeowner. The question is will owners finance this? Government borrowing would need to increase to fund the take up.

Air source heat pumps generally work for houses, but it is questionable how large will be the uptake for flat dwellers given the added complications of installation. Will metropolitan areas again fall behind in the proportionate installation of air source heat pumps.

It is interesting to refer to Chapter 7 on Technology regarding the process and timeline for first commercial deployment, to low cost and then widespread adoption. While solar pv (like wind power) is relatively mature, it is entering the low cost phase with widespread adoption forecast by 2040. In contrast, air source heat pumps are on a later trajectory. Installations are currently running at just under 30,000 per annum and forecast to increase to 45,000 by 2025. Given the residential sector has 25 million dwellings this is 0.18% of housing in 2025 and not enough to reach zero carbon in 2050.

Nuclear: The CCC in their Central Nuclear case recommends *"35 TWh of additional renewable generation alongside one additional nuclear plant beyond the Hinkley Point C project (25 TWh)"*. For Hinkley Point *"Since signing a contract in 2016 EDF - the developer - has progressed with the construction of the nuclear plant Hinkley Point C. EDF aim to pour the first nuclear island concrete in 2019, a regulator-approved milestone that indicates progress towards commissioning in the mid-2020s. Once fully operational it is expected to generate around 25 TWh of low carbon power per year."* EDF states itself *"The electricity generated by its two reactors will offset 9 million tonnes of carbon dioxide emissions a year over its 60-year lifespan."*

Again, the CCC *"In June 2018 the Government announced that it was beginning negotiations with Hitachi to support the Wylfa Newydd nuclear power plant. The proposed nuclear plant would provide 2.9 GW of capacity, capable of generating around 23 TWh of low-carbon generation. The proposed reactor design, the UK Advanced Boiling"* Water Reactor (ABWR), *passed the nuclear regulator's Generic Design Assessment in December 2017."* Hitachi decided to scrap these plans in early 2019, which calls into question the size of the Nuclear role in the strategy.

Nuclear can provide a bridge to a non-carbon future by providing baseload generation in the period until renewables and power storage fill that space. In contrast to other technologies mooted as the solution, nuclear is practical and scalable. Green opposition to nuclear per se continues, but the numbers support the need for it to be in the power mix to reduce carbon until storage supports renewables completely. The government needs to bite the bullet and enter into investment agreements to support the nuclear capacity recommended by the CCC.

Hydro poses two issues for the government to decide. In general, the planning regime (and our attitude to landscape) needs to be relaxed to permit small scale hydro both on rivers and offshore. Projects such as those by Simec Atlantis Energy and Whitby Esk should be encouraged and replicated. Using Hydro as Pumped Hydropower Storage (PHS) is relatively underused in the UK. At the end of 2017, the global installed capacity stood at 161,000 MW. This is known technology and a small example demonstrates the benefits. The power generated by a PHS project is linked to the turbine size and the energy storage capacity depends on the size of the reservoir. For example, with two Olympic swimming pools and a 500 metre height difference between them, a capacity of 3 MW storing up to 3.5 megawatt hours (MWh) can be provided.

In the UK there are four PSH facilities which amount to

2,828MW of total capacity and which have an energy storage capacity of approximately 26.7GWh. They were commissioned between 1963 and 1984. Since 1984 there have been no new developments, the potential include the announcement made by Scottish Power in early 2016 of their intention to upgrade the Cruachan pumped hydro power station in order to double its power output. The proposed new pump storage schemes Coire Glas, Balmacaan, and Glyn Rhonwy, the planned Sloy power station conversion into a pumped storage facility and two new PSH schemes announced under planning at Muaitheabhal 2 and Glenmuckloch.

Studies show that *"The role of the regulator for supporting the development of PSH is crucial and also that the open participation of PSH plants in liberalized markets seems unable to create enough incentives for the wide deployment of this technology. The investment in PSH plants requires long-term periods for recovering the Capex due to their capital intensity and the long construction times they require. The capital recovery process for PSH plants is then exposed to the risks created by unstable and short-term regulation, in addition to the risk due to electricity prices that are also heavily influenced by the ruling market regulation."* [clxviii] It is the lack of long-term contracts and a framework that does not adequately value the grid stabilisation services provided by the technology, which explains the lack of recent investment. Government needs to address this issue urgently.

Hydro can be used in tandem with batteries as is shown in the Nordic region. "Fortum (a Finnish company) is to deploy the largest battery so far in the Nordic region, a 6.2MWh system at a hydropower plant in Sweden

A further variant of this is being considered in Sweden, by *"using old mine shafts, Pumped Hydro Storage uses excess renewable energy from e.g. solar or wind power to pump water from the lower parts of the mine. The process can then be reversed when sun or wind conditions are lower, creating an underground water battery with energy potential by letting the water flow through turbines, generating electricity.*" All these variants on hydro use proven technology.

Bio Methane: In the section on Technology I commented that "*Currently the top producing countries are Germany, the UK, Sweden, France and the United States. A report in 2017 by Euractiv claims that by 2050 renewable gas could provide 76% of gas demand in Europe. This would require significant investment as current production produces 18 bn cu m out of a market of 450 bn cu m. This expenditure in production plants while large will allow continued use of the existing gas distribution infrastructure.*"

The CCC comment that "*Our central estimate of the available biomethane resource is around 20 TWh, which could displace about 5% of fossil natural gas in 2050.*" Against this forecast, a number of industry bodies argue for much higher figures. Cadent (formerly National Grid) which is responsible for gas distribution provides a much higher forecast. The Oxford Energy Report describes "*The UK provides a good example of how government policy can stimulate rapid growth in biomethane upgrading. In 2011, there was just one biomethane plant in the country. The introduction of Carbon Price Support from 2013, as well as a Feed-In Tariff per kWh of biomethane injected into the grid under the Renewable Heat Incentive, resulted in 20-30 new plants per year coming onstream between 2014 and 2016, and it is estimated that around 100 new plants could be in operation before 2018. The UK Renewable Energy Association points out that there is a need for clarity on policy beyond 2020/21 if major new projects are to be planned.*"[clxix]

The UK has 523 plants compared to 10,846 in Germany (2015). The rapid growth in Germany was largely driven by the use of energy crops, principally corn (maize), which provided around 75 per cent of the feedstock for biogas plants. This resulted in 8 per cent of German arable land, being used to grow maize as feedstock for biogas plants. There continues to be debate over whether this was good policy. The government needs to decide how biomethane fits into its decarbon-isation strategy in the UK given the implications for land use, and the other pressures if forestation targets are as high as recommended by the CCC. The balance between food produc-tion, forestry and biomass production needs to be decided.

Tidal: The Swansea Bay Tidal Lagoon project is another ex-ample of procrastination and vacillation. The current cost of £1.3bn is broadly the same as the overruns on the Elizabeth Line. It is insignificant compared to £40bn for Crossrail 2, and dwarfed by the HS2 budget of £80bn plus. In this context, the lack of commitment seems bizarre. The Labour Party ap-pears to support the project and a commitment to proceed is needed.

Conclusion Government policy should be to facilitate the in-vestment in these technologies on as short a timescale as pos-sible and certainly to make large strides in maximising the contribution of these emissions reduction methods by 2030.

Current Technology requiring further development

The Grid: A greater reliance on renewables poses new chal-lenges for power grids, compared to large scale production from fossil fuels. There will be re-engineering of the grids to adjust over time to different technologies and the rela-tive use of those technologies. Some are already operational with hydro storage of power. The use of intermittent renew-ables has posed new issues for grid management, as there will be much higher levels of intermittent power from wind and solar than the system today.

Reconfiguring the grid would, however, need more energy storage, different energy use patterns, and new technologies to keep the grid stable. It would require approximately quad-ruple the amount of energy storage (such as batteries) con-nected to the grid, to help balance out the irregular power supply from renewables and provide back-up if a large power plant fails. It would need about 1.3GW of energy storage, equivalent to that of the Sizewell nuclear plant, to safely operate an electricity system with net zero carbon emissions.

In addition, there will need to be change, to the demand and supply balance. While we currently generate to meet demand, going forward we will need to use technology to manage demand to meet generation by shifting part of demand to the times of high renewable production, through pricing mechanisms. Domestic appliances would operate on delayed programming, and moving demand to the night would access wind power in these periods.

A low-carbon system also needs new technologies to maintain the stability of the electrical grid and the frequency of the voltage. The cost of implementing a zero-carbon electricity system (including system costs) will therefore be significant.

Battery storage is a crucial element in harnessing the time volatility of renewables like wind and solar. This is a known technology being pushed in new areas and requiring dramatic upsizing. Chapter 7 focused on the challenges in changing to electric cars from the perspective of electric battery production. The same challenges apply to batteries for electricity storage. The key issue is supply of cobalt as the main component in batteries for cars and storage. The demand for batteries will produce competition for cobalt, and while supply and proved reserves are dominated by the DRC, supply will be stretched.

Given the pace of technical development, it is unlikely that technology will be the drag on development, but the supply constraints will need to be addressed unless solid state batteries assume a greater role. Having said this, the cost of battery storage is now 10% of the cost ten years ago.[clxx]

Developing technology

To reiterate the analysis from Robert Gross when considering the technologies which we have, which have not yet become scalable and the timescale to reach widespread adoption. This list would include:

Carbon Capture and Sequestration: CCS has been portrayed as the saviour of carbon since the early years of the century. Rio Tinto as a steam coal producer reviewed it and decided the risks were too great. The CCC report continues to hope that CCS will solve the problems of emissions from both industry and gas power generation.

The danger here is that it does not deliver on a commercial scale at the level required to remove emissions. For a technology which was being discussed in the early 2000s there has been very slow progress, if one compares this to the progress made in Solar and Wind Power. This is not to say that CCS will not make strides, more that the jury is out and that betting on this is brave. To put CCS in perspective, global emissions in 2018 were 33Btpa, CCS is capturing under 50Mtpa. The Climate Change Committee summed up the position: *Carbon capture (usage) and storage, which is crucial to the delivery of zero GHG emissions and strategically important to the UK economy, is yet to get started. While global progress has also been slow, there are now 43 large-scale projects operating or under development around the world, but none in the UK.*

Hydrogen: The fundamental problem with hydrogen is that at present the feedstock for production is carbon. A low carbon way to produce hydrogen does not currently exist. Experiments are ongoing to find a low carbon method to produce Hydrogen. Honda has been developing experimental home hydrogen stations powered by sunlight, as well as slightly larger stations that can be powered by waste or organic biomass. Toyota has taken more than two decades to perfect its fuel-cell car. The question with is whether hydrogen it can be developed in a way which isn't based on hydrocarbon and capable of widespread rollout in the timescale to 2050. This currently looks highly unlikely.

Given this both CCS and Hydrogen have potential, but that's as far as it goes. To repeat The Washington Post quote, "*we need a new emphasis from the research community on innovation beyond research and development. We need serious work on early deployment, niche markets, scale-up, demand and public acceptance*". The prudent base for a de-carbonisation strategy needs to be built upon known technologies which will deliver a transition which works rather than a hit and hope approach that something will turn up.

Personal decisions

Even if all this technology works and the investment is forthcoming, it won't eliminate emissions from all sectors as it is directed at either current electricity generation or additional electricity generation as a replacement for other fuel. It won't deal with emissions from agriculture, reduce aviation emissions (as electricity doesn't look able to power planes). These are two examples where the only way to reduce emissions is to change our behaviour. There are obviously others where we will have to accept change, as I have discussed in Chapter 18.

What we need to do

Having looked at the analysis of UK emissions, that there are some emissions which government regulation can remove. Primarily, what is required is government policy to facilitate the changes and investments needed, listed in Chapter 22. Politicians need to reach a consensus on these policies. It is equally clear, however, that this will not achieve zero carbon. We can only achieve this if we make personal decisions which do not delay reducing emissions (separate food waste collections) and, that actually result in reducing emissions. No government is going to dictate on issues of personal choice, it is up to us entirely whether we eat meat or fly.

		2017	%
Transport		125.9	27
Energy supply		112.6	24
Business		80.1	17
Residential		66.9	15
Agriculture		45.6	10
Waste management		20.3	4
Industrial processes		10.8	2
Public		7.8	2
Land use and forestry		-9.9	-2
Our Emissions		258.7	56

If we do not follow these twin paths, then we will need to increase the amount of carbon sequestration, beyond the targets proposed by the CCC to absorb the emissions which we cannot reduce. Additional offsetting would be possible, but it would have to be in addition to current plans to plant three billion trees. If we do not achieve zero emissions, then the amount of sequestration has to increase, and again the question will be, where the trees will be planted.

This twin track approach requires the issue of zero carbon to be discussed and debated, and a political consensus agreed as to the actions we need to take. As government action is urgent, this debate is too, and both politicians and the media have a responsibility to engage with this as a matter of priority. In this sense, the highlighting of carbon reduction by Extinction Rebellion is to be welcomed, but when their own members are interviewed and cannot agree on their policy towards not flying (BBC news 7 October 2019), it is evident that the changes we need to consider will be hard to achieve.

Conclusion

The decisions which need to be made are wide ranging and involve great change. Democracies don't cope with long term planning well and their political systems are not designed to take long term decisions of such great magnitude. There may well be considerable resistance to many of these changes, especially if we do this when other countries do not.

Decarbonising means a dependence on electricity as the dominant power source. Governments will be held responsible for the performance of electricity in a country. Given its dominance, protecting the grid from cyber attack, will need to be a high priority for the security services.

There is a danger that this is all too difficult, and that public interest declines over time as the media pursue other more acceptable stories. All of this will probably happen, but the scale of the problem and the solutions should not stop us.

This is Our Choice.

22 GOVERNMENT POLICY DECISIONS

The government policy decisions that need to be made include:

<u>Facilitating the switch to Electricity</u>

Remove planning restrictions on onshore wind new developments and repowering existing facilities.

Ensure that the planning regime supports small scale hydro both onshore and offshore.

Find price support mechanisms for solar pv (residential and commercial) that lead to new installations.

Find price support mechanisms for pumped storage schemes.

Support nuclear power development in terms of planning and price support.

Back Swansea Tidal Project

Accelerate roll out of electric vehicle charging points nationally – preferably with one standard nationwide.

Ban new gas central heating installation in existing properties and gas boiler replacement in existing properties from 2025.

Electrify remaining part of rail network.

<u>Sequestration</u>

Revise grant support for tree planting to facilitate planting target of three billion trees.

Restrict tree imports as part of a tree health policy.

Change the planning system to allow tree planting.

Increase training support for forestry workers.

Technology

Support commercialisation of geothermal and mine water domestic and commercial heating.

Direct technology support to the early deployment, niche markets development, scale-up, demand and public acceptance of technologies to achieve zero carbon including CCS, hydrogen, geothermal heating.

Signals

Set clear signals and timescales for the phasing out of carbon heating installation and use, carbon car sales and use.

Fiscal

Charge fuel duty and VAT on aviation and maritime. Introduce frequent flyer pricing of air travel.

Provide higher scale charges for carbon cars and council tax for properties with carbon heating to encourage conversion.

LAST WORD

Thank you for reading this far, and I hope
you have found the book useful.

You can follow Chris's blog at:

www.zerocarbonourchoice.com

Finally, if you have enjoyed this book, please consider
leaving a short review on Amazon and letting your
friends and colleagues know about the book.

Many thanks

[i] David Bowie. 1972. The Rise and Fall of Ziggy Stardust and the Spiders from Mars.

[ii] Financial Times Editorial Board. 2 May 2019.

[iii] 2017 UK GREENHOUSE GAS EMISSIONS, PROVISIONAL FIGURES Statistical Release: National Statistics 29 March 2018.

[iv] Financial Times 20 June 2019

[v] 2017 UK GREENHOUSE GAS EMISSIONS, PROVISIONAL FIGURES Statistical Release: National Statistics 29 March 2018

[vi] Bloomberg 8 May 2019

[vii] Official portal of Duchy of Luxembourg

[viii] Official portal of Duchy of Luxembourg

[ix] Assessment of climate change policies in the context of the European Semester Country Report: Luxembourg

[x] CLIMATE CHANGE ADVISORY COUNCIL IRELAND ANNUAL REVIEW 2019

[xi] CLIMATE CHANGE ADVISORY COUNCIL IRELAND ANNUAL REVIEW 2019

[xii] HOW GOVERNMENT SHOULD ADDRESS THE CLIMATE EMERGENCY. Greenpeace

[xiii] HOW GOVERNMENT SHOULD ADDRESS THE CLIMATE EMERGENCY. Greenpeace

[xiv] UK Committee on Climate Change Report 2019

[xv] THE GREEN TRANSFORMATION: LABOUR'S ENVIRONMENT POLICY 2019

[xvi] DG Energy (European Commission)

[xvii] IPPR Risk or reward? Securing a just transition in the north of England June 2018

[xviii] The Guardian 23 June 2019 Kevin McKenna

[xix] This Changes Everything Naomi Klein 2014 pg 21

[xx] UK Committee on Climate Change Report 2019

[xxi] European Investment Bank Survey 2019 Citizens perceptions of Climate Change and its impact

[xxii] U.S. Census Bureau, International Database.

[xxiii] Letter to Financial Times Ali Athar 6 May 2019

[xxiv] *Note on emissions sector categories:*

The global emission estimates described on this page are from the Intergovernmental Panel (IPCC) on Climate Change's Fifth Assessment Report. In this report, some of the sector categories are defined differently from how they are defined in the Sources of Greenhouse Gas Emissions page on the epa website. Transportation, Industry, Agriculture, and Land Use and Forestry are four global emission sectors that roughly correspond to the U.S. sectors. Energy Supply, Commercial and Residential Buildings, and Waste and Wastewater are categorized slightly differently. For example, the IPCC's Energy Supply sector for global emissions encompasses the burning of fossil fuel for heat and energy across all sectors. In contrast, the U.S. Sources discussion tracks emissions from the electric power separately and attributes on-site emissions for heat and power to their respective sectors (i.e., emissions from gas or oil burned in furnaces for heating buildings are assigned to the residential and commercial sector). The IPCC has defined Waste and Wastewater as a separate sector, while in the Sources of Greenhouse Gas Emissions page, waste and wastewater emissions are attributed to the Commercial and Residential sector.

[xxv] Financial Times 29 May 2019

[xxvi] Financial Times 22 April 2019

[xxvii] Nikkei Asian Review

[xxviii] OEC. AJG Simoes, CA Hidalgo. The Economic Complexity Observatory: An Analytical Tool for Understanding the Dynamics of Economic Development.

[xxix] OEC

[xxx] OEC

[xxxi] OEC

[xxxii] Wyoming Taxpayers Association

[xxxiii] Wyofile

[xxxiv] Wyofile

[xxxv] Energy and Climate Change Select Committee. UK Parliament

[xxxvi] EIA

[xxxvii] EIA

[xxxviii] EIA

[xxxix] BP Energy Outlook 2019 edition c BP plc 2019

[xl] Point Carbon. The MSR. Impact on market balance and prices.

[xli] EU Energy Roadmap to 2050

[xlii] Industrial Strategy. Building a Britain fit for the future. November 2017

[xliii] "How long does innovation and commercialisation in the energy sectors take? Historical case studies of the timescale from invention to widespread commercialisation in energy supply and end use technology" Robert Gross et al 2018.

[xliv] Research, Design, Development.

[xlv] The Renewables Obligation (RO) is one of the main support mechanisms for large-scale renewable electricity projects in the UK.

[xlvi] Financial Times May 28 2019.

[xlvii] Financial Times May 28 2019.

[xlviii] https://whitbyeskenergy.org.uk/

[xlix] This Change Everything. Naomi Klein. Page 137.

[l] Joshua Goldstein and Staffan Qvist. "A Bright Future"

[li] Joshua Goldstein and Staffan Qvist. "A Bright Future"

[lii] Joshua Goldstein and Staffan Qvist. "A Bright Future"

[liii] Nuclear Power Energy in a Clean Energy System. Fuel Report EIA. May 2019.

[liv] Nuclear Power Energy in a Clean Energy System. Fuel Report EIA. May 2019.

[lv] Nuclear Power Energy in a Clean Energy System. Fuel Report EIA. May 2019.

[lvi] http://theconversation.com/

[lvii] https://www.globalccsinstitute.com/

[lviii] https://www.globalccsinstitute.com/

[lix] UK Committee on Climate Change Report 2019

[lx] Washington Post. 24 February 2019

[lxi] https://ec.europa.eu/eurostat/databrowser/view/t2020_rd300/default/table?lang=en

[lxii] UK Committee on Climate Change Report 2019

[lxiii] "Solar action plan for London" (June 2018)

[lxiv] Wikipedia

[lxv] Areas of outstanding natural beauty (AONBs): designation and management. 18 June 2018

[lxvi] Areas of outstanding natural beauty (AONBs): designation and management. 18 June 2018

[lxvii] Energy Saving Trust responds to the Smart Export Guarantee consultation. 1 March 2019

[lxviii] The British Public supports onshore wind – why won't the government? Environment Journal 22 May 2019

[lxix] Quantifying the benefits of Onshore Wind to the UK. Vivid Economics. June 2019.

[lxx] Cornwall Insight 23 September 2019

[lxxi] Offshore Wind Asset development and ownership dynamics 2019. Wood MacKenzie. 26 June 2019

[lxxii] THE COSTS OF DECARBONISATION: SYSTEM COSTS WITH HIGH SHARES OF NUCLEAR AND RENEWABLES. OECD-NEA. 2019.

[lxxiii] The Costs and Impacts of Intermittency. UK Energy Research Centre. 2017.

[lxxiv] National Grid. Zero Carbon operations 1925. Page 2

[lxxv] OFGEN

[lxxvi] Naomi Klein. This Changes Everything. Page 136.

[lxxvii] UK Committee on Climate Change Report 2019

[lxxviii] UK Committee on Climate Change Report 2019

[lxxix] Crossover Utility vehicles overtake cars as the most popular light duty vehicle type. EIA. 19 July 2018.

[lxxx] Road Haulage Association

[lxxxi] Society of Motor Manufacturers & Traders

[lxxxii] UK All Party Parliamentary Group for British Biofuel. Report 17 July 2019

[lxxxiii] UK All Party Parliamentary Group for British Biofuel. Report 17 July 2019

[lxxxiv] Global EV Outlook 2019. IEA. May 2019

[lxxxv] "Charging ahead – the need to upscale UK electric charging infrastructure" PwC April 2018

[lxxxvi] www.energyreporters.com 22 November 2018

[lxxxvii] Financial Times. 11 June 2019

[lxxxviii] Green Car reports.

[lxxxix] Cobalt: demand-supply balances in the transition to electric mobility. Joint Research Group. 2018

[xc] Upscaling Electric *Freight* Vehicles. Frevue. September 2017.

[xci] Upscaling Electric *Freight* Vehicles. Frevue. September 2017.

[xcii] Business Insider. 8 May 2019.

[xciii] The Clean Growth Strategy Leading the way to a low carbon future. BEIS. April 2018

[xciv] NHS Energy Efficiency Fund Final Report – Summary February 2015

[xcv] Agriculture: Greenhouse Gas emissions statistics. Eurostat.

[xcvi] Healthy Diets from Sustainable Food Systems. Summary Report of the EAT-Lancet Commission.

[xcvii] Agriculture and Horticulture Development Board. 2019.

[xcviii] Food and Agriculture Organisation of the United Nations.

[xcix] Evaluation of the livestock sector's contribution to EU greenhouse gas emissions. Food Climate Research Network (FCRN)

[c] NFU 2019

[ci] Sustainable Food Trust. 26 January 2017.

[cii] Sustainable Food Trust. 26 January 2017

[ciii] European Environment Agency. EU Animal feed imports and land dependency. 10 December 2019.

[civ] Forbes. 2 August 2017.

[cv] Reuters.

[cvi] https://www.farmcarbontoolkit.org.uk/

[cvii] www.climatefocus.com

[cviii] https://carbonneutral.com.au/faqs/

[cix] https://www.greenenergyconsulting.co.uk/treeplant-

ing.php

[cx] The wrong kind of trees, Ireland's afforestation meets resistance. The Guardian. 7 July 2019.

[cxi] The wrong kind of trees, Ireland's afforestation meets resistance. The Guardian. 7 July 2019.

[cxii] Feral. George Monbiot.

[cxiii] https://ec.europa.eu/info/food-farming-fisheries/key-policies/common-agricultural-policy/future-cap_en

[cxiv] Feral. George Monbiot.

[cxv] Feral. George Monbiot.

[cxvi] http://evidence.environment agency.gov.uk/FCERM/Libraries/FCERM_Project_Documents/SC120015_case_study_8.sflb.ashx

[cxvii] Feral. George Monbiot.

[cxviii] Feral. George Monbiot.

[cxix] https://www.forestresearch.gov.uk/tools-and-resources/statistics/statistics-by-topic/woodland-statistics/

[cxx] www.forestresearch.gov.uk

[cxxi] https://findingnature.co.uk/what-types-of-deer-live-in-the-uk/

[cxxii] https://findingnature.co.uk

[cxxiii] Forestry Commission

[cxxiv] Now Research Fellow in Spatial Ecology, *Nottingham Trent* University

[cxxv] https://www.bbc.co.uk/news/science-environment-48155222

[cxxvi] https://www.theguardian.com/environment/2019/aug/07/part-of-german-soul-under-threat-as-forests-die

[cxxvii] having a random probability distribution or pattern that may be analysed statistically but may not be predicted precisely.

[cxxviii] Wiki

[cxxix] Meet the greatest threat to our countryside: sheep. George Monbiot. Spectator. 1 June 2013

[cxxx] UK Committee on Climate Change Report 2019

[cxxxi] Facebook group. Small Woodland owners group.

[cxxxii] Landfill Tax in the United Kingdom.Tim Elliott. The Institute for European Environmental Policy

[cxxxiii] "Bag it or bin it? Managing London's domestic food waste" February 2015. London Assembly Environment Committee.

[cxxxiv] Transforming wastewater treatment to reduce carbon emissions. The Environment Agency.

[cxxxv] BSRIA. https://www.bsria.co.uk/download/asset/wmi-flyer-for-wwhp18r2017.pdf. 2017.

[cxxxvi] An EGS typically involves the following processes. A borehole is drilled into the fractured rock to a depth where high temperatures will be found (~150–200°C). Water is then injected at sufficient pressure to ensure fracturing, or to open existing fractures within the developing reservoir and hot basement rock. This hydro fracturing generates shear along existing fractures. When the pressure is removed the fracture closes but due to shearing the two surfaces are now slightly offset and so the fracture is propped open enhancing the permeability. The developing fractured reservoir is monitored with micro seismicity. A second borehole is then drilled into the reservoir so that cold water pumped down the original borehole is heated by heat exchange in the reservoir and is abstracted to the surface where it is used for electricity generation and district heating schemes. Source Brit geothermal.

[cxxxvii] https://www.eurocontrol.int/platform/integrated-aircraft-noise-and-emissions-modelling-platform

[cxxxviii] https://www.atag.org/

[cxxxix] https://www.atag.org/

[cxl] https://www.icao.int/corsia

[cxli] http://www.airportwatch.org.uk/2019/09/foi-data-from-the-dft-shows-1-of-english-residents-take-20-of-overseas-flights/

[cxlii] European Commission

[cxliii] European Environment Agency

[cxliv] UK Committee on Climate Change Report 2019

[cxlv] https://ec.europa.eu/

[cxlvi] UK Committee on Climate Change Report 2019

[cxlvii] Quartz. https://qz.com/1608527/the-shipping-industrys-emissions-could-be-cut-by-slow-steaming/

[cxlviii] https://www.theguardian.com/cities/2019/oct/11/inside-copenhagens-race-to-be-the-first-carbon-neutral-city

[cxlix] OECD 2016 figures

[cl] https://www.oecd-ilibrary.org/trade/border-carbon-adjustment-and-international-trade_5k3xn25b386c-en

[cli] https://sandbag.org.uk/

[clii] https://poweringpastcoal.org/

[cliii] https://poweringpastcoal.org/

[cliv] Wiki

[clv] https://www.government.se/government-policy/taxes-and-tariffs/swedens-carbon-tax/

[clvi] https://www.government.se/government-policy/taxes-and-tariffs/swedens-carbon-tax/

[clvii] https://www.government.se/government-policy/taxes-and-tariffs/swedens-carbon-tax/

[clviii] Wiki

[clix] https://europeangreens.eu/news/eu-carbon-tax-agenda

[clx] https://www.telegraph.co.uk/business/2018/04/22/europe-gets-first-new-steel-factory-century-construction-starts/

[clxi] https://www.oecd.org/tax/taxing-energy-use-efde7a25-en.htm

[clxii] http://www.gmfus.org/publications/changing-climate-carbon-taxes-whos-afraid-wto

[clxiii] http://www.gmfus.org/publications/changing-climate-carbon-taxes-whos-afraid-wto

[clxiv] https://www.oecd-ilibrary.org/trade/border-carbon-adjustment-and-international-trade_5k3xn25b386c-en

[clxv] https://www.oecd-ilibrary.org/trade/border-carbon-adjustment-and-international-trade_5k3xn25b386c-en

[clxvi] https://www.oecd.org/tax/taxing-energy-use-efde7a25-

en.htm
[clxvii] https://www.greens-efa.eu/en/priority/group/climate/
[clxviii] http://www.british-hydro.org/
[clxix] https://www.oxfordenergy.org/
[clxx] Forbes

Printed in Great Britain
by Amazon